Crowning Glory

REFLECTIONS OF HOLLYWOOD'S FAVORITE CONFIDANT

By SYDNEY GUILAROFF

AS TOLD TO CATHY GRIFFIN

With an Introduction by

ANGELA LANSBURY

With grateful appreciation to Marvin J. Wolf
for his valuable assistance
with this project.

ISBN 1-881649-90-3

Printed in the USA

To my father and mother, Eugene and Anna Guilaroff,
and to my loving remaining sisters,
Eva Fieldman and Rita Loadman.

This book is dedicated
to the scores of men and women
who contributed to the wonder and excitement
that I have enjoyed for so long. They were glamorous film stars
and gifted directors, sensitive editors, insightful writers,
visionary producers, passionately committed set decorators
and designers, inspired clothing designers, dedicated crewmen
and a host of other friends and colleagues inside and outside
the film industry.

—Sydney Guilaroff

For John Casey and Jim Bullock,
who taught me a flawless love can and does exist.

And for my parents
Carrie and Grif, who live by Romans 8:28

—Cathy Griffin

TABLE OF CONTENTS

$\mathscr{A}cknowledgments$

My very sincere appreciation goes to my publisher, Quay Hays, at General Publishing Group. Despite modern bureaucracy, he had the foresight and perseverance to instinctively put together this book. An extraordinary, bright and gifted man with a great acumen for publishing, he has enormous charm and simplicity. A very special thank you also to the staff of General Publishing Group for all their efforts to make this book a very special one.

My deepest appreciation to my grandson, José Guilaroff, for his devotion and support.

Despite all our ups and downs, our laughter and our tears, Cathy Griffin remained steady, dedicated and loyal to my life story. Without her, this book would have never been possible.

Warmest thanks to Roddy McDowall and John Bryson for making their photographs available.

For those wonderful people who were helpful in refreshing my memory, a special hooray!: Margaret O'Brien (who gave us many hours of her time in a lengthy interview), Eva Marie Saint (we spent a wonderful afternoon sharing our memories), Nancy Reagan, Cyd Charisse, Ann-Margret, Roger Smith, Angela Lansbury, Peter Shaw, Jane Fonda, Katharine Hepburn, Stefanie Powers, Julie Powers, Shirley MacLaine, Jean Simmons (one of my dearest friends today), Esther Williams and Eva Gabor (a very warm friend now in Heaven).

I am appreciative of my advisers: my artist friend Yvonne Cross; her daughter, Allison Cross; her husband Peter Grossman and Frances Diaz, my dear neighbor and attorney—thanks to each of you for your valuable time.

For their efforts at the beginning of this journey years ago: thanks to Elizabeth Taylor, Jorjett Strumme, Debbie Reynolds and Irma Kuzely. Deep respect and best wishes to William Tuttle.

Thank you for your collaborative efforts Charlotte Purin, Paul Brogan and Molinda Karpman.

A note of gratitude to the Minnelli family: Judy, Vincente and my darling Liza, a generation of stars that made my career shine all the brighter. Liza, whom I consider my daughter, reached the apex of her life and career through the entire world with her enormous and unique talent. She definitely stands apart from anyone else in the world. You are my Liza with a Z. I love you dear.

A very special thanks to my very special and dear friend, Doris Carlyle, who herself was an outstanding theatrical agent in New York. We speak every day, and she always gives me tremendous moral support. My gratitude to George Schoenbrunn for his unwavering support and encouragement.

Last but not least, an immense appreciation and warmth to José's mother and aunt, Nela Rose de Santamaria and Gladys Leon, for their love and support through the making of this book.
—*Sydney Guilaroff*

Crowning Glory was a labor of love for me and all the many wonderful people who shared my passion for Sydney's story. I am extremely grateful to all those who assisted me in this collaboration, particularly my friend and personal assistant, Charlene Martin, whose loyalty went above and beyond the call of duty. She held my hand throughout this whole process, even going against her doctor's orders and staying extra weeks—almost up to the minute she delivered her son Kolby—to help me! Her tremendous organizational skills, insights and patience were invaluable.

Jim Pinkston, my agent and friend, provided advice and guidance and read the manuscript along the way. His willingness to listen to me and encourage me day and night will forever be appreciated.

Our editors, Peter Hoffman and Murray Fisher, are the unsung heroes. For their keen editorial input, enthusiasm and unwavering devotion to this project, I am truly grateful.

Inestimable gratitude to General Publishing Group publisher Quay Hays, for his belief and confidence in this project as well as his hands-on supervision.

The art department at General Publishing Group is par excellence! Many thanks to our art director, Susan Anson, for such a wonderful job.

To Sharon Hays and her publicity staff, especially Joni Solomon, appreciation for your creativity and going the extra mile to make this book a success.

Thanks to all the transcribers who put the many, many hours of my taped interviews with Sydney on paper, a tedious but necessary service: Bruce Dent, John Matthew, Richmond Chandler, Steve Berent, Rick Danenberg and Mary Deese.

Special thanks to Gavin Lambert for giving me his only copy of *Norma Shearer.*

My deepest appreciation to Denis Ferarra for always being there and for the many kindnesses and courtesies he always extends to me. Thanks to Liz Smith and Robert Osborne as well.

A dept of gratitude goes to Elizabeth Taylor, who was responsible for my meeting Sydney Guilaroff.

Jorjett Strumme deserves a huge thank you for her sharp instincts and immeasurable wisdom.

To my friends who listened patiently to my tears and fears, joys and triumphs throughout this challenging year, especially Riva Dryan. Warmest thanks to Jim Bullock, John Casey, Beverly Ecker, Mark Katz, Caroline Graham, Andrea Ioannidis, Karen Pascarella and Justin Davis.

Special appreciation to José Guilaroff for his numerous contributions to this book and his belief in me.

Finally, to that remarkable, great man who gave me this wonderful opportunity; granting me entry inside his heart, mind and soul. Thank you for sharing this marvelous experience, Mr. Sydney Guilaroff.

—*Cathy Griffin*

Introduction
BY ANGELA LANSBURY

Sydney Guilaroff was the first person to greet me when I reported to the makeup and hairstyling department at Metro-Goldwyn-Mayer studios in 1943. He made a very strong impression on me. This wonderfully handsome and attractive man invited me to sit down before a mirrored dressing table in a bare, white room. He immediately proceeded to take my hair in his hands, and with a few deft strokes transformed me from a 1940s teen to a Gay '90s parlor maid. His pleasing, cultivated English-Canadian accent eased my nervousness, and the fact that he was dressed in an impeccably tailored suit elevated my spirit. Here was an important fellow, I could see, and he was taking his valuable time to help me. I noticed that he never removed his jacket, even when working on hair, and that he always wore a beautiful gold wristwatch that wound twice around his arm, like a snake.

Sydney was at the studio before the crack of dawn to greet

all the actors and actresses. Cracking the whip, jollying his corps of lady hairstylists, joking pleasantly with everyone and all the while dressing the hair of the most beautiful women in motion pictures, he made me, a seventeen-year-old, feel comfortable and cared for. He roared with laughter at the audacity of my saucy character Nancy in *Gaslight* telling off the likes of Ingrid Bergman and Charles Boyer. He understood talent, encouraged it, nurtured it.

In those years, Sydney occupied a most elite and rare position at MGM. He was a designer of hair, but he was not a member of the union. Yet he was on the producer's roster and therefore allowed to work on the sets in the presence of union workers. For decades, he was the only male hairstylist in the movie business.

Sydney was the friend and confidant of every great star with whom he worked, and I know that he was at least partly responsible for their success. He knew how to present women and make the most of their natural attributes. Greer Garson, Katharine Hepburn, Joan Crawford, Marlene Dietrich, Judy Garland, Elizabeth Taylor—they all entrusted themselves to his discriminating taste and expertise. He reveled in period movies, and his wigs were the best ever seen on film. For instance, his splendid wig for Norma Shearer in *Marie Antoinette* was an imaginative study in unique coiffure design. Such great costume designers as Adrian, Walter Plunkett, Helen Rose and Irene felt his creations were the perfect accessories for their gowns. Sydney never said so, of course, but I imagine he felt it was the gowns that were the perfect accessories for his hairstyles.

He was persona grata in every executive producer's suite at MGM, and his suggestions on casting and scripts fell on grateful ears. Louis B. Mayer knew and understood Sydney's tremendous contribution to the films that were made during Mayer's tenure as head of the studio. In addition to the enormous respect he earned for his sensitivity and taste, Sydney got everyone's attention because he had been with MGM during the Thalberg years, so he knew where all the skeletons were buried! I watched him work on Lucille Ball in *DuBarry Was a Lady*, Ginger Rogers in *The Barkleys of Broadway*, Elizabeth Taylor in *National Velvet* and all the Judy Garland films of the forties. He also styled Hepburn in *Pat and Mike* and *Woman of the Year* and Greer Garson in all her great successes, as well as Ava Gardner, Deborah Kerr, Jean Simmons, Rosalind Russell and Lana Turner. For each of these glamorous women he created a new look to accompany their screen roles.

For *Harlow*, in which I played Jean Harlow's mother, Sydney worked overtime for Carroll Baker, creating a sensational platinum blond wig to transform Carroll into the "blond bombshell." It took days of experimenting with bleaches of every description to produce a wig that wouldn't turn yellow under the hot klieg lights. He also had to help calm and support a leading lady who was scared out of her wits because she knew she was totally miscast in the role. His patience and tenacity paid off, and Baker's performance won wide praise.

There are probably a thousand stories like that about Sydney. He worked behind the scenes, his name rarely before the public, but his contributions to the Golden Age of movies were tangible and enduring. He had a brilliant career, but even more important, he encouraged and cajoled and supported and befriended legions of young—and not so young—women. Sydney, one could never hope to have a better friend than you, and I am so proud to say that.

$\mathcal{P}rologue$

$f$or years I had been asked to write the story of my life as the head hairstylist at Metro-Goldwyn-Mayer from 1934 until the late seventies, an era of opulence the world will likely never see again. It was a time of ecstasy and sadness, of glittering beauty, of fantasy and reality, of teaching the world how to live, how to dress, how to speak. But I consistently declined the book offers because it seemed to me that there were many, many things the world needed more than another Hollywood biography.

And yet, deep down, I felt that what I had seen and heard and felt might be of interest to those who had not been fortunate enough to live through those times. If future generations were ever to make any sense out of that golden age of film, if my years at MGM could provide even a glimpse into that long-gone world—one in which I rose from a probationary hairdresser to head of the hairstyling and makeup department and eventually befriended and became a confidant of many of the greatest stars and moviemakers in the history of Hollywood—then I ought to make sure my story became part of the record. I also knew that I owed something to all those who had paved the way before me, comforted me in my failures and celebrated my successes. Reluctantly, I decided that it was up to me to make sure that all those wonderful times did not simply vanish when my life was over.

And so I began to recollect the more amusing or insightful anecdotes of my career, and as they occurred to me, I wrote them down. Although I had enough material for a book that would attract wide attention, I felt something was missing, but I couldn't quite put my finger on what that was. And as I continued collecting my anecdotes, I became more skeptical about the end result. I learned that publishers expected a "tell-all" book that would slander the dead and attract readers hungry for detailed descriptions of the sexual escapades of the rich and famous. I am totally against this approach. I believe in the truth, but I loathe the way most of today's biographies are based on character assassination, innuendo and exaggeration. Thus, when Kitty Kelley called one day regarding the unauthorized biography she was writing about Elizabeth Taylor, I told her that I didn't talk about anyone. Kelley, who revels in her reputation as muckraker, insisted, "Certainly you can say something nice about Miss Taylor."

"No matter what I say, you will twist it," I replied, "So I would rather not say anything." Then I hung up on her.

I was leaning toward abandoning my own autobiography when a close friend told me about *How I Survived AIDS*, by Niro Markoff. This book attracted my attention not merely for its uplifting story of a woman who, through spiritual means, completely healed herself of the killer virus, but also because by sharing her story, she surely inspired others to face the disease with more hope. This impressed me enough that I decided to write a book that might encourage those who are struggling down their own life's path. With this goal in mind, I began to envision my book and what it might offer readers, aside from the tale of my life.

What you are about to read is the story of a young man who came from nowhere with nothing but God-given talent and beliefs, who rose to be welcomed and respected everywhere. I like to think that this is still possible in any business, in any town, even in Hollywood. Among those who ascended to American royalty—including the dazzling screen stars who personified the dreams of many—I can say that I played a small part in their success. Their personal triumphs transformed my own life into a dream beyond imagination. As I approach my tenth decade, that life has nurtured a stream of wonderful memories. I have tried to tell them here with love and truth.

Sydney Guilaroff
Beverly Hills, California
July 1996

CHAPTER ONE

The Auction

*t*he year was 1970, and I was in Culver City to attend
an auction at the MGM studios. Everything was going on
the block: the soundstages, now decaying and obsolete;
the backlots of quaint streets filled with houses and shops
that seemed to have been uprooted from the four corners
of the globe; costumes—simple, ornate, bizarre, com-
monplace and everything in between—from the studio's
celebrated wardrobe department. Furniture of every style
and fashion and representing every period, some authen-
tic but most built by MGM's own artisans, was to be sold,
along with props that had turned cavernous stages into
palaces and skyscrapers and charming country cottages.
To the auctioneers it was just another sale of real estate,
furniture, clothing and equipment. But the deep sadness
in my heart told me that what was really being carted off
was nothing less than memories. It was these very items
that had transformed the studio from a mere film factory

into a city of dreams, a place where people could not only imagine a different world but become part of it forever.

Entire sections of the lot were destined for demolition and redevelopment; within months, a warren of condominiums would rise from their storied streets. I wondered if the families who moved into these units would ever find rest. Would their menfolk awaken in the windless hours before dawn to a phantom Charles Laughton cursing the HMS *Bounty*'s bold mutineers? Would young girls be jolted from their slumber by the spirit of Vivien Leigh stamping her pretty foot and mourning the loss of Tara and her gracious life? For the millions who worship the flickering idols of the silver screen, this is hallowed ground, forever a city of ghosts.

As the auction proceeded and as people carted off one treasure after another, the trickle of memories became a torrent. Closing my eyes, I took myself back 40 years, where in my mind's eye I once again strolled MGM's sumptuous lot. I saw and heard costumed actors practicing their lines. Stuntmen limbered up on the sidelines, then went through their routines at half-speed. Assistant directors scurried about, barking orders or shepherding extras, while gaffers ran colonies of cables and grips adjusted forests of massive lights. A horse-drawn carriage rumbled down a cobblestone street between the false facades of shops and homes that evoked the Paris of Louis XIV. A tractor slowly trundled over new macadam, towing huge flats of hand-painted scenery. Bit players in colorful costumes rushed from one set to another.

I smiled to myself as I remembered the thrill of the first time I was summoned to Greta Garbo's dressing room by the elegant lady herself. I recalled my embarrassment on that same day when she suddenly removed her blouse in front of her makeup mirror. Little did either one of us know that our relationship would blossom into a love affair lasting nearly 30 years.

My eyes still shut, I remembered my peppery lifelong friendship with the unforgettable Katharine Hepburn, from her free-living, free-loving early days in Hollywood through the years of her monogamous live-in liaison with the married Spencer Tracy.

I remembered my unbreakable bond of friendship with that tempestuous diva, Joan Crawford, through two of her four marriages and all her romantic flings.

I remembered with joy the 20 years of heartfelt devotion between me and the love of my life, Ava Gardner.

I remembered my weeks at the bedside of Elizabeth Taylor in the grief-stricken aftermath of her husband Mike Todd's death in a plane crash.

I remembered running into Lana Turner as she walked out of a Beverly Hills hardware store having just purchased the butcher knife her daughter, Cheryl, used later that very night to kill her mother's boyfriend, a two-bit hood named Johnny Stompanato.

I remembered the day my cherished, tragic friend Marilyn Monroe looked up at me and said softly, "You know, Sydney, I wish I had married you instead of Joe and Arthur. You've cared for me more than anyone I've ever known."

I would never be able to touch those times again. Opening my eyes, I found myself back on Stage 27, where an auctioneer was trying to arouse interest in a lamp that once graced the grand salon in the epic film *Marie Antoinette*. When it sold for a few dollars to a buyer who had not even been born at the time that bit of magic was immortalized on film, I realized yet again that glory and splendor always has its end. Powerful civilizations rise to dominate their world, then vanish into history. How could the glory that was MGM go on forever? Obeying the laws of our society, it inevitably succumbed to the burdens of success.

Nevertheless, as the visible remnants of my former professional home were carted off like so many trophies of the hunt, I felt the pain of the studio's dissolution more than ever. Today, I feel no better when I realize that most of the people who powered MGM from its humble beginnings at the dawn of the movie industry to its storied evolution into the world's greatest studio are also gone. One by one they fell, larger-than-life soldiers who lost the final battle against life and time. Joan Crawford, Ava Gardner, Clark Gable, Greta Garbo, Cary Grant, Marlene Dietrich, Ginger Rogers, Mary Astor, Judy Garland, Spencer Tracy, Gene Kelly, Errol Flynn, Lionel Barrymore, Fred Astaire and most of all, Louis B. Mayer, the dictatorial genius who kept all those egos in harmony. Their performances will live forever, but the performers themselves have returned to the dust.

Yes, that day back in 1970 was a sad one. Yet as the incredible tide of memories washed over me, I felt truly blessed, for destiny had taken me from rags to riches, from an unprepossessing childhood in Winnipeg and Montreal, to the starriest studio in the world of motion pictures.

CHAPTER TWO

Winnipeg

t he sidewalks of Saint James Place, in the Winnipeg, Manitoba, neighborhood where my family lived, were paved with railroad ties. One day, as I strolled down our street, I spotted something shiny in one of the spaces between the ties. Dropping to my knees, I peered down into the narrow crack. In the dirt below the sidewalk, wedged in a space too narrow even for my six-year-old fingers, was a 25-cent piece.

That was a lot of money for a boy in 1913. I ran home and returned with two of my mother's butter knives, and by gently imprisoning the coin between the two blades, I brought it nearly to the surface before it slipped out. I tried again, with the same result. But on the third attempt I met with success. Holding my prize in one grubby hand, I scampered home.

We were a household of nine: My brother, Theodore, and my sisters Olga, Dorothy, Vera, Eva and Rita shared a house with our parents. My father held several jobs and seemed to be working all the time to keep food on our table, so there never was much money for luxuries. This was very much on my mind as I brought my loot home to show my mother.

"Please, Mama, I want to go to the movies," I pleaded. "Do we have to tell anybody about this money? Couldn't I spend my whole quarter at the movies?"

My siblings also enjoyed films, but I was the only one who absolutely *loved* visiting the nickelodeon on Furby Avenue, where it cost only five cents to see a movie. My mother smiled and agreed that my lucky find would remain our little secret. And over the next several weeks I managed to see five movies—silent films featuring William and Dustin Farnum, Pearl White, Charlie Chaplin, Geraldine Farrar and the Gish sisters, Dorothy and Lillian, then mere children.

Movies became a rare treat for me. Sometimes I would beg enough for trolley fare and ride across town to one of the larger theaters, where I would see such grand films as *Intolerance*, D.W. Griffith's masterpiece. After returning from each performance, I would discuss what I'd seen with my mother. She was a fan of Chaplin, but I cared little for comedy and didn't see what all the fuss was about. Here was a little fellow with big funny shoes and a goofy walk. If I had moved like that, I'm sure my mother would have said something stern to me about it. And Chaplin was always dressed so oddly, carrying a cane but wearing a tight jacket that came together in front but split everywhere else. I thought he was more strange than funny.

I wasn't the only young boy who was permitted to visit movie theaters unaccompanied. Not only was Winnipeg a great city, but it was also a community where strangers respected one another and everyone looked out for children. Whenever I rode the trolley, for example, the conductor would help me board the high step. I had only to tell him where I was going, and as we approached the street he would pull the cord and a little chime would announce that we were stopping. And as I descended the steep steps, he'd again offer a hand in assistance.

As the sixth-born of seven children, I was raised as much by my older sisters as I was by my mother. It was Vera, the third-born, who took me to school on my first day. Although she assured me that I'd enjoy being with other children my age, I was very reluctant to leave home. When she headed off to her own classroom after dropping me at the kindergarten, I tried to follow her. The teacher told me to sit down, which I did. Then I began to cry. Later, when Vera walked past our door at recess, I tried to follow her again, and the teacher had to jump up, run after me and drag me back where I belonged.

I never did overcome that feeling of dread every time I entered a classroom. I hated sitting behind a desk, and my poor grades reflected it. Teachers wrote that I was well behaved but disinterested, that I was daydreaming through their lectures, gazing out the window or staring without comprehension. They were right.

Once, however, I got the whole class laughing. It happened during a grammar lesson, after our teacher asked us each to write a sentence to demonstrate the conjugation of a verb. The example she gave us was, "An apple a day keeps the doctor away," and I turned that around and wrote: "A doctor a day keeps the apples away." The others burst into laughter, but the teacher had no sense of humor, and I was sent to the principal's office for a strapping. I got another one that night from my father.

Although I earned poor marks in most subjects, I did earn better grades in a few, undoubtedly because I actually enjoyed them—history, poetry, music and drawing, all taught by visiting teachers who came every two weeks or so. I did exceptionally well in music, in part because singing and playing the piano were a big part of our family life. We had a modest upright piano, a Heintzman, that my four older sisters played regularly, taking turns at practicing their lessons. My oldest sister, Olga, who was sixteen years older than me, studied under Mr. Hungerford, a leading piano teacher of the day, and later became a noted concert pianist, earning recognition as Canada's finest artist of the day. Vera began playing the piano in movie houses—often getting me into the theater for free—and with her talent for improvising on classical scores, she went on to become one of the great jazz pianists of her time. In 1950 a selection of her records was sealed into a time capsule to be opened a century later as a definitive example of Canadian jazz music.

I, too, studied under Mr. Hungerford, but only for a few months. He then called Olga to say I was so talented that there was nothing more he could teach me. He suggested I try for a scholarship at a music conservatory, but my father thought it would be a waste of time. Despite my talent, he believed I would never become good enough to actually make a living as a pianist. That was the end of my music education.

This was a time when children were expected to be seen and not heard, and so we always listened carefully to my father's words. Long before Hitler, anti-Semitism was widespread throughout Europe, and to escape it my parents had emigrated from Russia to England before the turn of the century. I was born in London in 1907, but soon afterward we moved to Canada, where my father began working with the Baron de Hirsch Institute to resettle displaced Europeans. He found them jobs and sponsors and arranged for their entry into Canada. Lives were often at stake, as so much of Father's work was of a confidential nature, and he rarely discussed it. But he was a well-read man and was well informed about world events. He told us what was happening in Europe during and after World War I, then known as The Great War. There were evenings when he held forth at length on international leaders such as David Lloyd George, Woodrow Wilson, Georges Clemenceau, Ferdinand Foch, Kaiser Wilhelm and Otto von Bismarck.

My father was a man of principle and commitment. Despite our family's fondness for music, I was forbidden to attend any of the piano concerts given by Ignace Paderewski when he visited Canada. He may have been the world's greatest pianist at the time, but he was also a notorious anti-Semite, and my father wanted us to have no part of him. "They persecute Jews in Paderewski's Poland," he told us simply, and that was that.

I owe a great deal to my family for the life lessons I received from them. They also have my gratitude for fostering my creative side. It was Olga who first recognized my talent and suggested I take a class at the Ecole des Beaux Arts, a private school that taught music and the visual arts. When she told me about it, the summer break was only two months away, but I was allowed to enroll in a painting class that met in the early evening. All my classmates were adults—many in their thirties or older—but there was little muttering about my youth, and no one said anything to me about it.

For my first class I was given canvas and oil paints. After a few minutes a young man in a robe came in and mounted a podium in the center of the room. The teacher explained he'd be asking the man to turn his body from time to time so that each of us could have the opportunity to see him from every angle. And when everyone was ready, he took off his robe.

I had never seen a naked man before, and I was mortified. I was sure I couldn't paint him, but after a few minutes I looked at him again and decided that I liked his face. So I decided to focus on that, to forget that he was naked, to paint only his features and forget everything else. While I worked on this painting for the next two months, I glanced periodically at the canvases of my fellow students. They had captured every detail of the man's body, down to what was under his fingernails and, of course, his genitals. Then one night Olga dropped in, saw what I had done and remarked, "It's good training for you anyway, dear. You'll get better."

At the end of the class, each student was required to submit his or her body of work for the entire year. The others turned in their canvases, and I submitted my single painting. I was so sure they'd laugh at my efforts that I wrote a note in my childlike scrawl on the back of the canvas: "Please be kind enough to stand back ten feet and you'll see the meaning of my painting." I hoped the teachers would judge my work on its own merit, but I didn't have many illusions about my talent as a painter.

Despite my artistic leanings, the priority in our household had always been to bring in enough money for all of us to survive. In those days many children worked at part-time jobs, and in our family everyone contributed their wages to the common purse. It was soon after my eleventh birthday that my father began pressing me to find an after-school job. I found a position with a florist, running errands and delivering flowers, but I hated it. The boss kept complaining that I was too slow. Whenever I brought a bouquet or a wreath to someone's house after a death in the family, I felt terrible about it. And when the recipients tried to give me a tip, I always refused it because I felt so sad that someone had died.

As I began the eighth grade, my father began to talk to me about my future. "You should be interested in business," he said. "You should go on to high school, where you'll learn mathematics, geometry and business." But I wanted nothing more to do with school.

And as for business, I had looked around Montreal—where we had moved from Winnipeg—and there was little there that appealed to me.

After finishing the eighth grade, I took a couple of jobs. I didn't like the work or the people I worked for, however, and I soon quit. Finally I decided to give up on Montreal and try the opportunities I was sure to find in New York City. My parents weren't overjoyed, but they agreed that I could go if I really wanted to. So they bought me a one-way ticket, provided me with the address of my father's sister in Englewood, New Jersey, and gave me fifteen dollars to live on until I found work.

On a warm summer day in 1921, I boarded the train for my big journey. It was my first time away from the family, my first time out of Canada, and I was beside myself with excitement. I spent the day peering out the window at the unfamiliar landscape flowing by. The following night I was wide awake, sketching with pastel chalks, a present from Olga. All I could think about was what awaited me at my destination. I was sure that if the streets of Manhattan weren't actually paved with gold, at the very least I would find a job I liked, and in time I might even make a living. I might even make something of myself. Little did I suspect what an astonishing destiny lay ahead of me.

New York

My entrée to New York City was through Grand Central Station, an explosion of sight and sound and smell. Outside the station, the scene was even busier. Exhausted, my senses overwhelmed, I had no idea where to go or what to do. That night I slept on a bench in Central Park, then a safe and serene oasis surrounded by a city that never seemed to rest.

In the days that followed, I searched the want ads for a suitable job. Stretching my small stake as far as I could, I dined at the Horn & Hardart Automat, a Times Square restaurant that offered its entire menu in a vending machine. A nickel dropped in the slot bought several slices of bread and butter, almost enough to fill me up. Five cents more bought a small bottle of milk. Soup was a dime, and once in a great while I splurged, treating myself to 25 cents' worth of meat loaf or half a fried chicken. Still a growing boy, I was hungry constantly and remained very thin.

After a couple of days on the park bench, I found a bed in a Bronx boarding house for three dollars a week. My money was all but gone when I landed a position at Gimbel's department store. Easily the youngest, I was also the tallest and the skinniest kid working in the stockroom. But I was glad to have a job, any job, so I worked very hard. One day soon after I started, a lady came up to the ninth floor, where I worked. I don't recall her name, but I can still smell her perfume—it was enchanting. She asked, "Which one of you is Sydney?" and when I replied that I was, she said, "Well, you are a very good boy. The merchandise in this lot and the bill of lading are exactly in accordance." I didn't understand until she explained that this had never happened before, that there was usually something missing or the count was off. And that, of course, was because the other stockboys, underpaid and nearly starving like myself, often stole things. This was why we were searched occasionally. The only thing I had ever stolen was a pair of socks. I knew it wasn't right, but there were holes in my shoes and my socks were completely worn through.

The perfumed lady was a buyer, and from that day on she would always ask for me to unpack her merchandise when it arrived. It was a simple job, but I nevertheless took pride in doing my duties, no matter how insignificant.

I rode the subway back and forth to work from the Bronx. I hated that neighborhood—it was a cockroach-infested alley full of laundry-festooned fire escapes, with legions of diapers fluttering in the breezes that pushed through the narrow passageways between buildings. It was a lonely time for me: I could find no one to socialize with either at work or at home. My life was brightened only by the letters I received regularly from my loving family.

About six months after arriving in New York, I received a letter and a package from my sister Olga. The letter read:

"My dearest Sydney, you may not have thought you were very clever, but apparently the Beaux Arts Committee thought otherwise. Congratulations!"

I opened the package and was stunned: The expressionistic portrait I had made during my brief tenure in art school had won a silver medal! Tears of joy filled my eyes at the sight of it. This was perhaps my first realization that I had artistic talent, that by standing apart from the crowd I had distinguished myself as an individual. I fell asleep clutching the silver medal, and awoke the next morning with it still in my hand. Though 75 years have passed since then, I still have this medal and consider it one of my proudest achievements.

That night was a turning point. My self-confidence grew, and it showed in my work. As the Gimbel's buyers took note of my ability to follow through, I began to feel that I was already a success in life. Though I was not yet fifteen, I was learning the importance of working hard and of feeling good about whatever work I did, no matter how humble.

I might have worked my way up from the stockroom and into the buying department and perhaps gone on to top management at Gimbel's, but fate had other plans. One day, I was attempting to wrestle a heavy crate down from a high shelf. The crate fell and a metal band on the box broke loose. The jagged metal went through my shirt and sliced the flesh of my elbow almost to the bone. Bleeding profusely, I was taken to a nurse who stanched the bleeding and sewed me up. In those days there was no such thing as workmen's compensation or unemployment insurance. My wound needed time to heal, but there were plenty of boys eager for my job, so when the bosses at Gimbel's found I couldn't work, they let me go.

Without any income, my meager savings evaporated in a few days. By the time I was strong enough to look for another position, I was so broke that I couldn't afford even a two-cent newspaper. Each day I dug through trash cans to find one so I could read the classified ads, but no jobs turned up. Less than a year after I came to New York, I went back to sleeping in Central Park. That was against the law, but the beat cop looked the other way until the early morning hours, when he gently tapped me on the shoulder and said, "Sit up, son. Time to wake up." I knew that if I ever hoped to find work, it was important to stay as clean as possible, and I sometimes went to the YMCA to clean up. Fortunately, I didn't yet have to shave.

Were it not for my aunt Selina in Englewood, New Jersey, I might have starved to death. I got over to see her a couple of times on weekends, riding the ferry across the Hudson River to Hoboken, then catching a beat-up old tram called the Toonerville Trolley, and walking the rest of the way to her house. She must have known how hungry I was, because she always put out enough food for an army. After I'd gobbled down third helpings and was almost ready to explode, she'd ask, "Would you like some more?" When I said I was full, she'd ask, "Don't you like my cooking?" Later, I'd fall asleep. But even when I was too broke to ride the trolley, I never felt that I could ask my aunt for money. And although there were days when I went hungry, I never thought of going back home to Montreal. I was a dreamer and an idealist, and I knew I would make it.

Just after my fifteenth birthday, I saw an ad in the newspaper: *"Boy wanted for a beauty salon, the Hotel McAlpin, to clean up and help customers."* My arm was still in a sling when I interviewed for the job, and they hired me anyway. I was chosen for my quiet demeanor, even though I couldn't work to my full capacity until the sling was off. The McAlpin was respectable and its clients dressed well; everyone of substance did back then. In the summer, people donned hats and gloves, and ladies matched their handbags to their shoes.

As was my nature, I did more than was expected of me at the salon. I greeted each client warmly, took her coat and hung it neatly, then helped her on with it again when she was ready to depart. After about five months, the salon owner took me aside to say that although I was a very nice boy, I would never get anywhere if I didn't learn a trade. When I explained that I was too tired to go to school after working all day, he surprised me by offering to teach me his own craft: hairdressing.

Eager to learn, I started my training. The ladies working in the salon showed me how to give shampoos and oil treatments, and how to use vinegar and lemon rinses to untangle bleached blond hair. I was grateful for this apprenticeship as well as the raise in pay my new position brought me: fifteen dollars a week plus a fifteen-cent tip from most customers. In time, I was taught techniques for working with all types of hair, such as water-waving with my fingers and curling with an iron. This was around the time when permanent-wave solutions and dyes were being developed and introduced, so I learned how to dye hair. I also learned how to make wigs and how to ventilate the wig hair into the netting that fitted on the scalp. There was an artistry to all of it that intrigued me and challenged my curiosity. I soon found myself venturing beyond the basics to invent styles and colors that were far ahead of their time. It didn't occur to me then that this trade would become my fame and fortune.

One day an attractive young lady of no more than eighteen walked into the salon and was assigned to me. Her hair was cut in what was then called a Buster Brown style, curled under around her neck, and she said she wanted something different because the cut looked like so many other women's hair. I took a chance. Separating her hair into sections, I decided to shorten it drastically, and she loved the look. I cautioned her that the back would need to be shortened to match the front in what came to be known as a shingle. She nodded her assent.

This distinctive young woman was so elated with her new look that she summoned the manager and complimented me on my work. The cut cost $1.50—quite expensive for those days. She offered me a generous tip, but I was embarrassed and refused it. My reward was simply that she was able to walk out of the salon with a haircut unlike that of any other woman. A few months later, when I was at the movies, I was startled to see the same young woman on the screen: She was Louise Brooks! A silent-screen film star was wearing *my* haircut! I practically floated out of the theater.

My sixteen-year-old mind could not have imagined that this single event would eventually cause the *New York Times* to credit me with "starting the whole short-hair business." Nor could I possibly have dreamed that women in the 1930s would be running to their hairdressers in search of the same style. It was totally inconceivable to me that I would soon be trimming the tresses of Norma Shearer and Claudette Colbert, and that my career would become inextricably entwined with those of Greta Garbo, Cary Grant, Joan Crawford and Clark Gable, or that I would play an important role in the lives of stars still to be discovered: Katharine Hepburn, Judy Garland, Elizabeth Taylor, Lana Turner, Ava Gardner, Hedy Lamarr, Lucille Ball and Marilyn Monroe. Destiny would make each of these men and women living legends, icons to the entire world—and my closest friends.

CHAPTER FOUR

Antoine's

a few months after I began working at the McAlpin, I heard from a friend who had grown up on my street in Montreal. Joe Bambiger, a tall, handsome fellow a few years older than me, worked for the Victor Record Company in Montreal, but hoping that there might be more opportunities in the United States, he had come down to New York and had quickly landed a job. It paid fairly well, but Joe's fiancée was waiting back in Montreal, and he needed to save money. When he suggested that we share a small apartment in Manhattan, I eagerly accepted, not only to save money but also because I loathed the Bronx and, without any friends, I was desperately lonely.

We roomed together for several months, and Joe became a sort of big brother to me. We palled around, riding the subway to the beach at Coney Island, buying cheap, nosebleed-section seats to hear the world's greatest voices at the Metropolitan Opera House, double-dating now and then but mostly just working and hanging out together until he decided to go back home to Montreal.

Meanwhile, I continued to work at the McAlpin, where my clientele was slowly growing. At first I got just the overflow, women who came in without an appointment at a time when all our other hairdressers were busy. But after a while, certain customers began asking for me by name. I was still embarrassed each time one of these women insisted on giving me a tip. I needed the money, though, so I couldn't refuse them all. I asked my employer for a raise, but he said the shop couldn't afford it and that I was earning enough in tips. After that, as more and more ladies began to request my services, I felt his growing jealousy toward me.

On a summer morning in 1925, I left work to run an errand. I walked two blocks north from the McAlpin to a shop on 42nd Street to pick up my scissors, which I had left to be sharpened. Feeling a bit ill when I came out of the store, I started to cough and couldn't stop for several minutes. I was so weak that I had to sit down on the curb to rest. I coughed again, and when I put my handkerchief to my mouth, it came away bloody. A young man passing by stopped to offer help. When he saw the blood, he insisted that I go to the hospital. He was very kind and inquired if I had any money on me, offering to give me some if I didn't.

At the hospital they ran some tests. I had contracted tuberculosis. Because I had been undernourished for months, my body's defenses were down, and the disease had quickly gained a foothold. I called my boss to say that I was ill and would need a few days to rest before I could return to work. He abruptly told me that I no longer had a job.

In those days there were no medications that could cure tuberculosis. My only hope was to go someplace where, with proper rest and diet, I might recover on my own. The odds were not in my favor, however. Because I couldn't afford a private hospital in New York, I returned to Montreal and found refuge at Sainte Agathe des Monts, where there was a tubercular sanitarium. It was about 55 miles from my parents' home in Montreal, close enough for them to visit occasionally.

There was little to do except rest, try to build up my strength and hope to recover. The hospital was a depressing place. Every week my roommate, a very nice fellow who could barely muster the strength to get out of bed, looked a little worse. One day, as I stood before the mirror in my pajamas and robe to comb my hair, he said, "You know, you're a good-looking kid." I gave him the expected reply, "Thank you," but when I turned to look at him he had passed away.

After that I couldn't bear to stay in the room. Nor could I bear the thought of getting to know another roommate. I asked for a private room, but the authorities refused: They had far too many patients and too few rooms. Instead I asked if it would be possible to move my bed outside onto the balcony, and they agreed. When winter came, I often awoke in the morning to find several inches of snow covering my blankets. It was freezing outside, of course, but gradually I became somewhat accustomed to the cold. I never came inside except for meals and to exercise in the corridors.

Months dragged by. Finally, one summer day, I wandered off from the hospital. Some orderlies came looking for me, and when they brought me back I told my doctors that if I stayed there any longer, I felt I would lose my mind. I was discharged, feeling much stronger but still not quite cured. I returned to my parents' home in Montreal, but I became so unhappy that my mother and father loaned me the money to return to New York.

The fumes and congestion in Manhattan were too much for me in my condition, however, and I answered an ad for a hairdressing job in Greenwich, Connecticut. Greenwich was considered a bedroom community for the wealthy—mainly people who shopped or worked in New York. I turned up for my employment interview wearing a jacket, gloves and matching spats—the accepted fashion of the day—and was hired on the spot. The job paid $20 a week and was pleasant enough, but I was required to wear a white smock and to work in the front of the shop. Very few young American men worked as hairdressers in that era, and the young girls from a nearby school often paused at the window to stare and giggle. That irritated me, and I asked my boss to move me to the rear of the shop. One day not long after that, the manager escorted to my chair a lady by the name of Mrs. Highland. A striking woman about 35 years old, she was impressed with my work and told me I ought to be working in a famous hair salon called Antoine's at Saks Fifth Avenue.

I was incredulous: Antoine's was the most highly regarded beauty salon in New York City. "But that's where you belong," insisted Mrs. Highland. As it happened, she was friendly with Monsieur De Clairville, who managed Saks' entire third floor, which included both the salon and a couturier showroom where wealthy customers could view the latest Parisian fashions. Within about a week, Mrs. Highland had made arrangements for me to be interviewed at the salon.

After a brief conversation, De Clairville asked the salon manager, Miss Crowley, to see what talent I had, and she asked me to style the hair of one of the manicurists. Since I had no idea what sort of special cuts or perms Antoine's clients expected, I just looked carefully at the young woman's hair and face and gave her the best cut I could— exactly what I would have done to any lady who had entrusted me with creating a new look for her. Miss Crowley was very excited by the hairstyle and by the techniques I had used to achieve it. She called De Clairville in to look, and he remarked, "My goodness, he really is an artist, isn't he?" I felt my face blush when he asked, "When would you like to begin, Mr. Guilaroff?" He offered me $50 a week to start. I was dazzled. It seemed like a fortune. Never had I imagined that I would earn that much.

At Antoine's, wealthy, elegant women, including New York's 400 social set, were coiffed and pampered amid the opulence of crystal chandeliers and walls of mirrors. Fabulous French perfume wafted gently through the air, and their tresses were treated with exclusive lotions and shampoos shipped in from Paris. Sixty European hairdressers, each in an impeccably tailored smock, stood erect before their chairs. Each of them was addressed by his first name, preceded by "Mr." Miss Crowley suggested I adopt a more foreign-sounding name, preferably something French, or perhaps Italian or Spanish. I politely refused and was thereafter known on the premises as Mr. Sydney. As a London-born Canadian, I was as foreign as any Frenchman, but many of the wealthy who came to Antoine's didn't see it that way. A few even refused to let me work on their hair because it seemed to them that if I didn't have a foreign-sounding name, then I couldn't be a very talented hairdresser. I was just seventeen and this hurt my feelings, of course, but I never allowed it to show.

In time I began to acquire a following. One of my first weekly customers was Mrs. Claire Watts. She was quite attractive, a clever, bright and spiritual woman with a lovely way of speaking and wonderful manners. We soon became friends, and she introduced me to her husband and invited me to her home. She, too, wanted to tip me, but I always refused. I was by then making a good living and found tipping an embarrassment. I quietly explained to

Mrs. Watts why I didn't want to be tipped and began telling the same thing to the rest of my customers.

After I'd been at the salon about four months, Antoine himself finally returned from Paris for a visit. He had other salons in world capitals and traveled extensively, and he was paid a royalty by Saks for the use of his name on their salon. There was something a little peculiar about Monsieur Antoine, but I was still quite young and didn't understand at first. As soon as we were introduced, Antoine began to show an unusual interest in me. Whenever he had an especially wealthy client, he called me in to a private booth to watch him work. Then one night he sent word that he wanted to take me to dinner. Mr. White, a tall, skinny Englishman and fellow employee, said, "He's after you, Sydney."

"What do you mean?" I asked innocently.

"Well, he likes men; he doesn't like women."

"Well, I like men, too," I said. Then it struck me. "Do you mean sexually?"

White nodded.

I'm sure I blushed. "Well, it won't happen," I said.

That night, when Antoine himself asked me to go to dinner, I turned him down. He got quite angry with me, and I was offended. The next day I had a word about it with Miss Crowley, and she was quite sympathetic. But I wasn't willing to let things end there. I demanded to speak to Adam Gimbel, who owned not only the department store that bore his name but Saks as well. I called his secretary to make an appointment, and to my surprise he agreed to see me. There were several other items that I wanted to discuss with him: I felt that having to use the employee entrance, where I was required to punch a time clock on my way in and out of the store, was demeaning for a person of my profession, and while everyone else seemed willing to conform to this, it truly bothered me.

Another thing that I disliked intensely was having to wear a smock while cutting hair. I felt it wasn't the way I wanted to present myself to a client.

After I arrived at Gimbel's office, I began by telling him about Antoine, and he assured me that it wouldn't happen again. He said that he would have a word with Antoine and that Antoine was not my employer and had no authority over me. Relieved, I shared my experience of a few years earlier, when I was injured while working in the Gimbel's stockroom and was later fired without compensation. I told him about sleeping on a park bench and about catching tuberculosis and about the life of hardship I had endured because of losing my job. I asked that my spot in the salon be changed: I wanted to be at the very front of the shop, the first hairdresser each customer saw as she approached the appointment booth. Finally, I told him I refused to accept tips, and that instead of that sort of embarrassment, I wanted a raise in salary—$100 a week, double what I'd been getting. Mr. Adam Gimbel looked at me for a long moment. Then he smiled and agreed to give me everything I had asked for.

CHAPTER FIVE

Claudette Colbert and the Two Mrs. Fairbanks

At Antoine's, I began to cultivate a loyal following of customers that included old-line New York bluebloods as well as the nouveaux riches of the Roaring '20s. In time, a few of the other hairdressers became openly envious of my success, but I never allowed that to bother me.

There was one arena in which I didn't compete with my associates, however. New York in those days had quite a lively film business, most of it based on Long Island in and around the town of Astoria, where there were several busy studios. And the stars of this new industry, perhaps out of snobbery, seemed to prefer hairdressers with a European cachet.

Fate must have a sense of humor, though. Early one morning in 1928, Antoine himself rushed off to the Paramount lot to style the hair of Claudette Colbert. She had been cast opposite Maurice Chevalier in *The Smiling Lieutenant*, the charming French star's second film with Colbert. At Paramount, then the infant industry's leading studio, Claudette had already been marked for movie stardom, and after this role it would be clear to everyone that she was going to be a great star. But for some reason, Antoine's efforts didn't suit her, and she telephoned the salon the next morning, distressed. "I'm starting a movie, and I'm not pleased with Antoine's work," she told the receptionist, my friend Babs Bernachi.

Babs said, "We have a very talented American hairdresser here, Mr. Sydney. Would you like to make an appointment and come to the salon?" (I am, of course, Canadian, but perhaps to Babs the same side of the Atlantic was close enough.)

"Well," replied Claudette, "I'll take a chance."

I was quite excited; Claudette was already famous in New York for her stage work. I'd seen her on Broadway in *The Kiss in the Taxi*, and I knew she was a friend of a rising young composer named Johnny Green.

When she arrived early the next morning—wearing a full-length fur, tailored afternoon suit and matching leather gloves, bag and shoes—every eye in the salon was instantly riveted on her. And when she asked for Mr. Sydney, a number of my colleagues' jaws dropped in amazement. Rather than take my usual chair, she asked for the privacy of a booth, and I happily led her to one. She explained the plot of *The Smiling Lieutenant*. It was a romantic comedy, a ménage à trois co-starring Charlie Ruggles as the "other man." "I'd like something different," she told me. "I'm in your hands."

After carefully observing her from all angles, and noting that she had a somewhat low hairline, I said: "I'm thinking of a rather short cut, with bangs as the central focus."

"You know, I think you're right," she agreed. "That seems very modern. I'd like to try it."

I first styled the bangs, cutting her hair quite short. As

I worked, Claudette regarded me as though she was seeing me for the first time. "You have very beautiful hands," she said, and in my youthful embarrassment I turned deep crimson—I never have gotten accustomed to compliments. I pressed on with my work, and when I had achieved the look I was after, I used the curling iron to set it. Then I handed Claudette a mirror.

"Mr. Sydney!" she cried. "It's wonderful! I love it."

With that, I found myself catapulted into the movie industry: My creation became the hairstyle that Claudette would wear in all but one of her future films, and her "new look" was big news from coast to coast. Celebrity columnist Louella Parsons told her radio audience about it, and so did Walter Winchell. From Paramount's palm-draped Hollywood studio, publicists primed gossip columnists with reports of "Claudette's sensational bangs, which added a racy touch to the saucy star of *The Smiling Lieutenant*." While the wizardry of "Paramount beauticians" was officially credited for the hairstyle, most of Hollywood heard about "Guilaroff, the man with the golden shears," as Louella described me. When women saw Claudette on screen, many clamored for the same effect, and bangs were soon a nationwide trend.

Claudette, who became a close friend, enthusiastically spread word of my talent. She told her friends, and they told theirs; soon I was picking up a considerable amount of stage work. Gilbert Miller, then one of New York's leading producers, sent all his leading ladies to me. Among my better-known theatrical clients were Libby Holman and a beautiful, leggy blonde who danced on the stage of the Paramount Theater. Her name was Ginger Rogers, and in no time, it seemed, she was in Hollywood. To keep up with my sudden popularity, I came to the salon early and remained there, working hard until well after Saks closed its doors for the evening. For the next few years, my life was my work, a creative but lonely and exhausting existence that even now I find difficult to look back on.

My proverbial big break came in 1931. The wheels were set in motion when one of my regular customers, Beth Sulley Fairbanks, mother of Douglas Fairbanks Jr., wrote to her daughter-in-law in California to sing my praises. That daughter-in-law was Joan Crawford, and 1931 was to be the year she became a major star.

Joan was then making nearly a quarter of a million dollars a year at Metro-Goldwyn-Mayer and was well aware of her box-office appeal. She was a star, and she knew it, playing that part to the hilt offscreen as well as on. She never appeared in public in anything but her finest attire, and young women around the country imitated the way she dressed. Joan's wardrobe was designed by one of the world's leading couturiers, Adrian. When their artistic relationship began in 1929, he discarded the frills of the flapper period—emblematic of the "It" girl, Clara Bow, who had thrilled and inspired the youthful generation of the Roaring '20s—and cultivated for Joan a new sleek, tailored, sophisticated look. Padded shoulders and slinky, tight-fitting evening gowns and day dresses became Joan's trademark. More understated and self-possessed than Bow, Crawford defined glamour in both her professional and private lives.

It was during this period that Joan was showcased with Clark Gable in *Dance Fools Dance*, and their incandescent on-screen chemistry soon led to private trysts during location shooting in Northern California. As Joan admitted many years later, she proposed to Gable, saying, "Let's both get divorces right now." Joan was still married to Fairbanks, Hollywood's crown prince, and Gable's bride of a year was Rhea Langham, a wealthy Texas socialite seventeen years his senior. When Louis B. Mayer, head of MGM, learned of the affair, he moved quickly to end it, reputedly spreading $25,000 around the Hollywood press corps to hush reports of this scandalous romance.

Mayer also leaned hard on both stars. A terse studio memo informed Crawford that her next big film, *Letty Lynton*, which had been specifically written for her and Gable, would now co-star instead the happily married Robert Montgomery. To make things unmistakably clear, Mayer summoned Crawford to his office and ordered her to accompany her husband on an extended European tour—as he phrased it, "an extended and well-publicized second honeymoon." Gable, whose career was obviously his pre-eminent concern, backed off after the first gruff warning from the studio. But to make sure he stayed out of trouble, he was assigned to work on five films back to back, without a break.

No matter how much money the studio spent protecting its image, of course, there was no way to silence everyone. And it was just as rumors about her relationship with Gable began leaking out that Joan—a versatile singer and dancer as well as an accomplished actress and comedienne—was booked to attend a screening of her film *Possessed* at New York's Capitol Theater.

Beth Fairbanks immediately mailed a note to Crawford: "I know you'll be needing your hair done in Manhattan, and I have just the man for you: Sydney Guilaroff, who's considered the best stylist in New York City."

Joan telephoned Beth immediately: "Book me with Mr. Sydney at his first available time."

Although my clients at Antoine's by then included many stars, creating a new look for Joan proved to be the turning point in my career. The day she arrived at Antoine's, it seemed as if the whole world knew she was coming. Hordes of star-watchers gathered on Fifth Avenue, and when her limousine pulled up to the curb, she and her husband emerged to a crowd that parted before them like the Red Sea, murmuring and exclaiming in admiration at her beauty.

The crowd poured into Saks, filled all six elevators and followed their quarry upward. At the third floor, an MGM representative tried to protect the couple from being swamped by their onlookers, but as Joan walked to the appointment desk, they followed her step for step. She announced to the receptionist, "Hello, I'm Joan Crawford. I have an appointment with Mr. Sydney." As if the girl didn't know! I came out front to greet her. She looked stunning in a black silk suit and hat, high-heeled shoes and black silk stockings. Under her jacket was a white blouse trimmed in stand-up lace at the collar and cuffs, with a black ribbon laced through the eyelets and tied into a small bow at her neck. No less dazzling himself, Douglas wore a long camel-hair coat tied at the waist and a turned-down felt hat, which he gallantly removed before politely addressing the receptionist.

After I shook hands with Joan, she peered around and asked, "Oh, is your entire salon open like this?"

"No, Miss Crawford," I replied. "Come with me, please, and I'll show you to a private booth."

Every hairdresser and client in the salon watched spellbound as the glamorous Crawford and the suave, handsome Douglas strolled arm in arm through the salon. It was, of course, partly an act. I know that they truly cared for each other, but their marriage had become a highly prized commodity to the studio's publicity machine, and this little performance was calculated to allay any misgivings the public might have had about her rumored affair with Gable.

As we entered the booth, Douglas asked, "How long do you think this will take, Mr. Sydney?" When I estimated that it would be no more than an hour-and-a-half, he said that he had some things to attend to and would return. Then they kissed each other as though they expected to be apart for years, and he left the salon.

Alone with Joan, we chatted for a few minutes about her mother-in-law, and she smiled when I mentioned that Beth had told me all about her. As I always did with first-time clients, I asked Joan if there was any particular way she liked to wear her hair. She responded, "Please do whatever you think would be becoming on me. You have a wonderful reputation, and I would like to know how you think I should look."

Her hair seemed about the right length for what I had in mind. As I worked, she was conversational and extremely polite, replying to my queries with either "yes" or "no" and always adding "thank you." I would learn that this was not an affectation, that it was her natural manner. She spoke with affection of her life in California, of her lovely Brentwood home. As the time flew by, we grew a bit chummy. She confided that her stepmother-in-law, Mary Pickford—she and Douglas Sr. had long been considered Hollywood's royal couple—had frowned on her marriage to Douglas Jr. because Joan was a commoner, little more than a chorus girl at the time.

When her lovely dark brunette hair was dry, I removed the pins and started to brush out the curls. I parted her hair on the left and made a single wave on that side, then brushed it back behind her ear to fall in soft, flowing waves. The right side I brushed into a similar single wave, leaving the top of her head sleek and smooth. When I finished arranging it, she exclaimed, "Oh! I love it! Thank you, Mr. Sydney. I never looked like this before."

At that moment Douglas returned, and Joan asked him, "Don't I look wonderful! Isn't this a beautiful hairdo?" He nodded agreeably, then kissed her. She said to me, "Would you have time for me tomorrow? I would like to have this photographed and have a cameraman and publicity man in as well. I want to look like this for my new film, *Letty Lynton*." She then described the character she was about to play in the movie and said she wanted me to style her hair for it.

"It would be a great pleasure, Miss Crawford," I replied. "Come in whenever you like. I'm sure everybody would love to see you again."

Before she left, she invited me to join her and Douglas at that evening's screening of *Possessed*. As I walked her out, some of the crowd overheard her saying, "Mr. Sydney said he could fit me in tomorrow, if you please." Small wonder that an even bigger crowd was on hand the next day to watch Joan sweep in.

That night, as Joan and Douglas sat in their private box above the Capitol Theater's mezzanine, I was sitting beside them, thrilled. I knew that thousands of Joan's fans were outside waiting hours for the merest glimpse of her, and here I was in the seat next to her, watching her on-screen in *Possessed* and fully enjoying that wonderful moment. It also occurred to me that this wouldn't hurt my career. But despite this exciting introduction to Hollywood and the movie business, my career goals remained fixed on New York. And while I knew that I might not remain at Antoine's forever, I could hardly have predicted the circumstances that led to my departure.

It began innocently enough in 1931, in a conversation with Mrs. Odlum, one of my regular customers. She was attractive enough, but not really a beauty, and although she was married to one of the wealthiest men in the city, no one would have suspected this from the way Mrs. Odlum conducted herself: She was very down to earth, very approachable, very sweet and charming. I liked her immensely.

I was working on her hair while she was having her nails done. We chatted about her husband, and she confided that he had been working so hard lately that he was exhausted. He had decided, she said, to go on a cruise, and to ensure that he got his rest, he was going alone. Mrs. Odlum was the last customer of the day, and by the time we were finished, only she, Jackie Cochran, the manicurist, and myself remained in the shop. I escorted her to the freight elevator and told the operator to take good care of her and make sure she got safely to her car if her chauffeur wasn't waiting at the door.

When I returned to the salon, I found Jackie on the telephone at the appointment desk. This was unusual, and it was against the rules: Employees were required to use the pay phone. I reminded her of this, and she was rather sharp with me. "I don't care," she snapped. "I'll do as I please."

To my astonishment, Jackie was talking to somebody at the Bermuda Furnace Line, getting dates and sailing information about the very cruise that Mrs. Odlum's husband was taking. When she booked passage for herself on the same ship, I understood. I said, "I know what you're up to. You're going to go after her husband! You're very wicked to take advantage of a lovely woman like Mrs. Odlum!"

"It's none of your goddamn business," retorted Jackie.

"It *is* my business, and I don't like it," I said firmly.

Frankly, I didn't think she stood a chance. Jackie Cochran was a very ordinary-looking girl. But ten days later, after quitting her job, she was on that ship with Mr. Odlum—and somehow she captivated the man. Three or four weeks later, when they returned to New York, he announced that he was divorcing his wife to marry Jackie.

It cost the man a fortune, not only a bundle of money but his department store, Bonwit Teller, as well. After the divorce, the former Mrs. Odlum offered me a healthy raise in salary to leave Antoine's and take charge of Bonwit's salon. I took her up on it and brought my entire clientele along with me. When the story got around, a lovely and witty young woman named Clare Boothe Luce wrote a play about it, *The Women*, that established her as a Broadway playwright.

In short order, my salon became as famous as Antoine's had been. Among the ladies who followed me from Saks was Joan Crawford. For the next three years, before she made each new picture, she came first to New York for me to style her hair. Each time she went through the same procedure, with a still photographer and a cameraman capturing my creation on film for the studio's hairdressers to replicate.

Meanwhile, Louis B. Mayer, MGM's paternalistic studio chief, was becoming progressively annoyed with Joan. Such was his desire for control that he felt the need to know where his "children" were at all times. When Joan was about to leave once more for New York to have me style her for yet another film, Mayer demanded to know why. "I need to get my hair styled for my next role," she replied.

"What's wrong with the hairdressers here?" fumed Mayer. "Can't anyone here please you? We've got enough of them."

"There's no one quite like this man in New York. He is young and very creative, and you have no one here with his kind of talent. I just tell him the story of the film, and he knows exactly what to do."

"If he's that good, then we'll bring him here," growled Mayer, unwilling to give up a shred of control over his studio and everyone in it.

He was a man of his word. After reviewing still photos of Joan's hairstyles and comparing them to the lackluster coiffures worn by Norma Shearer in *Riptide* and *The Barretts of Wimpole Street*, by Myrna Loy in *Manhattan Melodrama* and by Jean Harlow in *Red Dust* and *Hold Your Man*, Mayer promptly told the studio boss, J. Robert Rubin, "Hire this man Guilaroff. Make him head of the hairdressing department."

So it was that in the autumn of 1934, I stepped aboard the Sunset Limited for the long journey to Los Angeles and the fabled studio called Metro-Goldwyn-Mayer. My entire life was about to change, but as I looked forward to Hollywood, I was just old enough to know that if a man's star could rise virtually overnight, it could fall with equal swiftness.

CHAPTER SIX

Metro

a studio limo with uniformed chauffeur was waiting for me at the curb outside Union Station in Los Angeles when I arrived for my new job at MGM. As we headed for the studio, I left the windows down to take in the summery sunshine of late November. At that moment I knew Manhattan pedestrians were holding umbrellas overhead, feeble protection from the sleet that was cascading down from an angry sky. But here, a warm wind carried the sweet scent of ripening oranges. The streets were lined with houses set back from generous green lawns, most of them adorned with colorful bird-of-paradise, gardenias, hibiscus and other lush blossoms. Torrents of red and fuchsia bougainvillea turned fences and walls into a glorious riot of color.

As I approached MGM's gilded gates, I caught glimpses of the studio's splendid backlot: Tarzan's jungle with waterfalls and banyan trees; a plaster-and-stone replica of old

Verona complete with cobblestones and exotic vines; and a replica of the Mississippi River that doubled as a Scottish loch or, with an appropriate change in backdrop, the Danube, the Dnieper or the Don.

Inside the gates was an entirely different world. On Soundstage One, Jean Harlow and Patsy Kelly were filming *The Girl From Missouri,* Robert Montgomery was wading through manufactured fog in *The Mystery of Mr. X,* and Hal Roach—one of a group of gifted producers contracted exclusively to MGM—was directing Laurel and Hardy amid oversize child's playthings for *Babes in Toyland.* MGM's empire, sprawling across five square miles, included seven enormous soundstages, a dozen office buildings and a glass-domed nursery featuring an astonishing array of flora: every sort of flower, shrub, bush and tree, from Louisiana bayou orchids to towering Ceylon rubber trees, each in its own pot so it could be easily whisked off to any section of the lot. Far in the back, trained leopards, chimpanzees, elephants and other four-legged actors shared a posh zoo with the studio's living symbol, Leo the Lion.

My destination was not this fairyland but the more businesslike executive office building, a vast complex overlooking the main studio entrance. There I reported to the dour Jack Dawn, head of the makeup department—he also supervised the hairstylists—a man with a thoroughly disagreeable disposition but a fine touch for cosmetology.

No one had bothered to tell me, but the studio was in the midst of an executive civil war. The source of this conflict was the rivalry between Louis B. Mayer and his one-time production chief, Irving Thalberg. Mayer was the money man, Thalberg the creative genius; together they had led MGM to the pinnacle of the industry. Paramount had more theaters around the country in which to show its films, but MGM's box-office grosses were unrivaled, and it had assembled a glittering galaxy of talent.

The brilliant Thalberg had been responsible for an unequaled string of artistic and commercial hits that included *The Divorcee*, *Dinner at Eight*, and *Anna Christie*. Though he personally oversaw every detail of his own productions, the self-effacing Thalberg never took on-screen credit for his work. Gentle and quietly authoritative—unlike many studio executives far less gifted and powerful—he was never overbearing or egotistical, and always took the time to confer creatively not only with his stars and his directors but also with the artists who worked under them, most certainly including myself. His only noticeable weakness was a not-unusual form of nepotism: He showered favoritism on his wife, the patrician Norma Shearer, who three years earlier had won an Oscar for her performance in *The Divorcee*. And Thalberg had chosen her to star in what would be the industry's most expensive film up to that time, *Marie Antoinette*.

As production chief, Thalberg wielded absolute power over each film. But he incurred Mayer's wrath with his predilection for overspending. Tinkering endlessly with each film, rewriting scripts, reshooting scenes, re-editing footage until he was completely satisfied with the product, Thalberg whittled away profits and unsettled the business people at Loews, Inc., the New York–headquartered theatrical company that owned MGM and to whom Mayer answered. When Mayer, who had brought Thalberg over from Universal back in 1923, attempted to curb these tendencies, he found that his protégé no longer took orders from him or anyone else.

But Thalberg had been born with a weak heart, and when he was felled by a heart attack at MGM's 1932 Christmas party, Mayer made his move. He sent Thalberg on a long European trip "to recuperate" and, in his absence, divided the production department under four sub-chiefs. When Thalberg returned in early 1934, he discovered that he was now merely one of five MGM producers.

Knowing nothing of all this, I was flattered when the great Thalberg himself took me on a grand tour of the studio, introducing me to various department heads along the way. He also offered some cautionary advice: "They are going to ask you to join the Makeup and Hair Stylists Guild, but ignore them. When we make you head of the new hairstyling team, union membership could stifle your creativity."

What he meant, as I would soon discover, was that if I was bound by the work rules negotiated between the studio and the union, I would be unable to work when and as I preferred. Worse, I'd be drawn inevitably into disputes in which the union would expect me to back even the most inept or lazy hairstylist as long as he or she belonged to the guild. Just days later, as Thalberg had predicted, Jack Dawn demanded that I join the union.

"I've been advised not to," I replied.

"Well, you won't work on this lot until you do," he warned. "You'll never set one curl." Then he showed me to an empty office and turned his back to me. As the weeks went by, I found myself in limbo. My paychecks arrived punctually, but I was not allowed to work.

At last, Joan Crawford began preparing for her next film, a glossy soap opera titled *Forsaking All Others*. She expected me to create her hairstyles, and when she learned about my situation, she stormed into Thalberg's office. "I brought him out here," she said, livid, "and I plan to use him. You'll have to work something out."

Thalberg's solution was to have me work in secret. Each morning, long before most of the other artisans reported, I slipped quietly into Crawford's dressing room and arranged her hair in one of the ten styles I used for the film. They ranged from sleek afternoon looks to dazzling evening coiffures. Because I had broken away from the finger curls and outdated flapper shags that many studio stylists still concocted, my contributions could hardly have gone unnoticed, but nothing was said. In fact, one of the styles I created for Joan, which clung to her head, then fanned out in the back, swept the nation as soon as *Forsaking All Others* was shown.

Norma Shearer was the first to comment publicly that Joan was getting special treatment. "If he can do it for Crawford, he can do it for me," she told her husband. Norma was scheduled to star in a series of pictures that demanded complicated costumes: *The Barretts of Wimpole Street*, *Romeo and Juliet* and the most epic of all, *Marie Antoinette*.

Before my arrival at MGM, Norma had made close to 30 films and was billed officially as "the First Lady of the Screen." Even with Thalberg's diminished power, she retained both her box-office status—number seven—and her choice of roles. Planning *Romeo and Juliet* as Norma's greatest showcase, Thalberg inflated the film's budget to $2.1 million. Still working in ostensible secrecy, I designed more than 20 coiffures for her turn as Shakespeare's greatest heroine. Each was based on my personal research into Renaissance hairstyles. Norma was 35, but the Bard's classic described the romance of two teenagers, so I worked to make her look as young as possible.

Still supposedly invisible to Jack Dawn and the union, I went on to create elaborate styles for Jeanette MacDonald in *The Merry Widow* and again for Joan in the costume film *The Gorgeous Hussy*. Then I began my study of French history in preparation for *Marie Antoinette*. I continued to slip from dressing room to dressing room, preparing original models that were photographed, then turned over to other hairdressers to copy. In reality, it was impossible to conceal such activities for long. Yet everyone, including

Dawn, turned a blind eye as I crafted most of MGM's star coiffures between 1934 and 1936.

The publicity department had already coined a phrase about MGM: "More stars than there are in the heavens," and nowhere were they more evident than in the Commissary, the studio's famous lunchroom. Clark Gable, Jean Harlow, Norma Shearer, Myrna Loy and all the rest, as well as flocks of famous writers, directors and producers, ate in this one room, along with legions of lesser-knowns. Even though I remained in official limbo, on occasion even I joined Joan there for a quick meal between takes on *Chained*.

The one star missing from the "restaurant roster" was the greatest of all: Greta Garbo. Just 29 but already a legend, she was MGM's biggest international box-office draw. She was equally notorious among her professional colleagues for seeming aloof and elusive. Despite her reign as the queen of MGM, her name was rarely mentioned on the lot. This was because she had quickly learned to detest publicity and was rarely seen out on the town. After reluctantly attending the wedding of Norma Shearer and Irving Thalberg, she said that would be her last public appearance, and for all intents and purposes, it was.

Even on the lot, Garbo was shrouded in absolute secrecy. Except for scenes that required her to interact with supporting players or extras, screens were placed around the set during shooting sessions. When it was time to film an intimate scene with Garbo alone or with a co-star, the set was cleared of everyone else except the cinematographer and the director. Many looked on this as temperament, but in truth it was only Garbo's intense shyness. Any outside interference, even the mere presence of others, completely shut down her ability to concentrate.

I would later learn firsthand that Garbo never felt like a star. Until her death in 1990, she remained a quite unwilling recipient of fame. She was amazed at her success and acted as if she had never really thought it through or even reflected on it at any length. I doubt that she ever fully grasped the immortality she had achieved. Instead of a blessing, her notoriety was a prison—but one that she herself had built.

Yet almost from the moment I first stepped onto the lot, I had felt Garbo's presence. I glimpsed her just once before we met formally. It was nothing more than a quick peek as she darted out of a dressing room to slip into her chauffeur-driven limousine, but to this day the scene burns in my memory because she paused for a moment to look at me. Never one to stare, I looked away and behaved as if she were merely another person walking by. My mind, however, was churning as I thought to myself, *That's the most classically beautiful woman I've ever seen.*

If Garbo's disposition lacked both envy or even inquisitiveness regarding her fellow stars, Joan Crawford was more than just a little curious about Garbo. So it happened that I became an unwitting accomplice to Joan's need for an excuse to chat with Garbo: When the two met by chance while strolling the lot, Joan seized the moment as an occasion to recommend my services to Garbo. "You simply must use Sydney," urged Joan. If Joan was your friend, she was your friend for life! Nevertheless, I was startled to learn sometime later that Garbo's response had been, "Yes, I have heard of this Mr. Guilaroff."

One day while I was in the makeup department, the receptionist called me to the telephone. The voice in my ear was low and husky: "Mr. Guilaroff, this is Miss Garbo speaking."

I thought it was a practical joke, that somebody was imitating her, so I said, "Yes, I know, and I'm John Gilbert."

But when she replied, "Mr. Guilaroff, you are very funny," I knew instantly that it was indeed Garbo. I apologized profusely. She laughed warmly, then asked if I could come up and talk to her about her upcoming picture, *Camille*. Although this period film would not be released until 1936, there were many details to be worked out, including, of course, its elaborate hair designs.

My heart was pounding as I hung up the phone. I had first seen Garbo on the screen in 1926 in *The Torrent*, a silent. It was plain to me even then that the camera worshiped her—and so did I. She was my favorite star, and I never dreamed that someday I would meet her and work with her, or that one day we would fall in love.

I rushed back to hair and makeup, where I had been chatting with Eleanor Powell and Jeanette MacDonald, and without saying where I was going, politely excused myself. At MGM, the female stars had separate dressing room suites. I went into the next building and up a flight of stairs to a door marked only with the letter G. I paused before knocking, so nervous and out of breath that I felt like I'd sprinted three laps around the entire studio. Finally, I summoned the courage to knock.

When the door opened, I beheld this radiant creature. Even without the camera's magical lens to enhance her looks, an aura of mystical loveliness enveloped her. To this day I blush to recall her first words to me: "Oh, you are quite beautiful, Mr. Guilaroff." This was an era when such a word was never applied to men. A man might be handsome or elegant or good-looking, but never beautiful. Her words took me by surprise. As I felt my face flushing, I stammered a reply. "Me? Beautiful? I think *you* are very beautiful."

"How charming," she said, and I took another look at her, equally astonished by her naturalness and the directness of her manner. I bent to kiss her cheek, the way one leans over to smell a rose, to catch its perfume. Accepting my kiss, she said, "Please come in. I need your help." I couldn't believe it. She was the ultimate star. What could someone like me do for her?

I was terribly taken with her extraordinary beauty: She was so different from anyone I had ever met. She looked sad even when she smiled, and this only added to the aura of mystery that surrounded her. I can think of only one way to express this most striking phenomenon: She looked as if she was sadly happy. When I said something amusing, her eyebrows knit together and she smiled, all the while looking infinitely vulnerable. It was her most touching quality.

Overcoming my own shyness, I soon got down to business. She described her upcoming role in *Camille* to give me an idea of the hairstyles she would need. *Camille* was a classic tragedy, among the most popular stories of all time. I had seen the two earlier versions myself, one of them with Alla Nazimova starring opposite Rudolph Valentino, the second with Norma Talmadge and Gilbert Roland. In this third screen version of the story, Garbo would play the title role, a courtesan dying of tuberculosis. George Cukor, the director, hoped that her compelling sadness would breathe new life into the role opposite Robert Taylor as *Camille*'s long-suffering beau.

We enjoyed a delightful discussion of Camille's hairstyles. I followed Garbo to her makeup table, where she took a seat before the mirror. As we continued talking, without warning and with no change of expression whatsoever, she removed her thin sweater, and suddenly she was nude from the waist up. Embarrassed and stunned, I stood behind her, facing the mirror, but unable even to look at my own reflection. I wonder now if she had bared herself to study my reaction, to see if I would be shocked or if I would accept her partial nudity as casually as she did. In any event, I said, "You know, I'm very uncomfortable this way, Miss Garbo. Would you mind putting something on, a dressing gown perhaps? I can't work like this."

She was very sweet. "It's all right," she replied, putting her sweater back on. We continued our conversation as if nothing out of the ordinary had happened.

Garbo was not, of course, the first unclad woman I had ever encountered. Although I have enjoyed many romantic relationships with women, my feelings about sex have always been that it is a beautiful but intensely personal and therefore extremely private act. I never tell dirty jokes or boast about my affairs, because that type of behavior serves only to degrade those who practice it. And so, while I respect and appreciate a beautiful woman for her loveliness, I do not become aroused merely by meeting her. Instead, I look beyond the physical. I enjoy more a woman's charm and the other qualities of her soul and intellect. Consequently, very few ladies have enchanted me, but the few who have done so have provided reason enough to maintain my standards and my self-respect.

This attitude was formed through my early romantic experiences with women. One evening at Antoine's, for example, just as the salon was closing, one of the Saks models invited herself to my apartment for the evening. This kind of frank invitation is all too common today, but in 1928 it was a bold move on a woman's part. In fact, few *men* of that era would have been so audacious. Yet I wasn't uncomfortable because in working together, we had established some rapport. We spent that night together, but in the morning I realized that it had been a mistake. Despite our intimacy, I could see that this young woman shared none of my passions or ideals. To be blunt, she was a beautiful but empty package; once you've removed the wrapping, there was little inside. We never spoke again.

The experience enlightened me, however. It made me aware that casual physical relationships are meaningless. If I was to enjoy the pleasures that lovemaking offered, I needed to bond with someone willing to share her soul and mind as well as her body. My thinking on this has never changed. It is not based on religion, and while it may seem quaint and old-fashioned, it is nevertheless the lifestyle I chose. In consequence, I have experienced intense intimacy in my romantic relationships over the years.

Being an individualist, of course, doesn't mean judging others with differing values. So when Garbo disrobed for me that day, I didn't discount her morals. Instead, I tried to convey that I had more respect for her than to stare in a manner that might have been seen as lustful. She was indisputably one of the most hauntingly beautiful and compelling women in the world, with a smoldering intensity far beneath the surface. From our brief first meeting I had already developed an admiration for her as a person, not merely as a screen icon. I wanted to make it clear that I had no intention of trying to take advantage of her.

Perhaps Garbo was merely testing me, trying to determine whether I was a homosexual. Or perhaps, having grown up in Sweden, she lacked the kind of inhibitions I had learned in my own Canadian childhood, when my parents insisted that everyone move about the house fully clothed at all times, even en route to the bathroom. Much has been written about Garbo, including flamboyant speculation about her sexuality. Some have even claimed that she had intimate relationships with both men and women. If she did so before we met in 1934, I will never know. What I can say with certainty is that from the very first day we spoke, I knew that she was truly one of a kind.

Aside from Garbo's dresser and her screenwriter friend, Salka Viertel, hairstylist Beth Langston was the only other person who worked with the reclusive star. I would have 30 years to examine this magnificent woman's features. I would learn that even for a filmed scene, she refused the services of a cosmetologist, preferring to do her own makeup. In a delicate manner, she applied a base of simple pancake, accenting her eyes by using dark eyeliner to draw a line in the fold of the eyelid from the inner corner to the outer edge. To cast a shadow over her face from the overhead lights, she applied dark brown mascara to her exceptionally long eyelashes. (So many actresses desperately longed for Garbo's long, plush lashes that they soon brought false eyelashes into vogue.) A light-colored lipstick completed her unique look. Fifteen minutes and she was done.

As I continued to work in supposed secrecy with Joan, Norma, Jeanette MacDonald and Myrna Loy, I felt Garbo's presence all around me. In part this was because many of the lavish sets built for her earlier films were so valuable that they remained intact on the studio's backlot, including the rococo love nest from *Flesh and the Devil*, the turn-of-the-century train station from *Anna Karenina*; the sixteenth-century sailing vessel from *Queen Christina* and the posh nightclub where Garbo collected World War I secrets in *Mata Hari*.

Now, new settings—just as lavish, just as costly—were being erected by an army of workmen in preparation for *Camille*. I had never expected to work with her; Garbo was a kingdom unto herself, and even Thalberg doubted that I would be able to work my magic on her. Nevertheless, in an effort to prepare myself to work with "the Swedish Sphinx," as some unkind observer called her, I steeped myself in her lore and in the history of the eleven-year reign at MGM that had begun when Louis B. Mayer imported Garbo and her mentor, Mauritz Stiller, from Berlin in 1925. Mayer fired Stiller almost immediately and forced Garbo to work with B-grade director Monta Bell on that lurid passion-and-orchids potboiler, *The Torrent*.

In spite of a poorly mounted publicity campaign, *The Torrent* swept the public. Audiences forgot about co-star

Ricardo Cortez, MGM's answer to Rudolph Valentino, whenever Garbo was on-screen. Viewing the film today, it's difficult to imagine what fans saw in the posturing, wide-eyed actress who moved like a sleepwalker. Yet at a preview in semirural Riverside, California, Irving Thalberg bore witness to the audience's reaction. "You could feel the electricity," he said. "People sitting all around me were enthralled."

Word spread through the Loews theater circuit that an international box-office legend was in the making, and demand for prints of *The Torrent* exceeded supply. But the crass publicity campaign for this picture scarred her for life, as I learned firsthand. As Garbo and I became close friends and I came to understand her, she began to regard me as a confidant who would never betray her trust with gossip.

One night she explained what had caused her to veto any studio promotion of her. "When I first came to Hollywood," she told me, "I was only 20 years old, but I had already made pictures in Europe. Mauritz Stiller introduced me to Lillian Gish, whom I revere as the greatest dramatic actress in the world. She taught me many things and warned me that I should maintain control of my image, as she had done. When I began working at MGM, I wasn't in a position to make any demands. But that quickly changed. After my first experience with their publicity men, I found it disgusting that they perceived me as this outdoorsy girl. They actually photographed me with an athletic trainer from the University of Southern California! I was made to wear skimpy shorts and a shirt, and to flex my muscles for a well-known athlete to feel. I was horrified. Right then and there, Sydney, I vowed that if I ever became a great star like Lillian Gish, I would never allow them to take pictures of me again."

For her second American film, *The Temptress*, cinematographer William Daniels used Chinese screens to seal off Garbo's sets so that the shy star was visible only to the camera, the director and her co-stars. Soon after that, she met the man who would shape her career, guiding her in a way that altered forever the nature of Hollywood star power. While making *Flesh and the Devil* opposite John Gilbert, Daniels introduced her to a nondescript man named Harry Eddington. Over dinner one evening at Gilbert's mansion, Eddington listened to Garbo complain about her paycheck—some $500 a week at the time—and voice fears that her stardom would fade. "You need an agent," said Eddington. "Let me help you."

Garbo agreed to let him deal with Mayer and Thalberg. "I don't like them, and they don't like me," she said bluntly. A week later Eddington met with Mayer and Thalberg for three hours. "There's one thing I think will work," Eddington said. "Since Garbo can't deal with the press anyway, why don't we cut her off completely—from the press, the public, even from her fellow stars. We will fashion her into an unknown commodity. The less people know about her the better. Nobody can resist that strategy."

Eddington even suggested that Garbo be known henceforth simply as the "Woman of Mystery." Mayer and Thalberg agreed, and Garbo promptly vanished from the public eye. Eddington scoured Beverly Hills and found a house as secluded as a Spanish nunnery, with a walled garden and a private road sealed by a gatehouse. Its address was a mystery even to the studio. Much later, when my life joined with hers, her habit of solitude remained.

Soon after Eddington took charge, John Gilbert and Garbo allegedly began an affair. MGM legend—probably another publicity fabrication fanned by the Hollywood scandal sheets that passed for fan magazines—had it that the two fell in love on the set of *Flesh and the Devil* while filming their first scene together. "It was mad, passionate love, not acting," said an MGM publicist. By other, more objective accounts, Gilbert did make an immediate play for Garbo, following her around the lot in his hussar's costume and begging for a dinner date or a night on the town. The flamboyant Gilbert, then Hollywood's leading male sex symbol, was a man of intense passions who drove flashy cars and cut a wide swath through the nightclub circuit, perpetually surrounded by a coterie of Hollywood friends.

Gilbert pursued Garbo with marriage proposals. He was overheard pleading his case during a private tennis match and during a dinner party at his own home attended by Jean Harlow, Paul Bern, Norma Shearer, Colleen Moore and many others. "She would never seem to understand what he was saying," Joan Crawford recalled. "I don't think she wanted to hurt his feelings."

There was nothing unusual about Gilbert's tactics: It was part of his public persona to make a play for each of his leading ladies. He actually married three of them.

In the midst of his campaign to win her heart, Gilbert actually went to Mayer's office and asked his permission to marry Garbo.

"You can go to bed with her all you like," said Mayer. "But you're not going to marry her. She's MGM property, and you're not going to jeopardize the value of my property."

"Well," retorted Gilbert, "they say all women are whores anyway."

Whereupon the indignant Mayer, that champion of family values, punched him right in the face.

Neither man had bothered to ask Garbo how she felt about it. Whatever her romantic inclinations, she detested the glare of publicity that surrounded Gilbert, and their affair was short-lived. She later told a friend that she had been "in love with Jack Gilbert for about fifteen minutes before the fleeting sensation evaporated."

Her disenchantment with MGM took a bit longer to develop, and it surfaced as her latest two-year pact was drawing to an end. Although the studio had the option to hold her for several more years, she went to Mayer's office and told him she was going back home to Sweden.

"Six hundred dollars a week is insufficient," she informed him, "especially for a star of my standing."

"What would you consider?" asked Mayer.

"Five thousand dollars a week will do."

Such a salary was all but unheard of except for the biggest box-office draws. A canny negotiator who possessed all the skills of a consummate actor, Mayer replied, "Well, Miss Greta Garbo, I brought you to this country, gave you a chance to star in American films and built you into a star. And this is how you repay us!"

Garbo continued to stare over Mayer's head, then slowly rose from her chair and turned her back on him.

"Where the hell do you think you're going?" he barked.

"Home. To Sweden."

True to her word, she entrained for New York, then boarded a ship for Stockholm. In short order, MGM capitulated. Cables promising to meet her every demand were sent, and she returned to Los Angeles.

From then on, MGM treated her like a rare orchid in a vast hothouse. Each of her directors had to organize his shooting schedules around her. When Garbo arrived, all her gowns were ready to be slipped over her head by the two dressers who always attended her. Her movements and positions in each scene had already been plotted with chalk marks on the floor.

A set where Garbo worked was more cloistered than Beijing's Forbidden City and was run in accordance with an hour-by-hour protocol that was seldom violated. When inconsequential things went wrong, such as a lighting failure, Garbo walked off the set, ordered her car and disappeared. Clarence Brown, who directed many of her films, told friends that the studio had created a monster when they caved in on the issue of her salary and contract. "Ever since she got her way, she has had the big head," he told Louella Parsons. "But if she can get away with it, more power to her. She's got them all scared around here. They don't dare scold or find fault with her for fear she'll turn around and go home."

Garbo's inflexibility increased over the years, and so did her paranoia. She was known even to imagine unauthorized observers on the set when there were none. "I know somebody is here. I can feel it," she once complained to Brown.

"I assure you, Miss Garbo, there's nobody here," he had said.

"I don't believe it. Turn on all the lights."

Not until the set was fully illuminated and Garbo could count each and every technician did she agree to continue the shoot. One afternoon a party of Washington bigwigs toured the studio as Mayer's guests. More than anything else, they wanted to see Garbo. While 28 people waited outside, a junior executive entered the set to plead with her.

"We can't keep these people standing outside," he said.

"All right, let them come in," she replied. "And I will go home." The subject wasn't broached again.

Between 1926 and 1934, the year we finally met, Garbo made 20 films. Her domestic box-office value, however, remained far below that of MGM's top star, Joan Crawford, whose pictures returned about four dollars for each one invested. Each of Garbo's films, with higher overhead resulting from her obsession for privacy, netted far less from U.S. exhibition. But overseas, her films grossed millions.

When MGM converted to sound in 1928, she feared it would spell the end of her career. After losing most of her savings in the stock market crash of 1929, she felt even more insecure. She even went to Thalberg's office and talked quite openly about leaving. "Silent, I'm a star all over the world," she said. "How will it be with dialogue? Can I handle it?"

Despite his own reservations, Thalberg reassured her. He knew that nearly all of Hollywood's foreign stars were finished the minute Al Jolson had appeared on the screen in Warner Bros.' breakthrough talkie, *The Jazz Singer*, to say, "You ain't heard nothing yet." Pola Negri made a few more silents, then headed back to Europe. Vilma Banky, Samuel Goldwyn's biggest moneymaker, who spoke English with a thick Hungarian accent, didn't even attempt the new medium, while Academy Award-winner Emil Jannings—star of *The Way of All Flesh*—never bothered to inform his agent that he was returning to Germany and relative obscurity. And macho John Gilbert, whose thin, high-pitched voice was not what his fans expected, was an instant failure in talking films.

But Greta Garbo was different. When she appeared in playwright Eugene O'Neill's *Anna Christie*, a story adapted for the screen by Frances Marion, her smoky voice and Swedish accent sounded exactly the way her fans had fantasized. By its fifth preview, the studio realized it had not only another talkie but a runaway hit. The ad campaign was unprecedented. "Garbo Talks" was shouted from thousands of billboards and blinked in flashing electric signs in New York and London. The slogan also appeared on life-size cardboard facsimiles of Garbo in her tawdry film costume. Her debut in talkies was a smash, but the insecurity she felt at the start of the sound revolution always remained with her.

"My range is really rather limited, and my audience is fragile," she once told Irving Thalberg. When he tried to disagree, she shushed him. "You know it's true. I know it's true. Without your support, my career would have ended long before now."

Because of her fear that each film would be her last, she preoccupied herself with the thousands of details involved in making a film. After 1933, Garbo had reduced her work schedule to one picture a year and exercised near-total control over her co-stars, screenwriters and directors. And because of her need for utter privacy, she worked at a snail's pace at a studio that turned out movies as regularly as a bakery punched out doughnuts.

Following our meeting in her dressing room, word spread quickly across MGM that Garbo had selected me to create her hairstyles for *Camille*. I was never one to boast, and I detest gossip. Until I sat down to write this book, I never discussed with anyone my relationship with Garbo—neither our professional alliance, the friendship that grew out of it, nor our later love affair. When our friendship grew we decided to call one another by pet names. She would come to call me Gilly, and I called her Gretala—the way my father affectionately added a "la" to the end of my sisters' names. But at this point in public, she was Ms. Garbo and I remained Mr. Guilaroff. Around MGM, however, news that I was out of limbo and working with Garbo quickly made the rounds. By the time I returned to the hair and makeup department after leaving her dressing room that day, I heard that Jack Dawn, who regarded himself as my arch-rival, had responded bitterly to news of my first official assignment. "That should take care of Guilaroff!" he said sarcastically. "He'll never be able to please Garbo."

The contract I had signed before leaving New York guaranteed that my name would appear on-screen for any film that I worked on. But as a member of the guild, Dawn was backed not only by its membership of hairstylists but by those of all the other craft unions as well. If

MGM dared to give me film credit, the makeup artists and hairstylists would walk out, and the electricians, carpenters, transportation workers, painters and all the other skilled workers involved in making movies might well refuse to cross their picket line. By holding the threat of a crippling strike over the studio's head, Dawn blocked my screen credit not only at MGM but also for films I worked on while abroad or on loanout to each of the other major studios. This bit of blackmail worked for years. But Dawn was wrong about his assessment of *Camille*: Working with Garbo was not the end of my career at MGM. It was only the beginning.

CHAPTER SEVEN

Garbo

at dawn on September 17, 1936, Jim Dawson, chief of MGM's private police force, strode to the base of the studio's flagpole and raised first the Stars and Stripes, then the bear flag of the State of California. After lowering both to half-staff, he wrapped around the bottom of the pole a black-on-black velvet mourning band that had been fashioned overnight by costume designer Adrian in the studio's vast wardrobe department.

MGM's massive office towers remained dark. Its sprawling soundstages were shuttered and silent. The only sign of life in this company town was to be found at its automobile garages. Soon, the studio's entire fleet of limousines fanned out from the front gate to collect Garbo, Harlow, Gable, Crawford and all the others—MGM's entire galaxy of stars—from their Malibu beach houses, their Hollywood Hills castles and their red-tiled Beverly Hills ranch houses.

Two hours later, all 75 automobiles, each flying a black flag of mourning in contrast to its distinctive blue MGM logo, reassembled at the enormous Wilshire Boulevard Temple. It was there that all of Hollywood had gathered to say goodbye to Irving Thalberg, the "boy genius" who had defined and personified the creative heart of filmmaking at MGM for more than a decade—and guided my own career during my first two years in Hollywood—until his congenitally weak heart failed at the age of 37.

Avoiding the temple's sweeping front steps, I slipped in through a side entrance and settled in a rear pew. Even after two years at MGM, I remained somewhat shy about the grandeur that was the essence of everything MGM produced, from spectacular musicals to lavish luncheons. This sad occasion was no exception. Jeanette MacDonald, the industry's reigning soprano, sang "Ah, Sweet Mystery of Life." A teary-eyed Grace Moore, the New York Metropolitan Opera star, gave voice to the 23rd Psalm. And all this was mere prelude to the eulogies and tributes that lasted for almost an hour. I caught only a glimpse of Norma Shearer, who sat hidden in a small chapel near the front of the enormous synagogue.

Garbo finally appeared, wearing a black jersey dress and looking even sadder than usual: Thalberg had guided her career since 1926, and he, more than anyone else, had made her an international superstar. MGM had taken in upward of $55 million from her 22 hits, and Thalberg had made sure that his star became the studio's highest-paid performer, with an income of $410,000 a year.

Now that Louis B. Mayer had total control of the studio, we both wondered if she would survive. As Garbo would later tell me, she was terrified that Mayer would stop casting her in high-quality prestige films and attempt to force her into glossy commercial productions, just as he had done with Joan Crawford.

Eventually the funeral cortege headed for the monument-studded hills of Hillside Cemetery. Now, in retrospect, it seems that besides honoring the departed Thalberg, that sad journey had a deeper symbolic meaning. The studio was setting a course for a new era, one that would drastically affect the future of every artisan on the payroll.

As it turned out, Thalberg's death would both make my Hollywood reputation and propel me into lifelong relationships with two stars he left stranded in the raging seas of studio politics: Greta Garbo and Norma Shearer. Back in 1934, Thalberg had confided to good friend Helen Hayes that he felt death approaching. This vision had caused him to put into preproduction two of the most expensive and ambitious epics ever attempted at MGM: *Marie Antoinette*, designed to be the glorious apex of his wife's illustrious career, and *Camille*, which he had planned as the ultimate vehicle for Garbo. His death left these two projects unfinished.

Because the scope of *Marie Antoinette* would require eighteen months of research, including a full year to prepare the costumes of eighteenth-century Versailles, Thalberg had rushed *Camille* into preproduction in March 1936. Putting all his prestige on the line while clinging to the last vestiges of his once total power, he had summoned me, director George Cukor, Adrian and art director Cedric Gibbons to work on the $2.1 million motion picture. Over dinner at his oceanfront mansion, Thalberg, Cukor and Garbo discussed the use of sumptuous costumes, hairstyles and settings to help tell the classic story of the courtesan who finally finds love, only to die of tuberculosis before fulfilling her dreams.

For this film, I worked with Adrian and Gibbons to achieve a look that suggested the slow erosion of Garbo's natural beauty and glamour. For early sequences, when

Camille is the most sought-after courtesan in Paris, Adrian designed elaborate gowns of white, including one fashioned from 22 layers of net scattered with 11,000 gilt stars. As her death approaches, the dresses she wears are first light gray, then dark gray. I achieved much the same effect with hairstyles. Working with Garbo day after day in her dressing suite, I fashioned descending coiffures, from complicated curls and bouffants for the first hour of the film, to stark, tucked-under styles for Camille's deathbed scene. After only a few sessions, I realized that Garbo's beauty needed no gilding; the simpler and cleaner the style, the more patrician she appeared.

When still photos of all nineteen styles were spread across her dressing table, Garbo took my hand. "Everything they had said about you is true, Mr. Guilaroff," she said. "They are even better than I had hoped."

She was particularly fond of the softness and maneuverability of my sample styles. "How do you do it?" she asked one afternoon. "I've always felt so constrained—as if weights were hanging over my head."

I explained that I never use sprays or the heavy setting gels then prevalent in studio hairstyling. "I want your hair to move with you, to compliment your natural grace," I said. I added that stylists, forgetting that hair should not compete or stand out, often create looks that would later be termed *overstylized*. After all the research I had done into Parisian fashions of the mid-1800s, I was striving not only to retain the feel of that period, but also to flatter Garbo's natural appearance.

Soon we developed an unspoken trust and a feeling of kinship, as if we had known each other for a long time. One morning, I gently suggested that she might try what then seemed a fairly daring approach to lipstick. At a time when makeup men concentrated on coloring the middle of the lips—a practice that had begun in the silent era—I wondered if she might look better with coloring and shade that extended from one corner of her mouth to the other.

"Show me," she said.

It required only a few strokes to redefine her mouth.

"That's very startling, Mr. Guilaroff, very startling," she remarked. In combination with her long lashes and un-plucked eyebrows, it was a natural look that set off her classic beauty, and she adopted it as her own from then on.

When principal photography for *Camille* began, Sound-stage Seven was turned into a lavish ballroom with everything from gowns to ceiling decorations decorated in white-on-white. Providing contrast were male dancers in black frock coats and full evening dress, each coat and suit made according to eighteenth-century patterns excavated from the archives of the Louvre in Paris. Thalberg, I remember, watched from a balcony as the dance sequence was filmed. Immediately afterward, he left the set, suffering, he said, from the flu, and was driven home. Six days later he was dead.

A few days after his funeral, I was with Garbo, adjusting one of her hairstyles, when there was a knock at the dressing room door followed by a gruff voice: "Miss Garbo, it's Mr. Mayer. May I come in?"

She caught my eye in the mirror, then put a finger to her lips, leaning in close to whisper, "See that closet? It contains a door to the outside. Stall him while I escape."

Moments after she had vanished, Mayer shoved open the door and shouldered his way in.

"Hello, Guilaroff," he said. "Where's Miss Garbo?"

"Gone to the set, I guess."

He must have heard Garbo's voice while he was outside the door, for he glared at me suspiciously. "Well, Guilaroff, tell her I came by, will you?"

"I will."

After Mayer left, Garbo returned with a smile, and neither of us said a word as I went back to work.

One of her greatest fears was that with Thalberg dead, Mayer would force her back into a publicity regimen. "Rather than do that, I would go back to Sweden," she would say, and I have never doubted her.

It was during the making of *Camille* that I came to fully appreciate Garbo's beautiful silver-brown mane; it was very easy to work with. As I styled her hair during breaks for costume changes, she always peered critically at her reflection in the dressing table mirror, using a hand-held mirror to inspect each angle after I completed my work. I was often rewarded with an approving smile from her. That was part of her charm. Despite her reputation for being "difficult" and her need for control on each film, whenever she made a suggestion to me, the director, the cameraman or anyone working with her, Garbo expressed herself softly, avoiding ultimatum and confrontation. I found that especially endearing.

As with everything in life, there were times when events on a soundstage didn't happen on schedule or as planned. Everybody tried to adjust to these situations as smoothly as possible, but now and then fate intervened to turn a mishap into something special. In those days, for example, every costume and hair design was tested and the director either ordered specific changes or gave approval before shooting began. One day the wardrobe assistant brought down a gown that hadn't been finished in time for testing; Cukor had yet to see it. She also brought a camellia, intending to attach it either to Garbo's breast line or atop a shoulder.

Looking at Garbo, I said, "The way the scene reads, you have been out with Armand and you become ill, so he takes you home. Once you are in your bedroom, you sit down on the bed. Instead of the camellia being attached to your dress, why don't you wear it in your hair? Then later, as you sit on the bed, the audience will feel your weariness as you slowly remove the blossom. That would be much more dramatic."

I knew Garbo could carry this off brilliantly. She was so skilled at using the slightest gesture to let the audience know exactly what she was feeling at the moment. I was delighted when she agreed with me. But when I accompanied her to the stage, Cukor immediately said, "I never saw that dress!"

I explained that it had arrived late, then described my interpretation of the scene. Hands on his hips, and smiling slightly but not enough to reassure me that he appreciated my idea, he responded, "Now, who is directing this picture, you or me, Mr. Guilaroff?"

I inclined my head respectfully to reply, "Well, you are, of course, Mr. Cukor. I am only your assistant."

He paused, then turned to Garbo, "Do you like it, Miss Garbo?"

She smiled sweetly. "Yes, I do, very much."

In no time at all the cameras were rolling. Cukor glanced at me, then winked. I sighed in relief. I felt a surge of satisfaction, but I cherished even more the thought that Garbo's confidence in my professionalism was blossoming along with our friendship.

Few knew that Garbo was an insomniac who paced her room for hours before finally falling into a feverish slumber. I soon became part of her ritual: She would summon me to her house or telephone me, and we would talk late into the night.

Later during the making of *Camille*, I noticed that the more tired she was, the more reclusive she became. Sometimes, during breaks in the shooting schedule, she withdrew behind an array of lace screens, where she sat on a chaise and tried to regain her strength. Often she invited me into her on-set refuge to discuss her techniques or her interpretation of the title role. Six weeks into production, as we sat behind the lace screens, she took my hand to say, "I think I can trust you, and I haven't really trusted anyone in Hollywood since Mauritz Stiller returned to Sweden. But with you, we seem to communicate without words, silently and soulfully."

At one point she consulted me about a love scene she was about to film with Robert Taylor as her youthful lover. "I want it to seem very innocent and tender. What would you do?"

"Why don't you try kissing him Continental style, with tiny kisses all over his face."

She brightened. "You know, I think you're right."

This love scene proved to be monumental—a classic. It was all done without body contact, yet Cukor later described it as "tremendously erotic. By suggesting passion, Garbo caught the eroticism beneath the surface."

As she and I became closer, she began to confide her innermost feelings. In keeping with her shyness, she had taken to heart the advice of Lon Chaney, who advised her that if "you let the public know too much about you, they will lose interest."

I quickly came to admire Garbo's determination to stand up for her convictions, one of several character traits we shared. And I learned that like me, she had been forced by family circumstances to give up part of her childhood and to forfeit higher education in favor of finding work. Garbo told me that she was only fourteen when her father died, and that to support herself she had found work in a barbershop, lathering men's faces. I confided in turn that at the same age I was surviving by sweeping up hair in a salon.

She also confessed embarrassment over her lack of formal education. Self-conscious about her poor spelling, she rarely wrote letters. But I recall one day many years later, when she looked at me rather wistfully. A furrowed line appeared on her forehead as she wondered aloud, "Gilly, you write to everybody else you care for, but you never write to me."

I answered, "Well, Gretala, when we aren't together, we talk on the telephone almost daily, and you don't write at all. So what's the point in writing you a letter and never getting one back?"

Smiling, she said, "Well, from now on I will write to you and you will write back to me, okay?"

When I nodded in agreement, she threw her head back and laughed in that delicate manner I loved so much. From then on, whenever we were apart, we wrote back and forth. I always signed my letters, "Love, Gilly." Once, just to tease her, I signed my name, then turned the stationery upside down and wrote, "...and John Gilbert, Leopold Stokowski and all the many other men you have been rumored to have been with over the years." She had a marvelous sense of humor and got a big kick out of that.

After *Camille*, I went to work on Thalberg's second great film legacy, the lavish *Marie Antoinette*, conceived as a tribute to Norma Shearer. Even when he was alive, it had been a controversial project, one that had exacerbated the studio war between Mayer and Thalberg. Four years before I came to MGM, the studio had purchased the rights to Stefan Zweig's best-selling biography of the doomed queen. Thalberg tried to keep the acquisition a secret, but word leaked out, and suddenly all the great divas on the lot were clamoring for the title role. Joan Crawford demanded the part, as did Myrna Loy and even Marion Davies, the gorgeous but stuttering mistress of newspaper mogul William Randolph Hearst.

Although the rumor mill said the role was up for grabs, Thalberg never actually considered anyone but his wife. When that got out, Joan declared bitterly, "Who can compete with Her Royal Highness Norma Shearer?" When

Norma later asked to borrow cinematographer William Daniels from Joan for a single morning, Joan screamed across the soundstage, "Tell Miss Shearer to get her own cinematographer. Mine is needed on this film. And tell her I didn't get where I am by making love to the boss."

I didn't agree with Joan's rudeness, and I told her so. "A lady doesn't act that way," I warned. "It's rude and it's crass. As an actress, your roles demand a lot of class. Why don't you show that in your personal life?"

Nevertheless, I sympathized with Joan. Norma's career had been carefully guided by her husband. She got all the prestige pictures; by the time Thalberg died, Norma had completed 37 films at MGM, including such silent classics as *He Who Gets Slapped* and *The Student Prince*. During her early years, she was often paired with big box-office draws John Gilbert and Ramon Novarro. Without Thalberg to protect and champion her, Joan and many others at Metro hoped that Norma's reign as "Queen of the Lot," with her choice of scripts and directors, was about to end.

Norma only added to the gossip and speculation about her future. For weeks after Thalberg's funeral, she remained cloistered in her beachside mansion, refusing all contact with the studio. Suddenly one day she telephoned me from her hideaway and shared a secret. "I'm dying to come back and film *Marie Antoinette*," she sighed. "I realize how much it has cost the studio to prepare and I know how hard you and Adrian have worked on this film. But I must play a waiting game at this point."

I confessed that I didn't quite understand.

"Sydney, not many people know this, but Mayer is trying to cheat me out of Irving's earnings from all the films he produced. I'm entitled to five percent—this was part of his deal with Mayer. They are claiming the deal ended with his death, but they owe this money to me, and I'm going to get it one way or another."

Dumbfounded, I didn't know what to say. Then she asked, "Can you suggest anything?"

"Well, Norma, they have already spent about $700,000 on *Marie Antoinette*, in addition to purchasing a handful of other screenplays for you to film. If you don't return, this money is all lost."

"You know, George Cukor told me much the same thing yesterday."

"Get a lawyer," I suggested. "And have him work this out."

Then and now, I was shocked by Mayer's attempts to pocket Thalberg's share of MGM's profits, which came to slightly less than $1 million. Perhaps he thought Norma was simply too naive to understand his maneuver. Instead, she took on the studio, prepared for a long battle. Her attorneys informed Mayer that she would return to finish *Marie Antoinette* only on the condition that all of Thalberg's percentages be guaranteed. While that was sinking in, she sent word that she wanted a new deal: six films at $150,000 each. Mayer and Loews, Inc., approved that overnight.

The next morning Norma returned to the studio for test shots for *Marie Antoinette*. That night she told Louella Parsons's vast radio audience that "I have to go back to work or face the poorhouse."

Because Thalberg had prepared everything in advance, preproduction continued smoothly at first. Set designers had already gone to Paris and purchased many expensive eighteenth-century antiques. Thalberg had delegated other details to Sidney Franklin, one of MGM's greatest directors. Franklin had selected the stages and sets to be used, assigned designers for the various costumes and put everything together.

When actual filming began, however, things moved at a very slow pace, and the production costs were enormous and growing. Both Mayer and Hunt Stromberg, a wonderfully capable producer, seemed to put the blame for the delays on Norma, and with no one to stand up for her, she was desperate. Then, two weeks into filming, Mayer fired Franklin and replaced him with "One Take Woody" Van Dyke, famed for directing action films in which he insisted on getting each scene right the first time. After learning of this change in a meeting with Mayer and Stromberg, Norma asked me to come to her dressing room.

"I'm heartbroken!" she cried." This is not what Irving had set up for the picture."

"Norma, dear," I replied, "I'm sure the man will compromise. You need to talk with him, see how he feels about it. See if he's read the script."

Since she felt I had earned her trust by helping her regain her husband's fortune from Mayer, Norma asked me to become her personal emissary to Van Dyke.

I went to Van Dyke and told him, "Norma would like you to read the script. It's very intricate."

"I've been so busy, Sydney," he said. "But get one to me, and I'll get back to you."

When he telephoned later that day, Van Dyke said he was looking forward to doing the film.

"This one might take a bit longer than those you usually direct," I cautioned.

"We'll get it done. Don't worry."

Whatever his feelings, Van Dyke had his marching orders from Mayer, and he began filming at a frantic pace, keeping cast and crew on the set six days a week. Agonizing over what she sensed to be a lack of attention to detail, Norma scheduled a meeting with me, Adrian and Woody.

She didn't want to make Woody feel as though we thought him unworthy, so we agreed beforehand that I'd tell him how she felt about the picture, about the love and the care that it required. Our concern was that although the studio wouldn't allow things to continue the way Franklin had handled them, the film nevertheless needed a good deal of conscientious effort. To help move things along, we agreed among ourselves to tell Van Dyke that once we had a successful take, we ought not to try to improve on it. What we *didn't* say was that in his entire career, Van Dyke had never made a costume epic like *Marie Antoinette*, and we feared he'd ruin it.

Norma asked me to open the meeting, and I began by noting that before his untimely death, Thalberg had prepared, arranged and designed everything and that we stood ready to continue shooting. Then I said to Van Dyke, "We know that you do shoot kind of fast on your Myrna Loy and William Powell pictures. But for this kind of film, it takes a little longer. It needn't be as costly as the route that Sidney Franklin was taking, but I'm sure you know yourself that this script needs more depth and quality."

Van Dyke seemed very agreeable, a good fellow. "You're right. And I love this script. I'm very proud to do it," he said.

At that point Norma chimed in. "I'm so happy to hear you say that. I didn't know whether you would like it or not."

Van Dyke made it plain that he was very anxious to make *Marie Antoinette* succeed. Though he never said so, it might have been because he knew it would move him into the realm of far more exalted pictures with bigger budgets.

With all our cards on the table, filming continued at a more reasonable pace. In Paris I had studied eighteenth-century French sculptures and paintings of the nobility and the court. Marie Antoinette had been a woman of extraordinary beauty, especially her face. But Norma Shearer looked nothing like her, so my challenge was to adapt the fashions of that period to a form that most complemented Norma's features, which had a regal quality of their own.

Because Adrian's costumes stressed contrast between black and white, I had to provide the same contrast in my wigs. This I accomplished by reducing the wigs' size while making them more ornate, in one case using beautiful black-and-white feathers and a strand of black pearls. In the interests of uncompromising authenticity, I chose a strand of real and extremely rare black pearls from Van Cleef & Arpels that cost $7,500. The studio balked, but when I explained that anything less would have compromised the authenticity of the film, my recommendations were accepted without question. In total I supervised the manufacture of 2,200 court wigs and consumed almost the studio's entire stock of hairpieces and swatches. From the wardrobe department I obtained jewelry, rings, flowers, earrings and all sorts of other objects to adorn them.

I also had to prepare wigs for 3,000 extras in the great crowd scenes that depicted the French Revolution. These wigs were the simplest to design, because they were intended for the poorly dressed and unkempt peasantry who were the bulk of the revolution. For these we used mostly what were called scratch wigs, old hairpieces with no dressing done to them.

The film's tragic climax is preceded by a sequence in which unruly mobs of disheveled extras demand death for the imprisoned king and queen. For one of the most touching scenes in all film history, Marie Antoinette's stoic ride over jolting cobblestone streets to the guillotine, I created yet another special wig. Made to resemble the queen's natural hair, it was streaked with just a touch of gray. Because the executioners didn't want her coiffure to get in the way of the guillotine blade, I cut it unevenly, as though it had been chopped with crude shears.

Once the cameras started rolling on *Marie Antoinette*,

my life was frantic: Night after night I styled wigs to pre-pare for the next day's filming, often working through the night, then dashing here and there to make last-minute adjustments. After scarcely more than a brief nap, I did it all over again. It was very hard work, but tremendously exhilarating.

Even as accustomed as I had become to the make-be-lieve world of filmmaking, the production of this movie was absolutely amazing to watch. I sometimes felt that I was living the entire history of the French Revolution. I was not alone in being chilled by the realism and the dra-ma; there were many times when Van Dyke said "Cut!" and there was complete silence on the set instead of the usual boisterous calls of "Hooray" or "That's a good take." As the crew began to set up for the next scene, it remained quiet, with only minimal conversations among those on the set.

Norma was thrilled with the finished film. It represent-ed the fruition of the years Irving had spent guiding her career, and because the movie's historic scope was fully re-alized on a grand scale, Norma's role was a complete tri-umph. When the picture was released—at one of the most glamorous and star-studded premieres in movie history—audiences marveled even at the wigs, which stand as land-marks in the history of costume design. I heard the audience gasp at some of the close-ups, and many uttered the words "beautiful" and "marvelous" during a scene in which an actor wore a wig dressed with a birdcage at the top, with what appeared to be a live bird inside. When the actor secretly pulled a hidden cord, the bird chirped!

Sometime afterward I was at Chasen's restaurant and ran into the actor Joseph Schildkraut, who had played Count D'Artois in the film. He caught my eye, then beckoned me over to his table, where he introduced me to friends. He got up, put his arm around me, then held up my hand.

"This man's hands are hands of gold. He made me look wonderful in *Marie Antoinette*." I was very touched, and although I always blush at such praise, I was very pleased to be recognized in such a warm and public way.

For Metro, *Camille* and *Marie Antoinette* were critically acclaimed box-office successes. For me, they were personal triumphs that marked my emergence as an artist whose work was recognized throughout the cinema world. The Makeup and Hair Stylists Guild's threats faded, and starting in 1938, as my original contract had specified, I received screen credit for every film that I contributed to, a first for a hairstylist. Eventually this innovation was recognized by the industry as a historic breakthrough.

CHAPTER EIGHT

The Adoptions

despite my steadily increasing success, the glitter and glamour of MGM did not fulfill me. Although I had many close friends, there were nevertheless many times when I felt acutely lonely. One day I realized the nature of my unfulfilled need: I missed having a family. I wanted to become a father, to raise a child, to experience all the joys of parenthood. There was no lack of women in Hollywood who might have eagerly borne my baby, but after seeing so many of my friends' marriages come apart, I had no illusions about the institution and little desire for the complications and commitments of matrimony. In those days, getting someone pregnant and then refusing to marry her while demanding custody of the child not only would have seemed grotesque but would have placed my employment in jeopardy: Everyone working for the studios was bound by the industry's infamous "morals clause."

So after thinking things through, in 1938 I decided to

adopt, despite the strictures of an era when unmarried men were virtually forbidden to do so. But the more I learned about the state's policies, the more determined I became to challenge them. Working through a legitimate agency, I found a beautiful, perfectly formed infant boy. The attraction was mutual: He smiled at me, and when I leaned down into his crib, he grabbed my finger. "This is it. He's the one," I decided.

In tribute to my friend Joan Crawford, I named him Jon, and my heart was overflowing with love as I drove home with him. At my house, a beautifully appointed nursery awaited his arrival, staffed by a carefully selected nanny to care for him while I was away at work. Whenever I looked at Jon, I knew that we belonged together.

Before he would become truly mine, however, I had to get through an adoption hearing. The first attorney I hired took a healthy retainer to study my case but soon withdrew, saying that it was hopeless. I found another, and he, too, accepted my money, then refused to continue. This happened twice more until I found Lloyd Wright, a lawyer who agreed to represent me but refused any fee. We soon learned that the state planned a strong challenge to my eligibility and had begun assembling evidence to show that I was an unfit parent. A lengthy and expensive investigation into my background and my friends, habits and vices, however, turned up nothing derogatory. Nevertheless, the state's attorneys prepared a motion declaring that my home was an "abnormal" one without a mother in it. I suppose the authorities suspected that as a man engaged in a profession in which most of its practitioners were either female or homosexual, I must be the latter.

The state of California dispatched a three-man delegation from Sacramento to Los Angeles County Superior Court, determined that I would never adopt a child. At the hearing they began their four-hour presentation with the words: "We cannot condone or allow this single man to adopt a child." Every legal precedent was on their side: I was the first never-married man in America to petition a court for adoption privileges.

My attorney replied, "Your Honor, I am not trying to praise myself, but I am not even charging for this case. What's more, if anything happened to me and my wife, I would be glad to name my client as parent and caretaker of my own children."

I was very touched by his tribute, but listening to the state present its case, I began to wonder whether the judge would be so moved. Gazing up at him, I thought to myself, *If they try to take this baby from me, I'll jump out the window with him and run as far away as I can.* Destiny had brought him to me, and no one was going to take him away, not even the court.

Although the state opposed the adoption on principle, one of their legal representatives nevertheless felt compelled to say, "As far as I can see, Mr. Guilaroff would be an excellent father."

Another admitted, "We think that he's more moral than most married people who want to adopt children."

The judge looked at me and said, "What do you think of that, Mr. Guilaroff?"

And I replied, "Your Honor, I just want to make one statement: The statute on adoption uses the term *parent*. It doesn't say *mother*. It doesn't say *father*. I am a good parent, and no one is going to take this child from me, legally or otherwise. He's mine, and I'm going to keep him with your blessing and your help—or without it."

The judge sat in silence for a few minutes. Then, glancing at the officials, he ruled: "Since we've heard testimony that you're much more moral than most married people, and since married couples have been able to adopt, I'm going to grant the adoption."

In court I showed little emotion, but inside I felt a tremendous elation, and an enormous weight was lifted from my shoulders. As much as I disliked publicity, I allowed MGM's publicity department to arrange a lavish article in *Look* magazine. Their magazine's photographer called to ask if he could come and take pictures of me and little Jon. When *Look* published our picture, the news of my adoption received worldwide attention, and I received a flood of propositions—marriage and otherwise—from women all over the world.

It also stirred an editorial in the *London Times*, marveling that such an event could have only happened in America. "THE MAN ACTUALLY ADOPTED A LIVE BABY BOY," screamed the headline.

About three years later, in 1941, I decided that Jon would be much happier if he had a brother to share his childhood. So when I heard about a little boy available in Reno, Nevada, I called and spoke to the doctor at the hospital where he was born. I made an appointment to come there and pick him up. After my experience with adopting Jon, I knew that there wouldn't be much information provided about this baby's birth parents. So I told the doctor only that I'd bring all the necessary clothes. "Just have his formula ready, and I'll feed him," I said. "I'll dress him nicely myself as soon as I get there."

The law in Nevada was very different from that in California, but I still needed permission to take an adopted child out of the state. Instead of a hearing this time, I phoned the judge, George Marshall. He said, "I've heard about your first adoption case, so I know who you are. Just come and get your baby."

I named my second son Eugene Dale Guilaroff, after my father.

CHAPTER NINE

The Feud

*h*ardly had my first son's adoption been granted when my professional life was threatened by a feud with none other than Louis B. Mayer. It began quietly enough in 1938, only two years after Thalberg's death. Mayer called me to his office, and when I remarked about the loss I still felt from Irving's untimely departure, he said, "I want to tell you something. Some of the photographers are complaining about your work. Your styles have changed the looks of most of the women, and the camera people don't like it." He explained that these men bemoaned my hairstyling because it meant that they could no longer backlight actresses.

I didn't know whether to laugh or cry. I had presided over radical changes in the styling of hair, and now Mayer was telling me they didn't like it because it meant they would have to change their ways! Yet the great movie photographer George Hurrell had recently praised me for revolutionizing the art of still photography by "freeing us from the outdated and antique process of creating the phony 'halo of hair' that was left over from the silent era."

My innovations had led the way for Hurrell's sleek, front-lit, light-and-shadow portraits of Joan Crawford, her face mysteriously shaded; of Norma Shearer, stunning in a hat and dappled light; of Garbo and her soft waves in brilliant profile. In time, these portraits would be considered classics of their era, a key component of Hurrell's enduring greatness. But Mayer, ever resistant to change, denigrated my achievements in the most offensive manner: "Guilaroff"—he was virtually the only one on the lot who never called me Sydney, and in return I was among the few who never called him L.B.—"we need the 'halo effect.' You're going to change back."

I'd already noticed that my styles were being slavishly copied at Paramount and Warner Bros. Apparently, Mayer was unaware of it. "No," I said firmly. "Have the still men light them from the front, as George Hurrell is already doing."

He turned on me. "You know, Guilaroff, you've got a big mouth, and I don't like it."

"Well, Mr. Mayer, I can't be a 'yes' man."

"I'm going to read your contract to you." he said. He called in one of the studio's attorneys, a man named Richard Hendricksen, who proceeded to read the first paragraph of my contract aloud. "Do you know what that means, Guilaroff?" asked Mayer.

"You tell me what *you* think it means, Mr. Mayer."

"It means that I can have the officer at the front gate monitor you, and he'll tell you every morning what time to come in and when you're free to leave at night. And he'll be your boss from now on."

"Mr. Mayer, nobody is my boss, not even you. I don't like the way you just spoke to me. I don't like to be insulted by anyone, and you are insulting me. I'll tell you one other thing: I'm leaving MGM. I don't want to be under contract. I don't want anything from the studio. I was a success before I came here, and I'll be a success wherever I go."

I rose from my chair and left the room. Among the hundreds of underlings Mayer had humbled, I was the first to walk out on him. I can't think of another person, except Garbo, and she was the studio's top star, who ever walked out on L.B. Mayer while he was head of MGM.

I went back to my office. While I was thinking about what had just happened, the telephone rang. It was Eddie Mannix, one of the studio's top executives. His distinctive, gravelly voice was instantly identifiable. "Hello, Sydney!" he said. "I hear you had a quarrel with L.B."

"No, we didn't have a quarrel. He was so damn insulting to me that I couldn't stand it. I'm quitting."

"Oh, no, you're not quitting," countered Mannix. "Don't pay any attention to him."

"I do pay attention to him. MGM *is* His Lordship, Mr. L.B. Mayer, and he insulted me, so I'm leaving."

That's just what I did, and I wasn't sure whether I would ever return. With some free time on my hands, I took my son Jon back with me to Montreal to meet my family. It was a warmer homecoming than my departure for New York had been so many years before. I think I had earned both their respect and admiration, and though I'm sure they would have preferred to see me married, they genuinely loved young Jon.

During this visit home I went into a tobacco store to buy some cigarettes, and there behind the counter, working as a clerk, was Jack Rosen. He didn't remember me, but I recognized him instantly as a childhood schoolmate who had been indirectly involved in a very painful experience from my early life.

My mother, Anna, visited my
Brentwood home a few years before
she died. When I was a child, she
always found a way to sneak me a
quarter to go to the pictures.

Above: I was 21 years old when this picture was taken. I returned home in my wingtip shoes, nice clothes and hat to show my parents that I had become a success in New York City.

Right: My father, Eugene, was a brilliant and compassionate man. He spent his entire life helping impoverished European immigrants settle in Canada and the United States.

My older sister Vera was always my friend. She became one of Canada's greatest jazz artists and many of her records and her sound equipment were sealed in a vault to be opened in the year 2020.

This picture was taken when I was 31. Although I was intensely shy, there was a time when I was encouraged to become an actor. On a visit to Los Angeles with Ann Sothern in the early 1930s, Universal even had me do a screen test. I was much more comfortable behind the camera.

*My marvelous career and one
of my most enduring friendships began in 1928 with
Claudette Colbert, my
first star client. I
cut her hair short
and convinced her
to let me give her
the bangs she wore
for the rest of her
career. I also styled
her hair for* The Two
Mrs. Grenvilles, *my last film.*

To Sydney
with my sincere good wishes
Claudette Colbert

I felt sorry for Joan when she told me how her husband's stepmother, Mary Pickford, disapproved of her. Miss Pickford may have been known as "America's sweetheart," but to me she will always be Mary Pitchfork for the dreadful way she treated my good friend.

I cherish this picture of Joan Crawford, which she autographed and gave to me in 1931, while she was a client of mine at Antoine's in New York. Three years later, she would be instrumental in my move to Hollywood.

For Sydney
My deep appreciation
never
Joan Crawford

Left: Greta Garbo and I developed an unspoken trust and a feeling of kinship. For years I had admired her on the screen. Never in my wildest dreams did it cross my mind that I would not only meet and work with Garbo, but that I would fall in love with her...and she with me.

Below: This is the only photo of Garbo and me together. Here we are on the set of her last film, Two-Faced Woman. *When the flash went off, I angrily said, "Who took that picture? Everybody knows that I never like to be photographed with a star." Garbo whispered to me, "It's all right, Gilly. I asked them to take the picture."*

I was 31 years old when I adopted my first son, Jon, named in honor of Joan Crawford. Three years later I adopted Gene, named after my father.

Norma Shearer in the Artist's Ball sequence of Marie Antoinette. *Since the picture was in black and white, it was difficult to bring out the vividness of the hair and costumes. The black pearls in Norma's hair are from Van Cleef & Arpels and cost $7,500 in 1938!*

Above: MGM discovered Hedy Lamarr in a European film. They had no idea what to do with her but signed her anyway; she was absolutely captivating on screen. Here we are with her maid on the set of Boom Town.

Right: Barbara Stanwyck was not an MGM contract player, but she was one of the few actresses who was allowed to freelance at the major studios. While not a classic beauty, she had an expressive quality which the public adored.

Marlene Dietrich in Kismet. *I look at this hairstyle today and wonder where my ideas came from. This particular style was inspired by costumer Irene who had the costume delivered to me saying, "Take this to the genius Sydney. He'll know what to do." I believe Irene was the greatest costumer of all time.*

Right: Marlene Dietrich was, indeed, the most glamorous star ever. Here I'm wrapping a long switch of human hair around her head for Kismet.

Marlene was still gorgeous in the 1960s.
This long coat was made of down
feathers plucked from baby chicks.
The coat cost $25,000 and weighed
a mere eight ounces.

*I escorted Ava Gardner to the
1951 Academy Awards.*

Ava sent this picture to me shortly before she died in 1990. She said it was her favorite
photo of herself. When she died, I felt as if a bullet had gone straight through my heart.
For the next two years, Gregory Peck, his wife Veronique and I attended church services
in Los Angeles to memorialize our precious Ava.

It happened in elementary school. The teacher had stepped out of the classroom momentarily, and the other children were laughing as I stared at the blackboard, tears streaming down my cheeks. One of the other boys had written: "The child most likely to succeed is Jack Rosen. The child least likely to succeed is Sydney Guilaroff." Finally, unable to take it anymore, I bolted from the classroom and out the front door of the school. The teacher caught up with me and said reassuringly, "They were very unkind to you. But let me tell you something, Sydney. You're different from all the others. You're more unusual than anyone else in the class. You're special."

Thirty years later, as I looked at Jack Rosen selling cigarettes, I felt proud of all that I had achieved. I still felt different from all the others. That's why I'd made a success of myself—and that's why I had stood up to L.B. Mayer.

Meanwhile, back in Hollywood, when word of my departure spread around the studio in a hurry, many producers were insisting that I return. Hunt Stromberg stormed into Mayer's office and screamed, "You may have discovered all the stars on this lot, all the producers and directors, but you didn't discover Sydney. He was the top man in New York City! He was famous! You've made a big mistake, and I want him back. I need him. I'm going to do *The Women*, and I need him for that right away."

Producer Arthur Hornblow Jr. also needed me to work on a picture starring his wife, Myrna Loy, and if it hadn't been for him and Norma and the others who protested, I would have remained in the east. When it turned out that everybody but a few lazy photographers was pleased with my work, Mayer finally gave in. I agreed to come back, but under different conditions. I had no intention of being insulted by anybody, so I refused to sign a contract. My salary continued, but for the rest of my career I was never again bound by the strictures of a studio contract. I could walk out anytime I liked, and the studio would have no leverage over me. Another fringe benefit of my new arrangement was that I didn't have to speak to Mayer again, nor he to me, for the next five years.

I had been lucky in standing up to Mayer. Whenever he was in one of his famous rages, everyone was in the line of fire, and everyone suffered—stars, directors, producers—but women were particularly vulnerable. I don't know how many stars he propositioned or if he even employed the so-called casting couch. But I do know that several actresses, including Jeanette MacDonald, were afraid to be alone with him.

One day she called me in my dressing room after everyone had gone to lunch. I was going to wash up before going over to the Commissary. She asked, "Do me a favor, will you, Sydney?"

"Yes, dear, anything. Tell me what it is."

"Mayer wants to see me, and I don't want to go by myself. He makes me nervous. Besides, I've already gotten out of my stage clothes and I'm in a dressing gown. Would you come with me?"

One of the world's great beauties, Jeanette had a wonderful voice, and she was among the first to bring music to the world on a movie screen in some of the loveliest filmed stage plays ever made. Most of her films were romantic; she exuded a distinctive charm and attracted a tremendous following.

When we arrived, Mayer seemed a little surprised to see me, but knowing that she could be very temperamental and easily upset, he didn't say anything. Jeanette was then making a film called *Smilin' Through*, and Mayer, who had screened the rushes—unedited film sent daily to the production office—criticized her for failing to show enough emotion. He said he felt that she seemed to be singing to herself instead of to her leading man, with whom she was supposed to be in love.

Jeanette listened as Mayer went on and on. Then he folded one hand atop the other and placed both on his chest. "You have to put heart into your singing," he continued. "You have a beautiful voice, but I don't see any heart."

Suddenly Mayer went down on one knee and began singing a lament from the Hebrew liturgy called "Eli, Eli." Jeanette glanced at me but remained silent, struggling to maintain her composure. I could see that listening to him was an ordeal for her, and since he was singing in Hebrew, she had no idea what the words meant.

Finally she stood up and said, "Well, L.B., I'll do better next time, but I really must go now. I haven't had my lunch yet. I'm wanted back on the stage soon, and before that, I'll have to get dressed."

As we left, Mayer thanked her extravagantly and even said goodbye to me. When we were safely outside, she burst out laughing. "Can you beat that? Getting on his knees and singing to me? In Hebrew? To show how passionate I should feel about a man?"

No matter how obtuse Mayer sometimes seemed, and no matter how eccentric or autocratic his ways, there was no denying that he had assembled the most talented team of moviemakers in the industry.

Not long afterward, I was both amazed and amused to learn that MGM had purchased Clare Boothe Luce's *The Women* and decided to bring this Broadway smash to the screen as a big-budget extravaganza with no men but 140 women and featuring 320 glittering high-fashion gowns. Based on a true incident, it involved a scheming manicurist, a middle-aged woman losing control of her high-roller husband and a secret phone call that changed all their lives.

This production was, of course, based on the spectacular seduction of the husband of one of my best clients, Mrs. Floyd Odlum, by Jackie Cochran, the scheming shampoo girl and manicurist at Antoine's. The stage play's success was enhanced because, within a few years of her marriage, Jackie Cochran Odlum outflew Amelia Earhart in a California race to become the world's most celebrated aviatrix and was soon rolling in money and personal glory.

I should add that while the playwright was herself among my regulars and apparently borrowed much of her bitchiest dialogue by eavesdropping on my other customers, she changed my character to a woman when she wrote her play. As a salute to my connection with the story, however, Mayer ordered that the salon in the film be named Sydney's, with set designs based on Antoine's actual look.

Every actress on the MGM lot, from the sultry Crawford to the patrician Shearer, bared their professional claws in a catfight over the major roles. When Norma was cast as the jilted wife, Joan Crawford set her sights on Crystal, the conniving perfume salesgirl. Mayer was appalled. He warned Joan that she would offend her loyal fans by playing a cold-hearted bitch. "I'd play Wallace Beery's grandmother if it's a good role," she shot back.

While Joan insisted publicly that appearing with an all-star cast would give her career a needed boost, privately she relished the notion of going head-to-head with Queen Norma, now without the protection of her late prince. Mayer disapproved of Joan's choice, but for once he didn't interfere. Instead, he told her that she would have to convince producer Hunt Stromberg and director George Cukor. The carefully chosen cast already included Shearer, Rosalind Russell, Joan Fontaine in her maiden role, Mary Boland, Lucile Watson, Ruth Hussey, Mary Beth Hughes, Virginia Weidler, Virginia Grey, Marjorie Main, Cora Witherspoon and even Hedda Hopper herself. Fearing that adding Crawford would upset this balance, Stromberg argued that Crystal was too small a part for someone of her stature.

"No part is too small if it's a good one," insisted Joan, who knew that the hard-boiled Crystal would stand out in marked contrast to a host of genteel society ladies. Reluctantly, Stromberg agreed to give her the role, but only if she could convince Cukor. She could and did.

With Shearer and Crawford cast in the same film for the first time, everyone at MGM braced for a delicious confrontation between the two actresses. It had been building for fourteen years, ever since Joan made her movie debut by doubling as the back of Norma's head. The younger woman had watched helplessly for years as Thalberg hand-selected his wife's vehicles and Joan got the rejects. Though she often socialized with the Thalbergs, she felt they treated her condescendingly as a former chorus girl who was beyond her element. Thalberg's death had seemingly left Norma vulnerable, and Mayer, perhaps out of remorse for the shabby way he had treated Thalberg, remained solicitous of her career. When he saw to it that Norma was cast opposite Clark Gable in *Idiot's Delight*, based on Robert Sherwood's hit play, Joan wept in frustration: She had wanted the role—a chorus girl who becomes the mistress of a munitions magnate—for herself.

And so everyone at MGM was waiting to see the sparks fly. Cukor directed *The Women* with extraordinary skill and cunning. His greatest challenge might have been what happened offscreen, and he kept the divergent temperaments in line with continual activity. Whenever the actresses weren't rehearsing or on camera, they were being fitted for costumes or tested with new makeup and hairstyles.

This worked well until Shearer and Crawford had their one face-to-face scene together, in which Shearer's Mary Haines confronts Crawford's Crystal in a couturier fitting room. The stage was hushed for the meeting of these rivals. The rehearsal was polite, and Cukor seemed to breathe a bit easier after he'd completed the master shot (the overall view of the scene). Then the camera moved in for Shearer's closeup.

While most stars retired to their dressing rooms at this point and allowed a script clerk or the director to feed their lines offstage to the on-camera performer, Joan, as usual, was prepared to deliver them herself. Positioning herself in a chair beside the camera, she took out a pair of long knitting needles and began working on an afghan. As Norma performed in front of the camera, Joan answered with her own lines, never looking up from her afghan. Her needles moved at a furious pace, clicking loudly.

Finally Norma had had enough. "Joan, darling, I find your knitting distracting," she said.

Joan pretended not to hear. As the scene continued, the flashing needles clacked louder and louder. Tension mounted as crew members' eyes darted from the irritated Shearer to the oblivious Crawford, then to Cukor, who looked like a deer caught in a car's blazing headlights. Norma began the scene again, only to be distracted by the whirring needles.

"Mr. Cukor," said Norma with icy control, "I think that Miss Crawford can go home now and *you* can give me her lines."

Furious, Cukor grabbed Joan's elbow and almost dragged her from the set. "How dare you behave so rudely?" he muttered.

"I'm paying the widow Thalberg back for her decade of ruthlessness," Joan snapped.

"I will not allow such unprofessional behavior on my set," replied the director. "You are dismissed for the day. And Joan, when you report tomorrow, I want you to apologize."

But Joan couldn't forget the years of playing second fiddle to Norma and being shunned by her powerful husband. No longer afraid of a studio reprisal, she went home, drank six martinis and sent a telegram to Norma informing her in no uncertain terms exactly what she thought of her.

Her relationship with Norma aside, one of the first scenes Joan filmed for *The Women* created a small sensation. Even though it was supposed to be a closed set, word somehow got around that she would be in a bathtub nude but thoroughly covered up to the neck in froth whipped up by a large Mixmaster. In the end, Joan disappointed everyone: When she emerged from the bubbles, she was wearing a skimpy bathing suit.

Crawford wasn't the only one who found cause to feud with Norma. After Rosalind Russell, in a bravura performance, stole a key scene from her, Norma went to the front office and demanded that Russell's name be listed below the main titles rather than above them. Since Rosalind's contract specified that only a man could be billed above her, MGM and Mayer dropped her name from the list of stars and co-stars and gave her the lowest of credits: "with Rosalind Russell." Outraged, Roz complained to Cukor, "I won't settle for that billing. I've already starred in a number of films, and I don't care to be demoted by Norma Shearer."

"Agreed," said Cukor. But there was little he could do about it.

"When it comes to a fight with management, the only thing an artist can do is refuse to perform," Roz would later say. "If an actress simply walks out on a production, the studio can force her back or sue her in court. But if a performer gets sick, what can the boss do?"

Accordingly, five weeks into shooting for *The Women*, Roz retired to her luxurious bed. "You couldn't pull that trick at the beginning of a film—they would just replace you," she said to me later. "I never attempted a ploy like that again, but I had a feeling I could make it work just this once."

Days went by. Despite personal requests from Mayer and Cukor, Rosalind's "illness" persisted. "I lay out in the garden, looking up at the sky," Roz said, "and every day Benny Thau, who was in charge of talent, phoned to ask how I was getting along."

On the fourth day of her strike, Thau telephoned to say, "Oh, Roz, something has happened. Norma Shearer says you're so good in this film, she's going to allow you to be starred, too."

"How perfectly lovely of her," Roz cooed.

There was a long pause on the other end of the phone. "Do you think," Thau said gingerly, "you'd feel well enough to come to work tomorrow?"

"You know, I'm feeling better this very second."

Rivalry among the top stars wasn't the only off-camera drama surrounding the *The Women*. When Paulette Goddard joined the cast at the last minute, she was assigned an assistant stylist. "No!" she screamed. "I want Guilaroff, just like Joan and Norma."

A few years before, while thumbing through an issue of *Vanity Fair*, the most elegant magazine of its time and not to be confused with the periodical which bears that name today, I happened on a photo of this stunning young brunette, who was then Charlie Chaplin's leading lady and a dabbler in high society. She had since married Chaplin and acquired a well-deserved reputation for being lively, friendly and wickedly witty.

Now that Hunt Stromberg had taken a professional fancy to Paulette, borrowed her from Paramount and added her to the cast of *The Women*, he summoned me to his office to meet her and discuss how her hair should look in the film. With Hunt's approval, I decided that she alone among the cast should keep her hair at its original shoulder length. With the others wearing their locks somewhat shorter, it would enhance Paulette's role as the ultimate *femme fatale*.

We decided to create a gallery of different styles and test them extensively, so I repeatedly had to set Paulette's hair and put her under the dryer. She somehow looked familiar to me. For a while I thought it was because of the photograph I'd seen a few years earlier in *Vanity Fair*. Then, as I was combing her out while she sat reading the script, I saw a tiny dark brown birthmark on the bridge of her nose. It startled me. I had seen that distinctive blemish about fifteen years before, but in those days, she had been using another name.

Mrs. Charles James had first appeared at Antoine's near the very beginning of my tenure there. She had beautiful eyes of deep blue, platinum blond hair and dark eyebrows and lashes. She was only seventeen, and I was enchanted just looking at her. She had a beautiful nose, and right in the middle of its bridge was a tiny birthmark. I wondered why she didn't use a touch of makeup to conceal it. Mrs. James came to the salon several times over the course of a month, then she disappeared without a word, only to return to Antoine's a few months later, still blond and even more beautiful. I was glad to see her and told her I had missed her. She seemed happy to see me, too, but I sensed a shadow of sadness beneath her smile. She said only that she'd been traveling; I never knew more than that. Soon she disappeared again.

One morning several months later, while reading the *Daily Mirror*, I came across a news story: A certain Mr. Charles James and his beautiful young wife had been arrested on a cruise ship in the harbor and charged in connection with a felony crime that was commonly referred to as the honey badger game. This is a confidence swindle that uses a pretty woman as bait for lecherous married men. It seems that while Mr. James was elsewhere, the lovely Mrs. James would flirt with a gentleman she met aboard ship. They might then take a stroll around the deck. If things progressed well, Mrs. James was soon disrobing with the gentleman in her cabin. Just when the man had achieved a compromising position, Mr. James, secretly watching or alerted by some signal from his wife, would burst into the cabin. If Mrs. James had flirted well, her inamorato would be both wealthy and thoroughly married. Threatened with arrest or a very public lawsuit, most of these "marks" would pay almost any sum for silence.

The New York police, however, were quite familiar with the badger game. Using a decoy, they arrested both Jameses in the act. But when her far-older husband jumped bail, charges against young Mrs. James were dropped on account of her age and inexperience.

Recalling all that, I lifted the dryer off Paulette's head and asked her if she had been the beautiful blond flapper known as Mrs. Charles James, who, by coincidence, had the very same birthmark on her nose.

She laughed. "Yes, you're right, you sly little thing. I was that Mrs. James." She got up, gave me a hug and whispered, "Please don't tell anybody. I was a poor Jewish girl named Pauline Levy. My mother and I had no money. I loved her and I would do anything to support her. She struggled very hard to make sure I got somewhere." Then a strange look came over her face, and she said, "Oh, well, never mind any of that. Look where I am now—and look where you are!"

I learned later that Paulette had a secret. She was always scheming during *The Women*. She immediately set her sights on a screenwriter named John McLean. Although he wasn't handsome, especially when compared to all the virile male stars who worked at Metro, he was a clever and prolific writer of powerful scripts. And apparently, all the women were crazy about him. He proceeded to become involved with Paulette.

On the set of *The Women*, she supplied the only witty moments. Earlier, Paulette had been rejected for the role of Scarlett O'Hara in *Gone With the Wind* and was secretly furious over the choice of Vivien Leigh to play Margaret Mitchell's antebellum heroine. One day, as I was preparing her for a close-up, I got a message from David O. Selznick. He wanted me to come over to his studio—they were having some trouble with Vivien Leigh's hairstyles. Before I could depart, Paulette cornered me. "You're not going anywhere," she said. "I won't do this close-up if you're not here to look after me! I'll hold up production. It'll cost thousands of dollars."

She declared this in front of everybody on the set. Joan Crawford, who hadn't even been considered for the Scarlett role, spoke up in sympathy: "Paulette, I wouldn't do the scene either if Sydney leaves!"

I stayed on the set.

Paulette's dressing room belonged to Jock Whitney, the New York socialite who had invested $220,000 in *Gone With the Wind* in hopes of helping her win the role. He often sent her gourmet food and made sure that she was comfortable. I can only guess, but I suppose that he was another of her beaux. Being married to Chaplin didn't seem to cramp her style, and Paulette appeared to have no shortage of lovers.

Or of friends. She even tried hard to make the crew feel special. She sent most of Jock's fancy food up to the technicians on the soundstage catwalks overhead. But she got something in return as well. Sometimes she'd call up to an electrician, "How are you doing up there? Give me some good lighting now. Make sure I look good. It's your fault if I look terrible."

Once, while I was resting in my dressing room, Paulette stormed in. She had a terrible hangover and couldn't work, so management had docked her salary $5,000. She stretched out on my couch trying to recover and said, "Don't ever tell Charlie I was fined $5,000! Let alone why."

"I wouldn't dream of telling him that," I said. "But as a matter of fact, Charlie just called me a short while ago."

She sat bolt upright on the couch and said in alarm, "What did he want?"

"He just asked me how I am, and then he said, 'Paulette's working today, isn't she?' And I said, 'Yes, she is.' Then he said, 'Well, I hope you had a nice time last night.' I said, 'Well, I didn't do anything. I just stayed at home.'"

"Oh, my God. Oh, my God, Sydney! I told him I was out with you last night!"

"I wish you had told me. Where were you?"

"I was with Johnnie McLean! Charlie will kill me!"

I just shook my head at her. But she was shocked sober, and I can only imagine what kind of trouble she got into when she got home.

I wish she had learned her lesson, but I remember another time I was invited to Charlie's house for dinner. When I arrived, Spencer Tracy was waiting at the front door. Just then, the door opened and there was Paulette.

Her face lit up as she saw him, and she gave him a kiss. He, in turn, handed her a small box, and seeing me behind him, she said, "Listen, Spence, why don't you join the others in the living room and I'll be right in." She winked at me to stay where I was, and as soon as he was out of sight, whispered to me to join her upstairs. She took me into a bedroom. I had no idea what she was up to this time, but she opened the box and there was a beautiful diamond necklace.

"Spence gave you this?" I asked.

"Yes, isn't it beautiful?"

"Of course, but what did you have to do for it, Paulette?"

"Nothing!" she said.

"Nothing?" I asked, dumbfounded.

"Nothing!" she repeated. "If you do something, you won't get anything. But if you hold out on a guy, well, you start getting all kinds of presents."

I shook my head at her again, but she said, "Sydney, I'm going to get older one of these days, and I'm going to start getting wrinkles around my neck. With enough diamonds, I can hide them before I get too old for anyone to care about me anymore."

"I've known you for years, dear," I told her, "and if I've learned anything about you, it's that there's no point in trying to tell you what to do or not to do. But I don't think you have to worry about getting older. You'll always be a prize."

I meant that, of course, in every sense. She was incorrigible, but I had always believed she was going to be a star, and that's just what she became. When her movie years were over, I was right again; she didn't have to worry about growing older. The great writer Erich Maria Remarque, known for such classics as "All Quiet on the Western Front," fell in love with her, and they married and lived happily and quietly together for the remainder of their lives.

CHAPTER TEN

Katharine

Katharine Hepburn blew onto the MGM lot in 1939, desperately seeking to revive her Hollywood career. Like Joan Crawford and Marlene Dietrich before her, she had slunk away from the film capital after being labeled "box-office poison" by motion picture exhibitors—the bosses of the big theater circuits that screened the films and sold the tickets.

Katharine had fled east to New York City, where Howard Hughes had purchased Philip Barry's play *The Philadelphia Story*, and turned it into a lavish Broadway production with her as its star. The play was a smash, and Louis B. Mayer, who attended the opening, vowed to purchase the film rights as a vehicle for Greer Garson. Unfortunately for Mayer, Hughes had already assigned the screen rights to Katharine. If Mayer wanted to make the film at MGM, his only option was to get them from Hepburn, who demanded in exchange not only the starring role but a contract with MGM. Mayer, who saw big numbers in the film's prospects, caved in and brought Kate back to Hollywood.

When she reported to the studio for hairstyling tests, I recalled how George Cukor had wondered aloud why the studio had even brought her out to California. He described Hepburn as "too skinny and too affected" and couldn't see anything about her that would make her worthwhile on the screen. Initially, I quite agreed with Cukor. Then I met her in the flesh. Fifty-five years later, I still remember our first meeting. Cukor brought her down to the hair and makeup department to meet me. The very first words that rolled from her lips amused me: "Oh, I've heard about you. When you sign your contract, they tell you about all the advantages, and you're supposed to be one of the attractions here at MGM."

"Well, I've heard about you, too," I reciprocated, "and it's a great pleasure to meet you at last." It was the beginning of a wonderful relationship.

As I worked on her hair, we chatted about her life in New York City. I had loved her performance on Broadway in *The Lake* and said so. "Oh, you saw that?" she replied. "I don't think I did too well in that."

We agreed to disagree: I told her what I had admired about the play and she told me why she had found fault with her own work. Despite all the critical acclaim she had garnered and the fame she had acquired among New York theatergoers, she was very modest about her own acting talents. And she seemed diffident about making the transition from acting on the stage to acting on the screen.

Everything about Hepburn—her looks, her manner, her voice, even the way she moved—was totally unlike that of any other movie star. The same applied to the way she lived. Despite the morals clause that was strictly enforced on all the stars at the studio, Katharine was very much the captain of her own ship, and as we got to know each other, she told me more and more about her private life. Something of a pioneer in her personal morality, she had been married to socialite Ludlow Ogden Smith, called Luddy, in New York. They were divorced in 1934, and she thought nothing of carrying on romantic flings with the biggest womanizers in Hollywood: her agent, Leland Hayward, a married man, screenwriter John McLean and entertainment lawyer Greg Bautzer, who was already involved with Joan Crawford when he and Katharine began a short-lived affair. As a matter of fact, there weren't many of her leading men in the 1930s and 1940s who failed to become her bed partner, including Cary Grant during the filming of *The Philadelphia Story*.

"In order to be a good actress," she told me once, "you have to be very selfish, and I am selfish. I'll do exactly as I want to do." She made this statement not in a haughty way but very simply and directly, just as she said everything else. She was unconventional in every sense of the word, and nobody ever challenged her sense of entitlement to live the way she wanted to. She would have done it anyway, and everyone just accepted it.

Even her hair was unruly. She washed it each morning before she came to the studio, and it was so straight that I had to use very, very small paper rollers to impart the slightest curl, and even then I would lose that curl almost instantly unless I treated it carefully. At lunchtime, while everybody else went to eat, she and I remained in the hair-dressing room, toiling together to put some body back into her hair. If I forgot and made a date for lunch, I was invariably called to the Commissary telephone: "Sydney? I'm waiting!" Katharine would say.

I soon found out that there was another reason why Katharine's burnt-orange hair was always in strings. Like her sometime-boyfriend Howard Hughes, she was terrified of germs. She brushed her teeth frequently and took as many as eight showers in a single afternoon, forcing me to work overtime to save her hairstyles.

Katharine's affair with Hughes went on for several years. They even lived together for a while, but their relationship was always rather stormy. They were both highly opinionated. Somebody had to give in, though, and it was almost never Katharine. The one exception was an afternoon when she wanted to join him in a new plane he was test-flying. He wouldn't let her, and it was just as well: That very day he crash-landed in Beverly Hills. Miraculously, Hughes walked away from the wreckage, but if he had been carrying a passenger, she might not have been so lucky. "Destiny," she said later, recalling the incident, "was kind to me that day."

Katharine was unconventional even when I threw parties at my home. They were formal affairs: Men were expected to come in black tie and ladies were to wear evening gowns. I always answered the door myself, because I never hired help for my gatherings, not even people to open doors or park cars. This had the intended effect of making my friends, who included film stars and many other celebrated people who valued their privacy, feel safe and at ease. So relaxed and enjoyable was the atmosphere that Marlene Dietrich even played waitress at one of my parties. But I find trousers on women distasteful under any circumstances, and my invitations usually specified, "No slacks for women."

Nevertheless, Katharine came to my house one night in pants. It was a nice outfit that included a jacket and a very beautiful blouse, but I had my standards, so when I greeted her at the door I politely but firmly said, "I told you that it was going to be formal and to please not come in trousers. It upsets me, dear."

"Well, that's all right," she replied in her direct manner.

"Don't worry about it." And without another word, she turned around and went home, leaving me to think, *If that's the way she wants to do things, what's the use in trying to stop her?* But after an hour, she returned in a fancy evening gown, looking marvelous!

Katharine's determination to break the rules and act individualistically also extended to the screen. During production of *Woman of the Year*, I was summoned by producer Pandro Berman. After shooting wardrobe tests for all the costumes, Pandro decided that he hated a particular outfit that she especially liked. "Kate insists on wearing it," he said, exasperated, adding that of all the costumes in the picture, this was the one he liked least.

We went to a projection room, but before we screened the wardrobe tests I made a request. "Don't tell me which one you don't like. Let's see if I can pick it out and if I agree with you." When the lights came back on, I said, "I think I found the one you're upset about. Please, will you run the film back and I'll tell you when we come to it."

The test was rerun, and when one particular outfit was on the screen, I said, "That's the one I don't like."

Pandro concurred. "Yes, that's the one. But she's determined to wear it, and she can't understand why I don't like it."

"I can tell you why. Because she looks beautiful in everything else. But in this one, instead of seeming slender and pretty, she just looks skinny."

"That's it!" he exclaimed. "That's what's wrong. But I don't understand it, because it's the same body, the same underwear, the same everything except for that dress. So it has to be the dress that's making her look skinny."

A little later Pandro went down to the set, and when Katharine had finished her scene, he discussed the dress with her. "That dress that you like so much, that you're determined to wear," he said, "I know now what's wrong with it."

And she said, "Oh? And just what's wrong with it?"

"Sydney had the answer. You look beautifully slender in everything else, but there's something about that particular dress that makes you look too skinny."

She was furious, but instead of displaying her full anger, she merely stamped her foot. "We'll see about it later," she said tartly, and turned on her heel.

At lunchtime, as usual, Katharine came into the cavernous makeup department, a deserted space at that hour. "Sydney? Sydney!" she yelled. "You know, Sydney, you have a lot of nerve, telling Pandro that I look skinny in my favorite outfit!"

With equal volume, I replied, "First of all, I was invited to look at that dress. Now, listen to me. You're always telling everybody else what to do. You are forever minding everybody else's business instead of your own. I don't mind telling you, Katharine, because that's the way you are."

She seemed quite taken aback, but she said, "You have a lot of goddamn nerve telling me I look skinny. A lot of nerve!" By now, we were shouting at each other.

"Maybe so," I said. "But let me put it to you this way: you don't just look skinny in that dress—you look like a damn scarecrow in it."

She looked at me defiantly. Then, suddenly, a smile spread across her face. "You know something, I think you're right. Come on. Let's go do my hair, shall we?"

Katharine's long and stormy relationship with Spencer Tracy began in 1942 and lasted through the nine films they made together until his death 25 years later. While they were filming *Woman of the Year*, their first collaboration, rumors were already circulating that they were involved with each other. She had adored him from the moment she laid eyes on him and considered him one of the finest screen actors of all time. I can't say that I ever understood her attraction to Spencer; frankly, I never figured out what the public saw in him either. He certainly wasn't attractive, nor was there anything dashing about him. It was really puzzling to me, because he was considered one of MGM's greatest stars, and he certainly proved that at the box office.

Spencer was a married man and a womanizer, but he fell in love with Katharine and she with him. He and his wife were devout Catholics, and they had a son who was born deaf. So instead of getting a divorce, he continued to support his family in the style to which they had become accustomed, but he moved out of the home and in with Katharine. They led a very quiet life; there was never any gossip about it, never the slightest remark passed by a gossip columnist. I think everyone respected the fact that Tracy hadn't abandoned his family to run off with Katharine. Even Mayer accepted their arrangement, which was remarkable because it was a time when stars were expected to be circumspect in their personal lives. It was all such hypocrisy. Mayer tolerated their affair because there was nothing he could have done about it except fire them, and that would have cut into studio profits.

Ever the nonconformist, Katharine didn't feel the need to be married just for the sake of it, but was committed to Spencer and settled down with him. She gave up her freewheeling social life and, I believe, remained true and faithful for the rest of their years together.

To me, the real mystery of their relationship is why Katharine tolerated Spencer's alcoholism. I would have thought that someone with her refined upbringing would have been disgusted and miserable being around someone who was always drunk. I don't know how she managed, but for better or for worse, they lived like a married couple until the day he died of a heart attack in 1967, just three weeks after they made their final picture together, *Guess Who's Coming to Dinner*.

Katharine and I are still friends after all these years. I

treasure the frequent notes she sends me, and she always brings a smile to my lips when we talk on the telephone. In a phone conversation not too long ago, she asked, "By the way, how old are you now, Sydney?"

I said, "I'm 87," and she exclaimed in her uniquely brisk and brittle voice, "My God, you're old!"

"Well," I replied, laughing and remembering that we were born the same year, "that makes us even. At least we're still here, and we can still enjoy each other."

"Yes, and it's certainly better than the alternative," she said.

CHAPTER ELEVEN

Joan

When my first son, Jon, was about two, I took him to swim at Joan Crawford's pool with several other children, the sons and daughters of Joan's friends. Jonnie was a little shy and didn't mix with the others, preferring to stay near me. Joan sat down next to us and after playing with Jon for a bit, she sighed, "Oh, how I wish I had a child of my own."

I knew that she couldn't have children, so I said, "I know somebody who can help you. If you really want to adopt a child, she'll show you how to get one."

I introduced her to Mrs. Anson, who worked with unwanted children and an adoption society. She had helped me to find Jon and, later, Eugene, so I had no hesitation about asking her to help Joan. She located a lovely little girl, whom Joan adopted and named Christina.

Aside from her new role as a mother, Joan had reached a crossroads in her career by the early forties. She had enjoyed conspicuous cinematic success since 1925, first as the female personification of the Jazz Age, then as the archetypal hard-luck, working-girl-makes-good of the Depression, and finally as successor to Greta Garbo and Claudette Colbert as the epitome of glamour. By 1940, though highly-paid and respected, Joan had all the laurels of Hollywood achievement except one: She had never been nominated for an Academy Award. That void was starting to gnaw at the edges of her career.

One night, after reading that arch-rival Norma Shearer had been nominated a fifth time, for 1938's *Marie Antoinette*, she told me: "It doesn't matter how brilliant an actor's performance is. The Oscars are a reward to the studios, not recognition of an actor's best work. There isn't even a fair vote; whoever wins the award, no other actor at their studio has a chance the next year."

Joan knew whereof she spoke. For several years she was not only an active member of the Academy of Motion Picture Arts and Sciences, but also, as daughter-in-law and stepdaughter-in-law, respectively, of Academy co-founders and powers-that-be Douglas Fairbanks Sr., and Mary Pickford, privy to the Academy's intimate machinations. It was beyond denial that she had been abused not only by the Academy but also by MGM. For eighteen years she'd had to content herself with roles rejected by Norma Shearer. Even when she sparkled in a film, as she did in *Grand Hotel*, the studio saw to it that its Oscar nomination for Best Actress went to the likes of Shearer, Garbo or Marie Dressler.

I have little doubt that if they had chosen to do so, those who ran MGM could have ensured Joan at least a nomination and very likely an Oscar. By 1935, the Academy was financially dependent on the major studios for the Oscar program as well as for most of the organization's other activities. The studio bigwigs associated with the Academy weren't reluctant to make their wishes known, and the functionaries whose salaries and careers depended on pleasing the moguls were rarely so foolish as to cross swords with any of them.

I understood Joan's frustration, since her quest for a nomination was much like my own battle to achieve screen credit. When it came to Joan, however, Louis B. Mayer and many of the executives working for him simply didn't care. Even after her success in *The Women* and her standout portrayal of a distinguished beauty in *A Woman's Face*, no one championed an Oscar nomination for Joan.

She made several official complaints to the Academy, but after failing to receive even the courtesy of a reply, Joan asked me what further course of action I could recommend. I suggested that she resign from the Academy in protest, and so she did. Then she marched into Mayer's office and demanded that he cancel her contract. Joan had made some 50 films at Metro, and they had made quite a lot of money for the studio, so Mayer put up a long struggle before agreeing to let her go. And though he told friends that her career would crumble without MGM's protection, Jack Warner grabbed her only a month later for a fee of $100,000 a picture.

At Warners, Joan knew that she had to become more selective in her choice of roles, since not every script would give her the opportunity she needed to stand out. "Joan realized," said Isadore Freeman, a studio publicist, "that this was a comeback for her, that she would sink or swim on the strength of one picture." For two years, she proceeded to reject every script Warners offered her as unacceptable to an actress of her stature. That's a long time for any film star to be offscreen, and especially long for a woman approaching middle age, when her looks were sure to fade. Without movie roles, the studio publicity mill couldn't promote her, thus compounding her plight. Joan had to carefully maintain her public image by supporting herself in the grand style that Americans had come to expect from their stars. Without income, she barely survived a calamitous third marriage to actor Philip Terry, that depleted her savings even further.

Then, finally, she read James M. Cain's novel *Mildred Pierce*. The story of a woman who builds a modest hash house into a business empire, it had strong parallels with Joan's own life. Playing the title character would be a clear departure from her dozens of glamorous roles in which she portrayed screen goddesses so exalted that no ordinary person could identify with her characters. "This is it," she told Jack Warner. "This is the right role." He heaved a sigh of relief: Bette Davis had already turned it down, so Crawford's decision solved two problems at once.

The film opened to long lines at the box office in Los Angeles and New York, and the next day Warner ordered the studio to start an all-out push to win Academy Awards for this production. It began with a series of ads unprecedented in the eighteen-year history of the Oscar race. As soon as I saw them, I thought Crawford would win. So did Jack Warner—and ironically, so did Louis B. Mayer.

But I knew it would be an uphill fight. Shortly after *Mildred Pierce* opened, I began my own six-month campaign to win Joan a Best Actress nomination by going to Johnny Green, then head of the Academy's music branch and a future Oscar-winner himself. We'd been friends since I was nineteen years old and he was writing songs for the Broadway stage. I said, "She earned this recognition a long time ago, Johnny, yet the Academy hasn't even recognized her."

I doubt that my support made any difference in the final decision; it was something I felt I had to do as a friend. Joan was indeed nominated. Then came the hardest job: convincing the Academy to give her the Oscar. Hollywood's bluebloods had looked down their noses at her since she arrived at MGM as Lucille Le Sueur. But long after her rivals—Norma, Garbo and MacDonald—had vanished from the screen, Joan had returned in triumph in *Mildred Pierce*.

Five days before the awards ceremony, she was stricken with the flu, and gossip columnists immediately began speculating about "Crawford's mysterious illness," intimating that she was suffering from nerves or was too fearful of losing to show up in person. I knew otherwise: She really was ill, and her condition was worsening with each passing day. But Joan was a Christian Scientist and refused to consult a doctor.

Arriving at her fabulous white-on-white mansion the evening of the ceremony, I was shown to her bedroom, where I found her sitting up in a beautiful gown and satin robe—albeit absolutely furious. "Jack Warner doesn't think I'm really ill!" she moaned. "I might as well be back at MGM. The studios just don't trust me. They believe I would use my illness as an excuse, so they're sending the doctor over to make sure."

At that moment the doorbell rang, and Warner's studio physician arrived. I went downstairs while he examined her, and after several minutes, he came down to say, "Her fever is pretty high. She shouldn't go out under any circumstances."

It was a long evening. I was alone with her in her room, and when dinner was served, Joan could only pick at her food as we listened to the radio broadcast of the Oscar presentations (the ceremony was not televised until 1953). Finally, presenter Charles Boyer, from the stage at Grauman's Chinese Theater, announced the nominees for Best Performance by an Actress in a Leading Role: Ingrid Bergman for *The Bells of St. Mary's*, Joan Crawford for *Mildred Pierce*, Greer Garson for *The Valley of Decision*,

Jennifer Jones for *Love Letters* and Gene Tierney for *Leave Her to Heaven.*

When Crawford's name was read as the winner, her eyes grew moist, and she said, "This is the greatest moment of my life." I knew she meant it.

The next morning Joan was feeling well enough to greet her public, but she wasn't about to leave home. Banks of congratulatory floral displays lined the front steps and filled the entryway, and over a thousand telegrams arrived, including one from Louis B. Mayer. I arrived to style her hair and saw legions of photographers jamming the entrance to her mansion. When they were finally allowed to come in, they found her sitting up in bed. Those photographs, and the interviews she gave from her boudoir—not to mention the Oscar itself—put her back on top.

Joan's private life, however, was still a mess. She was in the midst of a long and stormy affair with Hollywood attorney to the stars Greg Bautzer. I innocently joined them for dinner one evening, and she gave him an expensive pair of beautiful Perry Foster cufflinks, gold inlaid with diamonds and rubies. That same night, though, Joan began accusing Greg of cheating on her—with none other than Katharine Hepburn—and they quietly argued through dinner. On the drive home she became very angry and agitated. She snapped, "You've got a hell of a nerve to accept my gift tonight when you won't tell me who you've been cheating on me with."

"Why don't you just calm down?" retorted Bautzer. "This is all going to wear off anyway." They continued to quarrel until we arrived at her home in Brentwood. She turned to him and yelled, "You're a son of a bitch for cheating on me!"

Removing the cufflinks, he grabbed her hand and shoved them into her palm. "Keep the goddamn cufflinks," he told her. "I don't need them." And then he left.

She was still steaming when I said goodnight and drove home. I learned the next day that after I left, she was so angry that she flushed the cufflinks down the toilet. In the morning, however, she had second thoughts and called a plumber to dismantle the pipes and retrieve them. Eventually she and Greg made up, but she never returned the cufflinks to him; they were too grim a reminder of their bitter quarrel. Bautzer showered her with gifts as well, including a gold cigarette case with rubies and engraved "Forever and Ever," which was from a song she had sung in *Mannequin* in 1938.

Although Greg might have been unfaithful, he was nevertheless Joan's most solicitous beau. As Rosalind Russell put it: "He treated her like Joan Crawford, a star." He opened doors for her, and when she entered a room, he remained a few steps behind, carrying her dog or the knitting bag that Joan took everywhere. At the table, Joan expected him to hold her chair, place a napkin in her lap, light her cigarettes—everything except feed her. When they had company for dinner at her home, she usually let her help go home early and got Greg to serve and clear the table afterward. Not many men would put up with this kind of thing, yet Greg did, and without compromising his masculinity.

Joan, however, eventually moved on to other relationships. Years later, in 1953, she returned to MGM to make *Torch Song*, a musical. For this film she wanted her hair cut quite short, and despite my misgivings—I thought the style would make her look less feminine—I bowed to her wishes. After cutting her hair in front, I layered it and, again with misgivings, made a shinglelike cut down to her neck. She was quite happy: "It suits parts of me, and it suits my part in the film." And in the end she was right.

It was Joan's way to give small but expensive gifts to the

directors of her films, and to everybody whom she especially liked. She liked Chuck Walters, the handsome young director of *Torch Song*. Her usual routine began with cufflinks, followed by a gold bracelet or perhaps a gold watch. Then, halfway through the picture, when Joan started to entertain amorous thoughts and believed that Walters had grown as fond of her as she was of him, she learned that he was homosexual. That was the end of the gifts, although she had the grace not to ask for them back.

Throughout her career, Joan was almost always playing the field until she met Clark Gable. I really believe he was the love of her life, but it was a turbulent affair, and her feelings for him remained strong even after he married Carole Lombard in 1939. I will never forget the bitterness between him and Joan while we were filming 1940's *Strange Cargo*. He was drinking quite heavily at the time, and although there were no outbursts of emotion, she must have been whispering things that irritated him, because he would walk away from her, furious. She would remain cool until she reached her dressing room, and then she'd burst into laughter. The tension between them was so thick that everyone on the set found it almost unendurable, and I finally asked to be taken off the picture because it upset me so.

While Joan and I remained good friends until her untimely death in 1977, our relationship was mostly by telephone after she moved to New York City. That was when her acting career was behind her and she had married Alfred Steele, who ran Pepsi-Cola. Joan was very clever and had a wonderful sense of humor. Steele made her head of marketing, and when he passed away she took over management of the entire company and did quite well at it.

Joan came out of retirement in 1962 to do Warners' *Whatever Happened to Baby Jane?*, with Bette Davis. I found it quite shocking to see the two of them up there on the screen. For their entire careers they had always appeared beautiful, immaculately groomed and costumed and coiffured, and now they looked just dreadful, like ugly, terrible old hags. But of course they were both still magnificent actresses, and one had to admire their courage in taking on such roles.

After she stepped down from Pepsi-Cola, getting in touch with Joan became a bit complex. One had to telephone a message service, leave a number, and then wait for her to call back. She always called me within a few minutes. One day while we were talking, Joan said she wanted to send me a swatch of her hair, which was gray, so I could design a new style for her. When I said, "Gray? You shouldn't have done that," she sounded as though she was very hurt. She never did send that swatch.

We spoke about a week later, not long before her death. I think she knew that she didn't have much longer, though as a Christian Scientist she wouldn't acknowledge her illness and wasn't speaking to doctors. Instead, someone came over to give her religious instruction. I said I hadn't received that hair swatch yet. She replied, "It doesn't matter, dear, it doesn't matter at all. I'll wear my hair the best way I can."

"I wish I lived closer to you," I said. "I'd be able to be of some help, like I was when you won the Oscar. Do you remember that night? "

"I do, and I remember you with love." She sounded sad and lonely. It felt as if she was saying goodbye.

Immediately after we ended our conversation, she called her longtime assistant, Betty Barker, who then telephoned me to say that Joan wouldn't be taking any more calls, including Betty's. A few days later she was gone. I was the only one of her Los Angeles friends to fly out for the funeral. I volunteered to be a pallbearer, only to discover that Joan had been cremated, and there would be no interment, only a church service. It was a sad ending to a re-markable life. I will never forget her, and neither will millions of fans. She was a great star, one of the greatest I ever knew. But I would miss her even more as a friend.

CHAPTER TWELVE

Gretala

*t*he Japanese bombs that fell on Pearl Harbor on Dec. 7, 1941, not only sank America's vaunted Pacific fleet but helped scuttle Greta Garbo's career as well. Along with millions of others, her life, and mine, would change forever.

Even after the Nazis marched into the Sudetenland of Czechoslovakia, even after the blitzkrieg conquest of Poland and the merciless bombing of London during the Battle of Britain, MGM films continued to play in Europe's first-run theaters. In fact, Adolf Hitler himself paid MGM's Berlin agent $50,000 to "rent" a print of *Camille* to screen for guests in his palatial new Reich Chancellery. His ambitious girlfriend, Eva Braun, bragged that she "and Greta will be friends after we conquer America."

Then came Pearl Harbor. With flames still licking at the shattered hulks of America's fleet, President Franklin D. Roosevelt demanded a declaration of war against both Japan and Germany, and Congress eagerly complied. Europe and the Far East were now closed to American films, and MGM lost more than 40 percent of its worldwide revenues literally overnight. For stars such as Garbo and Marlene Dietrich, who had been even more popular abroad than in America, this was dire news.

In January 1942, L.B. Mayer handed Garbo a new contract for three films at $150,000 apiece. He was determined, in his words, to "remake her into an American star, to tailor her for audiences in this country."

To me and the others in makeup, hairstyling and costuming, this meant a complete change in Garbo's appearance. Her very next film, *Two-Faced Woman*, was the preposterous story of a "modern woman" caught up in a romantic merry-go-round set against a backdrop of socialite hangouts and elite ski resorts. The script called for her to play twins, one a natural athlete, the other a fey, flirty club girl who could rumba with the best of them.

I soon realized that we'd been handed the deplorable and thankless task of deglamorizing the most glamorous woman in the world. I was able to satisfy Garbo with new hairstyles, bobbing her hair and curling it in a style modified from that of ancient Rome: classic scallops and a ski-style pulled away from her face. It was a compromise between the classy coiffures from her earlier costume pictures and the modern look Mayer had decreed.

Adrian, the studio's head costume designer, fared less well. Mayer went so far as to decree that Garbo would wear a swimsuit in the film despite the heaviness that the camera added to her hips and thighs, features that directors had always taken great pains to disguise. "If she doesn't like the swimsuit, tell her to lose weight," Mayer barked to Adrian, who proceeded to create outfits using stretch fabrics that would emphasize her curves. He even designed a ski suit. His wardrobe for her, cut too low in the front, totally lacked the understated elegance that had once displayed Garbo's ethereal beauty like a jewel in a simple setting. The moment she read the script, she told me she wasn't going to wear the swimsuit. "I'm not a cheap bathing beauty. I won't do it," she said.

George Cukor, who was at the helm of *Two-Faced Woman*, was under the gun; both Mayer and scriptwriter Salka Viertel, one of Garbo's closest friends, adamantly wanted the scene to remain in the film. Desperate, Cukor called on Katharine Hepburn in New York to help convince Garbo that she would look satisfactory despite the revealing suit. Cukor recalled that a specially designed bathing costume from the couturier Valentina had worked out well for Hepburn in *The Philadelphia Story*, and he convinced Kate to mail it to the West Coast, where he offered it to Garbo in the privacy of her home.

"The suit might do," Garbo told Cukor. "But I still do not like the scene or my lines."

"That you will have to discuss with Viertel," he stated.

Garbo came to dinner with me soon afterward. She was close to tears. "Just ask Salka to rewrite the scene," I suggested.

"It's not as easy as that," she said. "I haven't liked any of her contributions to this film, and I told her so. I told her I wished to have another writer on the project. But she threatened to expose the nature of our relationship during my early years in Hollywood."

I saw fear in Garbo's eyes. Still naive about many things, I asked, "What sort of hold could she possibly have on you?"

"Never mind," she muttered. "It was something I did with Salka when we were young and foolish. Something unfortunate. But, Mr. Guilaroff, I must do this film. I must read her lines. I have to."

She was painfully torn over the desperate need for a rewrite of *Two-Faced Woman* and her inability to demand one. In years to come I could only watch helplessly as various secrets from Garbo's past ruined her career, her confidence and eventually her lifestyle.

Back then, however, she went ahead meekly with the film. Viewing the first rushes, it didn't seem so bad to me. I remember one sequence with great fondness: a graceful rumba that Garbo performed on a crowded dance floor to the tune of a new Latin song, "Doing the Chica-Chaca." Watching her move with the music, my hairstyle gently tossing and Adrian's dress moving beautifully, I thought it was the most subtly erotic thing I had ever witnessed. During a break in filming, I asked her if she would take a turn on the dance floor with me. Cukor signaled the orchestra to reprise the song, and we rumbaed around the set, earning applause from the extras and bringing an infectious smile to Garbo's face.

"Sydney," she said, "you're a marvelous dancer."

I must have blushed, because Cukor slapped me on the shoulder and roared with laughter.

This was about the last laugh anyone enjoyed over *Two-Faced Woman*. It wasn't just a flop, it also sparked a furor of criticism over its provocative plot—and Garbo's performance. Actually, it was an innocuous comedy about a wife who teaches her husband (Melvyn Douglas) a lesson in fidelity by pretending to be her own twin. But the National Legion of Decency, the Roman Catholic church's watchdog of public mores, described it as "un-Christian towards marriage...impudently suggestive...dangerous to public morals...in all, a film which should be shunned by Christians everywhere." My wild, curl-laden hairstyles and Adrian's rumba gown were described by the Legion as "salacious and degrading even toward Miss Garbo herself." Film critics were even harsher. Cecelia Ager wrote in the newspaper, *PM*, "It makes Garbo into a clown, a buffoon, a monkey on a stick."

Unfortunately for MGM and sadly for Garbo, from that moment on both she and her studio bosses lost interest in her career. There were half-hearted attempts to develop the second and third films in Garbo's three-picture deal, but enthusiasm was in extremely short supply. At dinner several weeks after the premiere of *Two-Faced Woman*, Garbo said simply: "Sydney, I will never, ever make another film. It is over for me."

We soon learned that it was over for MGM as well. I have read with deepening dismay over the years the many accounts of how Garbo walked out on her contract, that she voluntarily forfeited her MGM deal. This is not true. Behind the hoopla of announcing a high-priced three-picture deal, the actual contract was essentially a picture-by-picture arrangement that the studio could cancel at whim literally overnight. Mayer abruptly invoked the cancellation clause and terminated her relationship with the studio.

Despite her protestations to me, I don't think Garbo ever had any intention of leaving MGM for good. She had been there too long and had too many good years left. She knew it and I knew it. Mayer and Metro, however, felt otherwise. One afternoon in 1942, Garbo telephoned me at the studio. "Sydney," she whispered, "I just had a call from somebody—I won't say who—telling me that they have taken all my things out of the dressing room and sent them in boxes to Colleen Camp, the matron who takes care of the dressing rooms. They told me that they needed my room for Lana Turner."

She sounded so depressed that I wanted to give her time to collect her thoughts, so I sat silent for a minute. Finally, I said: "I can't believe it. As much as I loathe Mayer, I doubt even he would do that."

Through tears, she said, "Will you find out if it is true?"

"Yes, I will, dear, and I'll call you right back."

I dialed Colleen. "Is it true about Miss Garbo's things?"

I asked as gently as I could.

She was crying as well. "Yes, Mr. Guilaroff, it's true."

"Who told you to do this?" I demanded.

"Oh, I don't want to say."

"I must know who ordered this shame—this degrading way to let a great star go. You must tell me."

After a long pause she answered in a quiet voice, "It was Mr. Mayer."

I am as shocked today as I was then. It showed me the crass nature of the men at the top of the motion picture business. One can rise to such heights as Garbo and then, suddenly, the moguls have no use for you anymore. In deep sadness, I collected Garbo's things and drove them out to her. She accepted them without a word, but I could see the pain in her eyes. Later on, the studio would treat Joan Crawford, Clark Gable, Spencer Tracy, Lana Turner and many, many others with equal contempt.

The only bright side of the studio's casual cruelty was that afterward Garbo and I were free to begin a love affair. One evening not long after her unseemly ejection from the studio, we went to a quiet Beverly Hills restaurant. After dinner, I escorted her up the walkway to the door of her home. She didn't ask me in, but she was very sweet and pleasant. She said, "I am going to say goodnight to you in the nicest way I can." Then she kissed me gently on the lips.

It was very touching. I said, "That's a very nice goodnight." We let it go at that, but from then on she wanted to hear from me often, and our relationship began to blossom. We never went out very much, and Garbo sometimes stayed with me in my Ambassador Avenue home in Beverly Hills.

Hedda Hopper lived only one street north of me, but miraculously we evaded her and everyone else for quite a while. Then gossip columnist Army Archerd wrote, "Greta Garbo is visiting her good friend, Sydney Guilaroff," and Hedda's antennae went up. She obviously thought that she could simply traipse over to my home and catch Garbo there. Although Hopper was relentless, she needed a lot more than nerve to find her quarry. Whenever my doorbell rang, no matter what time it was, Garbo always hid upstairs. One day, when she was staying with me, she went over to the home of Gaylord Hauser, a mutual friend, for a visit, and while she was gone, Hedda dropped in to say, "Sydney, I hear Garbo is here in town."

"Really!" I said.

Just as Hedda was leaving, Garbo and Hauser pulled up to the house, but when he saw Hedda at my door, Hauser drove on. A few minutes later, Garbo came inside, quaking with fear. It was the first time I had seen her that upset.

"Are you friends with her?" she demanded.

"No, I can't stand her," I said. In fact, I had once been quite rude to Hedda, telling her, "I can't stand gossip reporters." Later, Hedda and I managed to become a little bit more friendly, but it was many years before she found out about my relationship with Garbo.

Though we were very much in love and she was deeply tender with me in private, Garbo despised any public display of affection, no matter how subtle. Once, while I was in New York City making a movie, I took her to dinner with Joseph Vogle, head of Loews, Inc., and his wife at the home of some mutual friends. As we were chatting among ourselves, I did something very unusual for me: Underneath the table I discreetly, gently touched Garbo's hand with mine, simply patted it to make sure she was enjoying herself. She stiffened and moved her hand away, unwilling to betray the real nature of our relationship even with a touch or a look. Later she told me never to do that again, that it was "too much." And I never did.

For many years, whenever I had to go on location, she

usually came along. We were never apart more than a month or two at a time, and we talked constantly on the telephone. Whenever she was in New York, she never answered her phone unless she knew who was calling. Our signal was to call, let it ring once, hang up, wait three minutes, then dial again and let it ring four times before hanging up. When I called the third time, she would know it was me and pick up the phone. She never called me, and I never expected her to do so.

In 1950 I went to Rome to work on *Quo Vadis?*, my biggest film up to that time. Robert Taylor and Deborah Kerr were the leads in a story about lovers in ancient Rome. Deborah soon became unhappy with her Italian hairstylist and called director Mervyn LeRoy to ask if I could come over. I was happy to be going to Rome for the first time in my life.

Producing this film was such an enormous undertaking that even Garbo became interested, so I brought her with me—very, very quietly, of course. She managed to blend in; the way she dressed while in Rome, she could easily have been mistaken for a penniless waif. Most of the time she stayed alone in our hotel suite. She was soon bored, however, since I had a lot of work to do, and she decided to return to New York.

In addition to hairstyling on *Quo Vadis?*, I also became involved in the care and feeding of the 5,000 extras in the film. Many of them were destitute people who had lost everything in World War II. I was appalled to discover that a production associate, Henry Hennigson, was hard on the extras. He didn't seem to care whether or not they were given any water, and although they were to get one hot meal at the end of each day, there never seemed to be much food to go around. This meanness was very irritating to me, since the craftspeople and crew had plenty of food for ourselves.

There was a camp atop Cinecitta studios for displaced persons. Conditions in the camp were appalling, so I took some of the children out of it long enough to feed them. One day inside the camp, a beautiful woman appeared with her child, a thin but lovely girl of about fifteen. They said something to me in Italian, and the gate guard, who spoke a little English, translated. He said, "They are hungry, and they need work."

I arranged to hire the mother and obtained special permission for her daughter to accompany her. That first day I offered this beautiful girl most of my own lunch. I didn't learn until much later that the child was none other than Sophia Loren. I was sorry that Garbo had left without meeting her.

When I returned to London in 1960 for the filming of *Cleopatra*, Garbo and I took an apartment rather than stay in a hotel, where people would stare at her coming and going. The flat was in Westminster, one of the oldest parts of the city, with winding cobblestone streets so narrow that cars and trucks weren't allowed. It was a charming area, but for some reason, whenever I mentioned to English friends that I lived in Shepard Market, they laughed. In time I discovered why: The street was known for its brothels, and their workforce trolled the narrow lanes in search of business. The little mews house in which I rented the two top floors was flanked on both sides by such establishments.

Garbo was traveling, as usual, under the name Harriet Brown, and she settled in. One summer evening as I sat quietly reading, she leaned out our window into the gloom and struck up a conversation with a man in the street below. Then she pulled her head back inside and said teasingly, "Gilly, guess what? I got attention from a man."

"Please don't do that anymore," I replied. "This is the only respectable house in the neighborhood."

Instead of shutting the window, Garbo said, "Let's see if I can do it again."

She took one of my silk scarves and tied it around her head before sticking her head out the window again. After a few moments, she pulled back inside to say, "Gilly, I've got another customer! Business is awfully good in this neighborhood."

"Where do you think you are?" I asked incredulously.

As we laughed together, a male voice came from below: "Are you still there? You're very pretty and I'd like to come up!"

We broke up in laughter. I went downstairs to make sure the door was locked, and when I returned I said, "If you're going to keep this up, we might as well go into business together!"

Garbo liked the fun of seeing how others lived, and she had a marvelous sense of humor that she rarely shared with others. But she was still intensely shy. One weekend we strolled over to a London flea market, where we passed a group of three or four boys, all in their early teens. "Oh, there's Greta Garbo!" said one in his thick Cockney accent. Garbo recoiled, and the kids continued to stare, which made her feel very uncomfortable.

"These kids are just showing you respect," I said quietly. Your films are running in Britain now, and here's a four-teen-year-old who has seen them and knows who you are, even though those pictures were made 30 years ago. I think that's wonderful, that it's a most sincere compliment to have another generation admiring your work. Why won't you be nice to them?"

"I don't know, Gilly," she said in a soft voice. That was just her way. But once in a great while, she would surprise and delight me with a gesture of appreciation. A few years later, on a Sunday afternoon in New York, we encountered an extraordinary couple. Usually, when you see an exceptionally handsome man, the woman he's with isn't quite in the same league, and vice versa. But these two, walking arm in arm like old marrieds, were quite perfectly matched in looks. As we passed them just before we turned onto 57th Street, the woman smiled at Garbo in recognition.

I said to her, "That's very sweet."

"I like that," agreed Garbo.

We walked on a bit, then stopped and for some reason turned around to glance back. The couple was still on the corner, and then the woman blew us a kiss. "You should kiss her back," I said, and Garbo did just that. I was surprised and pleased.

Although she shunned newcomers, Garbo maintained the friendships she had. One time, while we were in Paris, we went for a walk. Suddenly she glanced around and said, "Would you care to meet a friend of mine?" I responded that I would be very happy to meet any of her friends, and she told me that we were going to pay a visit to Cecilé Rothschild.

"You mean the Baroness de Rothschild?" I said, wondering how she might have met the wife of the fabulously wealthy and cultured French banker. We met the baroness for tea at the Ritz, and I sat quietly while Garbo and Cecilé chatted in French. I knew, of course, that Garbo's French was excellent, but I had never had occasion to hear her speak at such length. Finally, Garbo switched to English.

"Isn't he handsome?" she commented, and I turned my head and glanced around. I didn't see anyone who suited that adjective, so I looked back at Garbo questioningly. "I don't see anyone particularly good-looking," I said.

"I'm talking about you!" she exclaimed, and I blushed, stunned that she could be so intimate in front of someone else. She must have been quite close to the baroness.

I did ask Garbo to marry me at one point, and she refused. She didn't want to marry anyone. Our relationship became a marriage of its own without that piece of paper. We each had our lives, and mine was exceptionally full because I was not only working steadily but also a single father. We exchanged vows of fidelity, agreeing never to become involved with anybody else. And despite what has been written elsewhere, I am perfectly satisfied that we each remained faithful to our vow.

Yet Garbo could be secretive, even with me. Once she asked me to take her to Palm Springs, and when we got there she wanted me to let her out of the car at a certain spot. She wouldn't tell me where she was going. I later discovered that she had a brother who was living in Palm Springs. But I was quite annoyed at the time, and the idea that she was so clandestine about it both vexed and pained me.

As I came to know her well, however, I accepted Garbo's ways. We never had a spat or an argument. I was aware only of being in love with her. If people stared at her on the street, I didn't give a damn. But there were times when her fame, and her shyness about it, put me in an awkward position. There was a time in New York, for example, when I walked into a store with Garbo and there was actress Polly Bergen, who gushed, "Oh my God, there's Garbo, with *Sydney!*" and rushed over. I stepped away and told Polly that Garbo didn't like to be introduced to anybody, so I would appreciate it if she understood and didn't insist.

Despite her intense desire for privacy, Garbo loved to take walks. She and I wandered up and down the entire length of New York City over the years we were together; the shopping areas, the antique stores, the theaters—we walked, walked, walked. Looking back through the decades, I have the most romantic memories of those lovely outings: strolling under the chestnut trees in Paris, walking along the banks of the Thames in London, and trudging on the sand in Malibu with the Pacific Ocean lapping at our feet.

Most of the time Garbo wore a jersey cap pulled down to her eyebrows so no one would recognize her. She had a knack for looking inconspicuous in the most expensive clothes. If she found a pair of slacks she liked, she might buy two or three identical pairs so that she'd always have one while the others were being cleaned.

One day she asked me, "Would you like to see me very dressy, in a nice hat?"

"Yes, I would," I answered, and she put on the most beautiful silver fox hat. We walked through Manhattan outfitted like movie stars.

Garbo and I remained in love through 1964, sharing a bond that transcended passion, an unspoken devotion to one another. We did not show it to the world and we did not talk to others about it. She was never passionate in the traditional sense, but she was loving, tender, sweet. Like all enduring relationships, it wasn't all excitement. Mostly it was just natural, as natural as having a meal. At the end of each day we would say goodnight to each other, and sometimes, when Gretala was in the mood, we would make gentle love together. Ours was a blending of hearts and spirit and bodies, a once-in-a-lifetime experience.

As I became a fixture at MGM, outlasting Mayer, who left the studio in 1951, and many who followed, Garbo expressed a lingering curiosity about her old studio. One day in 1962, while I was working on *How the West Was Won*, she asked me to take her to lunch at the Commissary. I made a few arrangements, calling ahead to the hostess and asking her to keep it quiet and to reserve a table for us against one wall. When we arrived and were seated, director Clarence Brown sent a note over, asking if he could come say hello to Garbo. I received a similar note from George Cukor, and another from Robert Taylor.

Soon the whole place was in an uproar: The queen had returned. She took it all graciously, but I honestly can't say if Garbo enjoyed the attention or not. And she never told me why she wanted to go back and visit MGM.

In her later years, Garbo became increasingly withdrawn and eccentric, afflicted with hypochondria and worried about her health. Although she expected me to listen attentively to her worries and ruminations, she didn't seem to have much patience for other people's illnesses. When her friend, actor Clifton Webb, became ill, she asked me to go with her to visit him. "If he gets me on the phone, he always has to tell me about his troubles," she complained. "When I say, 'Hello, how are you?' he tells me about every little ache and pain. I can't stand it."

Eventually Garbo's self-preoccupation, and her preoccupation with privacy, deepened into an all-consuming obsession, and she became almost suffocatingly reclusive, unwilling to leave her apartment for long periods. Yet my love for her never withered. One night in 1964, I went to dinner in Los Angeles with Garbo and one of my few friends who knew the intimacy of our relationship. We had talked about going to the theater or a concert, but Garbo didn't want to go. My friend told her, "You know, I think you're very selfish. Sydney is so in love with you, yet you constantly say no to every little suggestion he makes. Why do you treat him this way?"

Garbo became very upset, but she said nothing. I was silent, too, knowing that she wouldn't want the conversation to get out of hand. I thought I would have an opportunity later to defuse the situation, but when we got in my car to go home, her whole attitude and her body language made that impossible. Once home, Garbo told me that she thought I should have reprimanded my friend for insulting her. I protested that if I had done that in the restaurant, it would have caused a scene. But she remained upset and called a friend to come pick her up. She refused to spend another night under my roof and said she was going to stay with friends in Santa Monica before returning to New York. I begged her not to leave. "Please don't do this," I said. "It will only spoil the relationship between us." She left anyway.

I telephoned that same night to say, "I don't know why you let him disturb you that much. He had no right to say what he said."

"He was insulting to me and *you should have said something!*" she said.

"He didn't matter to me. You matter to me! It was out of respect for you and loving you that I chose to keep silent."

"Gilly, I don't like thrashing things out, and you know it. So I'm not going to say any more about it, or about anything, I'm just going to say goodbye!"

She hung up. When I put the receiver down, I felt as though I had been shot. I was in complete shock. All I could say was, "Oh my God." I sank down into a chair, realizing that we were through. Tears came to my eyes as I wondered what life was going to be like for me now.

I have had more than thirty years to consider the irony of that scene: The woman who prized her anonymity above all else, who avoided publicity and confrontation at all costs, sacrificed our love because I would not defend her in public. Afterward, deeply wounded, she refused to discuss the matter, yielding to her own undeclared emotions.

For a few days following the day of our parting, I considered telephoning Garbo, but I knew she wouldn't answer her phone. She was never one to change her mind. As with everyone else, when she said goodbye, she meant goodbye, once and for all. I had never dreamed that it could happen to me, but it did.

Some years later I was visiting my friend Shirley

MacLaine, who had an apartment on the same block as Garbo's in New York. I confessed, "Every time I walk by here I just hope that I might see her one more time." Without quite realizing it, I had somehow joined the legions of Garbo watchers who expressed their love for her by hoping to catch the merest glimpse of an unhappy and reclusive legend.

Shirley said, "You'll get over her someday. You won't talk about her anymore. The loss was hers, it's not yours."

But I did see Garbo one last time, about a year before her death in 1990. As I came out of the Beverly Hills post office, I saw her walking on the sidewalk with another woman. She looked dreadful in dark glasses with long, whitish gray hair. As we passed each other, I said, "Hello, how are you?"

She looked at me for a moment, then looked away without answering. I felt sad for myself, but most of all I felt sorry for her, sorry that she, who had once epitomized glamour, now cared so little about her appearance that she would go about looking as she did. I was sorry that she had chosen to spend the last years of her life in isolation when the world would have given her anything, when I would have given her anything.

It was a bittersweet time for me, this passing of a nearly 30-year commitment, but whereas Garbo had turned inward, into a lonely world of her own, my world was still a place filled with challenge, excitement, adventure—and eternal promise.

CHAPTER THIRTEEN

Marilyn

*I*t was one of those glittering Hollywood parties that Hedda Hopper used to call star-studded. All the top people in Hollywood were in attendance, seemingly from wall to wall. The most famous and beautiful leading ladies of the screen were present. But the one who caught my eye, clinging nervously to the arm of Johnny Hyde, one of the town's most powerful agents, left an indelible impression on me. *That girl has something,* I thought. Though she wasn't a breathtaking beauty in the classic cinematic sense, she nonetheless exuded both an expressive quality of wistful longing and a spark of inner strength and depth. She was also one of the most powerfully erotic women I had ever seen. Her name was Marilyn Monroe.

As she stood on the fringes of the crowd, she seemed to be contemplating all those famous faces, realizing that she was out of place yet wishing almost visibly to become part of the scene. She was nakedly ambitious, yet almost achingly vulnerable, the sort of girl who might easily be broken by Hollywood's brand of casual cruelty. I wondered if she would survive long enough to have a chance at what passes for success in this town.

I dismissed the beguiling blonde from my thoughts until several weeks later, when I got a call from Arthur Hornblow Jr., the producer of *Gaslight*, *The Hucksters* and *The Major and the Minor*, among other important films. He told me to expect a girl named Marilyn Monroe to test for *The Asphalt Jungle*, a gritty underworld drama. "I would like you to make her look more ladylike," he instructed.

"Send her over," I replied, adding that I knew her.

"But how would you know someone like her?" said Hornblow with a nasty quality that seemed to imply that this girl was somehow vulgar, an impression he confirmed by making a few salacious observations. But like so many others who met Marilyn early in her career, Arthur had misjudged her. She was never vulgar, never cheap or coarse. The very qualities—her curious combination of sex appeal and vulnerability—that would ultimately lead her to stardom initially caused many in the industry, including producers and executives who should have known better, to underestimate her.

With a couple of hours to kill before she arrived, I sent for the script of *Asphalt Jungle*. Marilyn's character was Angela, a creature of great sensuality, yet mentally and emotionally an innocent. This was the best starlet cameo I'd seen in years, just the sort of role that could lead to stardom, if director John Huston could find the right actress. During my years at MGM, I had developed a good sense about what we called star quality, the phenomenon of sensing what kind of an impression someone made on movie audiences. In the silent era, it was called flesh impact. Studying the planes of her face, the way she carried herself and the way she radiated her feelings, I became convinced that Marilyn had it. After reading the screenplay, I knew she was born for the role.

When she arrived, Marilyn was terribly nervous. More than merely emotionally insecure, she seemed overwhelmed at the mere notion of being tested at MGM. I guided her through makeup, where I had Charlie Schram, the cosmetologist, apply subtle shades of make-up, then personally cut and styled her honey-blond hair, opting for understatement. I trimmed her hair carefully, curling it under in the beginnings of a pageboy, but leaving it free to move and shift with Marilyn's motions. It was an original style, much shorter than the standard length at that time and structured to follow the contours of her face. It was the look that would help make her famous and become her trademark.

While she was under the dryer, I polled my assistants on what they thought of her looks and potential. They concurred that she was "nice looking, but nothing special." I thought they'd all sold her short. "She's way above average, and I think the camera will love her," I predicted.

But all that was in the future. At the moment I knew only that in most newcomers' screen tests, an actress was shoved onto a soundstage and ordered around by underlings of the sort who seemed to derive satisfaction from bad manners and studied callousness. Such a test can end a career before it's even started. The way Hornblow and my staff had casually dismissed Marilyn as ordinary prompted me to make a radical decision: I took over her test personally.

She was competing against eight other actresses, including Lola Albright, a brash newcomer who MGM's management hoped would become a star. Only an outstanding test could get Marilyn the part. Accordingly, I recruited the best cinematographer I could find and personally made sure that the lighting was perfect. Then I stood in the darkness off-camera and coached her through every move. Costumed in a white shirt and sweater, Marilyn was soon hypnotized by the camera—she loved it as much as it loved her—and by the sound of my voice.

"Take it very, very slowly," I said. "If I told you a joke right now, what would you do? You'd be smiling, wouldn't you?"

"Yes," she answered, breaking into a smile. Just above her, peering through the lens, the cinematographer also smiled. Her emotions registered beautifully.

"Now think a little seriously," I continued. "Think about something bad in your life, something that happened to you." Her look broke your heart. Of course, I couldn't know then about the indignities and abuse this girl had already endured. I knew only that she was a natural, that she could convey all that sadness and vulnerability to an audience.

"Try to appear sensuous, Marilyn," I called softly. "I know you have that sensuality, and so do you. But show it now in a very quiet way." I put her in a swivel chair and told her to twirl around, to gaze back at me standing next to the camera. "Just look over your shoulder," I whispered. "Now, lean forward on your crossed leg. Then smile at me." She did, and the effect was unsettling in its erotic impact.

The test went on for almost half an hour. In the last five minutes, we did the close-ups. When your face appears on a screen 30 feet high, when the slightest imperfection is magnified dozens of times, that is the greatest challenge, the biggest barrier to movie stardom. Perhaps only one in 10,000 people have the necessary quality, the indefinable look that rivets an audience. As we filmed Marilyn's close-ups, we knew instantly that she was one of the chosen few. When John Huston saw the tests two days later, he was amazed. "What vulnerability—sexy without being crude or coarse," he raved. This is what audiences eventually saw, and it was what made her a star.

While filming *The Asphalt Jungle*, Marilyn sweetly and subtly ingratiated herself with everybody. She even charmed Huston and eventually Hornblow, who only weeks earlier had dismissed her as "common." Word quickly got around the studio that there was a new blonde in town, one with "that certain look." That whiff of stardom in the air brought agents, producers and casting agents to the set to watch her. Whenever Marilyn saw me, she hurried over to ask how I thought she was doing. As a newcomer and a lesser character in a big film, she was barred from the nightly screenings, but when she begged to see the rushes, I took her to see them. I worried that seeing herself this early would make her nervous and overly self-conscious, but to my surprise she liked what she saw, and a bit of self-assurance was born.

In the end, when the film was released in 1950, the only jury that counts—the audience—was impressed. MGM's front office, however, didn't offer Marilyn a long-term contract. The business people figured that because the studio already had one sexy blonde—Lana Turner—it didn't need another. For a while, at least, Marilyn would have to settle for working as a $50-a-week "floater," a young starlet who wanders from studio to studio and from small role to small role in hopes of being noticed. Feeling fatherly and protective, I made it clear to her that I would be available to do her hair and supervise her makeup for readings and tests wherever she was working. Arranging with MGM to get her a drive-on pass, I ordered my staff to treat her like a star.

The first time she called for advice, however, Jane Shagru, my principal assistant, said to me, "Breathless is on the phone." I let it pass. But the next time she used that line, I said, "Jane, don't ever say that again. Even with your hand over the mouthpiece, you never know whether she can hear what you're saying. Just say 'It's Marilyn Monroe' and hand me the telephone."

This was just one of the things I did to bolster Marilyn's confidence and her sense of self-worth. I knew she would need it to handle the pressures of stardom, and I never doubted for a moment that she would become an actress of the first rank.

One day she telephoned with the exciting news that 20th Century-Fox had agreed to test her for a role in *All About Eve*, starring Bette Davis. If she got the part, said Marilyn, then a studio contract would probably follow. She was scheduled for both black-and-white and color screen tests. "Can you supervise my hair and makeup?" she asked.

"I'd be glad to," I answered, "but let me handle the negotiations." I phoned production executives at Fox and said that for a one-time fee of $5,000, I would do her hair. I added that I thought Marilyn would become a major force in Hollywood, perhaps one of the greats. This was not an act of avarice; I didn't need the money. But I believed that demanding such an unprecedented amount for a mere test would awaken the powers at Fox and force them to look at Marilyn as an extremely valuable property. To my surprise, my offer was accepted without a whimper of protest.

After creating a new version of the *Asphalt Jungle* hairstyle that was both curlier and lighter, I once again guided Marilyn through her screen test. Two days later she won both the part and the contract. Even Darryl Zanuck, Fox's top production executive, told me, "Sydney, I think we've got a star here."

Marilyn dropped by MGM to thank me, taking my hands in hers and, with tears in her eyes, murmuring, "Sydney, I want to thank you for everything you've done for me. If I become a star, I'll want you to do every picture with me. Make your fee as high as you wish. I'll make sure they pay it."

Just before *All About Eve* was released to standing-room-only audiences, Sidney Skolsky, the Hollywood columnist, telephoned early one morning. "I'm calling about a girl named Marilyn Monroe," he began. "I know she's a starlet at Fox, but she's shy and refused to talk about herself. She said, 'If you want to know anything, call my dear friend Sydney Guilaroff at MGM.'"

I asked, "Do you know much about Ava Gardner?"

"Of course I do," said Skolsky.

"Well, you know what she's like, her style of acting, her beauty, her sex appeal and her sensuous seduction of a movie audience. And you must know Lana Turner as well, the appeal she has."

"Sure," said Skolsky, "I know Lana Turner very well."

"Well, let me tell you that in her own way, Marilyn Monroe has everything that both of those two stars have. But she also has something even more valuable: a quality of innocence that is absolutely enchanting. Where Lana and Ava exude sensuality, Marilyn's is built-in, but in a very innocent manner, because it's completely natural. She was born with it."

After *All About Eve's* glowing reviews appeared, Marilyn was on her way.

When *Niagara*, a dark melodrama with Marilyn in the lead role, opened in 1952, her star was rising from coast to coast. Moreover, her stardom was created by public demand rather than as a product of studio politics or the casting couch. Because she owed her success not to the faceless men who controlled the studios but to the ticket-buying public, she was able to demand the hairstylist of her choice, no matter what the cost or how many difficulties it raised for the studio. For her role as a disturbed bride in *Niagara*, I designed slightly unruly blond curls that gave her a seductive yet somewhat menacing appearance—beautiful but troubled. This was the first of what became a new wave of cinematic looks that I created for Marilyn's films. Once these appeared on the screen, they swept the nation and much of the moviegoing world.

A year later, for her role in *Gentlemen Prefer Blondes*, I created a very loose pageboy coiffure that was unique in movie history. Some of the style's loose, sleek lines were dictated by the production's rigorous musical numbers, particularly "Diamonds Are a Girl's Best Friend," a sequence in which Marilyn dances down a staircase and is lifted and carried about by a troupe of male dancers. Marilyn's hair had to bounce and sway to accentuate her natural sensuality. The color I chose was a subdued platinum that framed her face and offset the vivid stage makeup she wore, which had been designed to shimmer like the diamonds she sang about in the song.

For the film's premiere at Sid Grauman's Chinese Theater, I re-created one of the classic glamour styles of the 1930s—the ultimate movie star look. Marilyn and that cut were immortalized by the 44 still cameramen and 20 newsreel photographers who surrounded her and Jane Russell as they put their handprints in the cement in front of the theater. In just three years Marilyn had become a full-blown superstar, and finally she had the mud on her hands to prove it.

Over the following years she soared to dizzying heights, marrying America's greatest sports hero, the Yankee Clipper himself, Joe DiMaggio, and appearing in a string of hits: *How to Marry a Millionaire, There's No Business Like Show Business, The Seven-Year Itch* and *The River of No Return.* But an undercurrent of tragedy blighted Marilyn's career as well as her personal life. After walking out on her contract at Fox, she flew to New York and announced that she was forming her own production company with photographer Milton Greene. Fearing that her fame was due entirely to her physical attributes, she decided to begin cultivating her mind by associating herself with famous writers, poets and artists.

A whole new world opened up to Marilyn as she devoured every scrap of quality literary work she could get her hands on.

One day she telephoned me about the possibility of her playing one of the roles in *The Brothers Karamazov,* adapted from Dostoevsky's nineteenth century novel about a Russian family. I agreed that this would be a wonderful vehicle for her to demonstrate her talents as a dramatic actress. But it would be two years before we discussed the idea again, because while she was in New York, Marilyn fell under the spell of Lee Strasberg and his wife Paula. Strasberg was the founder of the Actors Studio, a theater workshop that had become hugely popular in the Fifties with alumnae such as James Dean, Marlon Brando, Paul Newman, Montgomery Clift and Shelley Winters. Lee and especially Paula swooped in on Marilyn and clutched her tightly under their suffocating control.

I wasn't fully aware of Paula's hold on Marilyn when I joined her in 1956 for the filming of *The Prince and the Showgirl*. MGM agreed to loan me out to do Marilyn's hair on the condition that she agree to attend the upcoming premiere of *Gigi*. After letting her out of their grasp a few years before, Metro now knew the drawing power Marilyn possessed wherever she went.

Marilyn had by now divorced Joe DiMaggio and married playwright Arthur Miller, who represented her own unfulfilled intellectual aspirations. I was instantly aware that this marriage was coming apart at the seams when I arrived at the small cottage she had rented for us during the filming. At a press conference for the movie, Miller was asked what it was like to be married to Marilyn Monroe. "Like living in a goldfish bowl," he snapped. Her face fell, and I leaned over to whisper in his ear: "Arthur, you could have lived your whole life and never said a thing like that. Look what you did to her. You should be proud to be her husband. You wouldn't be here if if weren't for her."

As much as Marilyn was looking forward to working in *Showgirl* with Laurence Olivier—who was not only co-starring but producing and directing the picture—the experience turned out to be an unhappy one. I sensed Sir Laurence was irritated because his co-star was coming across far better on the screen than he—and he was no doubt jealous of all the attention she was receiving in his homeland. Even though I respected him as the director, he seemed unduly critical of every aspect of Marilyn's appearance, from her hair to her costumes, and he nixed one dress in particular because he considered it too low-cut. But his real reason for rejecting it was because it was an eye-catcher and he knew that people would be watching Marilyn in that dress.

One night we were invited to a party and Marilyn decided to wear the gown he refused to let her use in the movie. It was a beautiful white linen dress with little loops for button holes that went from the breast line all the way to her feet. Arthur and I were already dressed in our tuxedos when she came onto the upstairs balcony.

"Oh, Sydney," she said, "I don't know what to do. The maid is so nervous about dressing me that she can't get me buttoned up. We're going to be late for the party, and I don't want to arrive late for a big party. I want to show up on time just like everybody else."

"Marilyn, don't worry," I called to her. "I had sisters while I was growing up, and I had to help them all with their buttons on many occasions."

So I hopped upstairs, two at a time, until I reached her, and went to work. There must have been 70 button loops on that dress.

I said to her, "Breathe out. Just let the air out of your body until I get this top button."

She was quite bosomy, and it took some time, but I finally got that first button through the loop. Every time I needed her to hold her breath, I was able to get five more loops. To button up the bottom part of the dress, I had to go down on one knee, and I looked up at her.

"My, my," I said, "you've even got me on my knees."

She patted me on the head and said, "Well, you're a darling for doing this, and I'll kiss you when you get up." When I was finally done, she did just that, and we were off to the party.

During the evening, Marilyn was asked by many men to

dance, but she told everyone she was so tired that she was saving up her energy for just one dance with her good friend Sydney Guilaroff.

As we began to twirl around the floor, I said to her, "I remember when I was a child in Canada, my mother used to read aloud the society columns about some of the very people who are here tonight. And here I am—and here you are. Look at all you have achieved. Both of us have gone from nowhere to somewhere." She smiled at me as if everything was finally okay. That sweet moment between us was interrupted when someone commented on how lovely her dress was.

She winked at me as she replied, "Why, thank you. Don't tell anyone, but it's a reject from the movie."

In 1958, Marilyn was back in Los Angeles to start filming *Some Like It Hot*. By this time, her temperament had become grist for the industry's rumor mills, and she was still unhappy over not being taken seriously as a dramatic actress. Adding to her depression was the news that Maria Schell was starring in *The Brothers Karamazov*. I had pleaded with Richard Brooks to give Marilyn the role, reminding him that Doris Day had been hugely successful playing Ruth Etting in *Love Me or Leave Me* to show that Marilyn too could make the cross-over from comedy to drama, but he refused to listen.

When the film finally wrapped, I attended a sneak preview in Westwood. When the lights went up, sickened by the sycophants who gathered around Brooks, I walked out of the theater without a word. As I entered my home, the telephone was ringing. It was Brooks.

"Sydney, you son of a bitch!" he bellowed. "You walked out on me, didn't you?"

"No, I didn't. And Richard, don't you ever call me a son of a bitch again. We've always been good friends, and I want to continue to be friends. But I told you to give Marilyn Monroe a chance by testing her for the role. She would have agreed to a test even though she's the biggest star in the world. But you said no, and now you have to see how wrong you were. The film we saw tonight lacked the electrifying magic that only Marilyn could have brought to it." Brooks strenuously disagreed, of course, but I was proved right when the picture failed at the box office.

Back on the set of *Some Like It Hot*, Marilyn was sparring daily with co-stars Tony Curtis and Jack Lemmon. I was a witness to this because I created the hairstyles for this picture, including the wigs for Curtis and Lemmon, who appeared in drag. One day, after exchanging harsh words with director Billy Wilder, Marilyn refused to leave her dressing room unless I joined her on the set.

"She wants you to come over," said one of Wilder's assistants, so I went down to the location on Coronado Island near San Diego as quickly as I could.

When I met with Wilder, he said, "Mr. Guilaroff, we're holding up the production because Marilyn won't do anything until you get here. Can you tell me why she had to have you here to watch the shooting?"

I told him she simply found my presence reassuring, so I went in to find out what was wrong. The minute I walked into her dressing room, I knew what—and who— was the problem. Inside was Paula Strasberg, whom I called the "black spider" because she always dressed in black from head to toe.

I happened to know that Paula was angling for screen credit as "Drama Coach to Marilyn Monroe," and I also knew that no studio would grant such credit. Even Marilyn knew it, yet out of misplaced loyalty to Paula, she was holding things up.

I raised the issue and Marilyn promptly told Paula, "Every time you come on a picture with me, you get me into trouble, and I can't do anything about it! And I'm in trouble enough as it is. Look at the way Tony Curtis talks about me."

"What about Tony Curtis?" I asked.

"He's always saying unkind things about me—that I drink too much, that I'm late to the studio." Then Marilyn lightened up for a moment. "I think he's jealous because I look better in dresses than he does."

After we had a big laugh, I explained to Paula that she could hold up production and get everyone angry at Marilyn, but she still wouldn't get her name on the screen.

"It's never happened, and it never will," I said. "Every studio has plenty of drama coaches. Since they don't need you, and what you teach is not a style that the studios prefer, I suspect that you're here only for personal gain. By remaining here, you only hurt Marilyn."

I told Marilyn I would go out and offer some explanation about why she had refused to work. "But you must not get into more of these discussions with Paula," I added. To Paula I said, "Just watch it, that's all I'm going to tell you. Because one day it will explode."

I kissed Marilyn goodbye, then went outside to find Wilder. I told him, "Marilyn's trouble is personal, and I can't tell you about it, but she's ready to return to work now and I'm certain she'll be just fine. Before I leave, I want to ask you something else. How long have you been shooting now?"

"Exactly three weeks," said Wilder.

"She's been late before?"

"That's right."

"What does she look like on the screen? Does she look good? Is she doing well?"

"Oh, she looks marvelous. She's doing wonderfully."

"Well, then, please don't worry about her being a little late sometimes. If she's registering that well, your picture will do very well, too."

So Wilder, a masterful director, gave Marilyn a little leeway, and the movie not only got made, it was a smash hit.

Although Marilyn had a natural flair for comedy, she could also play serious roles. During the scorching summer of 1960, I journeyed to the desolate high desert near Reno, Nevada, to work with her on *The Misfits*, her first dramatic role since *Niagara* eight years earlier. I realized instantly that she was doing this film only to please her husband, Arthur Miller, who had written the screenplay. Word had it that since their marriage, he had produced nothing worthwhile except this script, written specifically for Marilyn. This put her under a great deal of pressure: She believed that the future of her marriage was riding on the success of this film.

The only bright moments during this picture came from Marilyn's joy over working with her idol Clark Gable. She had personally requested that he be cast in the film. Gable bore a striking resemblance to a photograph of her father that her mother had once shown her. I suspected that she fantasized that Gable might indeed be her natural father.

A great deal has been written about how upset Gable was at Marilyn's lateness during the making of *The Misfits*, since he was always punctual, but I saw how enchanted he was with her. The real irritant to Gable was his other co-star, Montgomery Clift, who bumbled his lines so badly in a scene one day that Gable told him during a break in shooting, "If you weren't such a little runt, I'd smash my fist into your face." I too had had my fill of Clift in 1956 during the filming of *Raintree County*, when I had to fish him out of the river after he fell into it face down, apparently passing out from some kind of substance abuse. Elizabeth Taylor had to carry many of their scenes together in that picture because he was too overcome by drugs to deliver his lines.

On the set of *The Misfits*, marital problems between Marilyn and Arthur Miller had climbed to a fever pitch. In public, Miller played the role of adoring husband, but, away from the media, he was barely civil to his wife. He was already involved with still photographer Inge Morath, whom he would later marry after divorcing Marilyn in

1961. Putting on a brave front, Marilyn pretended that nothing was going on, though she knew differently.

In the first shot of the film, a crowd scene, Marilyn's character is arriving for a divorce hearing at the Reno courthouse. Director John Huston pulled the camera back to capture the crowd milling about as a backdrop. Marilyn, a commanding figure with her long, silver-blond hair and dazzling black dress—"a portrait of fire and ice," as critic Bosley Crowther would later describe her.

Then Huston moved the camera forward, closing in on Marilyn for a crucial line. Marilyn's character was waiting to finalize her divorce, and the script called for her to say, "If I'm going to be alone, I'm going to be by myself."

But when Huston bellowed, "Action!" a cloud of emotion came over Marilyn's face, and instead of speaking, she began to tremble. Instantly I knew what was troubling her: The script was too close to the reality of her own life. Earlier, as we sat in her dressing room, she had confided that she and Miller had discussed divorce. The notion terrified her. Wanting desperately to be loved, Marilyn had concocted a fantasy of her life with Miller. She had even purchased an idyllic New England cottage where she dreamed of raising a family with him.

Marilyn's line of dialogue, however, had brought her face-to-face with both the failure of her marriage and the death of her dream. Huston ordered the camera to stop, then looked away. In the oppressive silence that settled over the set, I ran to her side.

"What's the matter, dear? Is anything wrong?" I asked.

She lowered her eyes. "I'm so lonely," she sighed. "So lonely, so alone."

She seemed like a lost child. I wrapped her in my arms. "Don't cry anymore," I said. "As long as I'm alive, I'll be here for you. I don't want you to be lonely, dear, not ever!"

"Thank God you're here, Sydney," she said.

While I comforted her and John Huston nodded sympathetically, Miller and Paula Strasberg remained on the sidelines, impassive and apparently unconcerned.

Not long after that, I was doing her hair on the set. She was very unhappy that day. "You know, Sydney," she said to me wistfully, "I wish I was married to you. You're so kind and so sweet to me, and you understand me better than anybody else does.

I said, "Marilyn, I could be your father."

And that's the way our relationship remained from then on—strong and pure—like the love of a father for his daughter. I tried to remain always no farther than a phone call away, hoping to provide a bulwark against her ongoing struggle with loneliness and depression. But until much later, she wouldn't share even with me her greatest heartbreaks—and only then, it seemed, in the moments of her greatest need.

In the winter of 1961, after Marilyn and Miller's divorce, her press agent, Pat Newcomb, was my date at a party hosted by Robert Wagner and Natalie Wood. She was late and apologized profusely, saying that she had been delayed by Marilyn Monroe. There was something about her tone I didn't care for, so I pulled Pat aside and asked, "What made you say you were held up by Marilyn?"

She seemed annoyed. "Well, I couldn't stay. She was in tears when I left. I'd have been there all night."

That made me angry. "What sort of friend are you, leaving her in tears?"

I immediately telephoned Marilyn at her Beverly Hills Hotel bungalow. "What are you doing, dear?" I asked.

"Nothing," she mumbled.

Marilyn's soft, quavering voice gave her away: She had been crying. I asked jauntily, "What's a lovely girl like you doing home on a Saturday night?" She laughed weakly.

Gossip columnists had been reporting that Marilyn had

shut herself away in the bungalow for weeks, living on room service food and remaining in her dressing gown for days at a time without bathing. They also gleefully described the rumored activities of the Beverly Hills Hotel's other famous bungalow recluses: Howard Hughes, Woolworth heiress Barbara Hutton and, at times, Elizabeth Taylor.

Determined to lure Marilyn out of her depression, I said, "I don't want you to be alone on a Saturday night. Come with me to Trader Vic's for dinner." Marilyn always struggled against herself. Should she trust someone and come out for the evening, or just sink back into the loneliness that had enveloped her since she was a child?

After what seemed an eternity, she answered: "Oh, Sydney, I couldn't do that. I look dreadful."

"You've never looked dreadful in your life."

"My hair is awful, too."

"You know, dear, your hair is naturally curly. The only reason I do it at all is for the movies. I love the way you look when you haven't had it done. Why don't you just put on a little lipstick and I'll pick you up."

Reluctantly, she agreed. To avoid the teeming lobby, with its constant parade of the rich and famous, she used a side entrance on the lush tropical grounds and slipped into my car. She wore a simple black sheath and just a touch of lipstick and trailed a black scarf in one hand. We walked through the doors of Trader Vic's and into its wonderfully hokey paradise of gilded fish nets and bubbling fountains. Every eye in the house followed her: As beautiful as Marilyn was on the screen, in person she was stunningly graceful and feline. Writer Adela Rogers St. John observed, "When you first see her in person, she takes your breath away; she leaves you speechless."

Even Norma Shearer, also at Trader Vic's that night, motioned to me for an introduction to Marilyn, who remained totally oblivious to the effect she had on others.

That evening she seemed utterly lost in her inner turmoil. Trying to make small talk, I said that I'd read in the papers that she was seeing DiMaggio again.

She became angry. "I visit Joe because I love his children. I would do anything for them. As for Joe, I don't like a man who beats me."

Shocked and distressed, I asked, "What do you mean?"

Marilyn explained that after Joe had beat her up, she had warned him, "Don't ever do that again. I was abused as a child, and I'm not going to stand for it." Nevertheless, after watching her film a sexy scene for *The Seven Year Itch*, Marilyn said, "Joe slapped me around the hotel room until I screamed, 'That's it!' You know, Sydney, the first time a man beats you up, it makes you angry. When it happens a second time, you'd have to be crazy to stay. So I left him."

DiMaggio had hit her so badly that special makeup was needed to hide her bruises and contusions from the camera so that filming could continue. As we finished dinner, Marilyn said sadly, "I don't know what makes a man beat a woman. I just don't understand it."

Then and now, I wondered how many other secret hurts she was hiding from the world. Yet somehow Marilyn managed to keep going in 1962, a year of revolutionary change in Hollywood. As the last of the great moguls departed, the studio system was collapsing into commercial and artistic turmoil. The musical, long a staple genre, was dead. A pack of sexy young stars, including Lee Remick, Carroll Baker and Ann-Margret, began crowding out such established cinematic queens as Kim Novak, Jayne Mansfield and Lana Turner. Through it all, however, Marilyn remained a box-office favorite. After *The Misfits* she was offered starring roles in no less than fifteen films, including several with salaries of $500,000 or more, a fortune at the time.

Unfortunately, she still owed 20th Century-Fox a final film, a bit of hokum titled *Something's Got to Give*, co-starring Dean

Martin and Cyd Charisse. Fox brought me in to orchestrate an entirely new style for Marilyn. For the first time, she would portray a fairly well-to-do mother of two children with an unlimited choice of couturier clothing. A yearlong diet had slimmed her down, and Marilyn's earthy sex appeal had evolved into an astonishing glamour. I created for her a series of styles, slightly bouffant and occasionally upswept, which would sweep the nation when they appeared in *Life* magazine.

When we met at Fox in February 1962, I had no idea that Marilyn had now fallen under the spell of a Svengali named Ralph Greenson. Without Marilyn's knowledge, he had been hired by the studio to guarantee that she would finish *Something's Got to Give* "on time and within budget." From the outset, Marilyn felt that this film would never become memorable in any way. But finishing it would allow her to escape Fox after a dozen years of what now felt like slavery to her. Everything proceeded well on the set until Paula Strasberg reappeared, preaching her insidious brand of drama coaching and on-set control. She haunted the set, and she sometimes used hand signals to secretly direct Marilyn under director George Cukor's nose. As I had during the filming of *The Prince and the Showgirl, Some Like It Hot* and *The Misfits,* I warned Marilyn, "Get rid of Paula! You're the one with the talent." But she wouldn't listen.

As far as I was concerned, Paula was the worst kind of parasite. Marilyn became so dependent on her that she felt she could barely read a line without her coaching. One afternoon, I sat nearby while Marilyn was on the phone to New York. "Why aren't you here, Paula?" she asked. "You know I have to begin principal photography for this picture. You should have been here a week ago. I don't know how to read my lines."

Dumbfounded, I said, "Marilyn, put your hand over the mouthpiece for a second." She did, and I continued:

"Why are you begging her to come? Already she's making you miserable and unhappy. Look how she's affected you during this brief conversation. You're trembling. Get rid of her!" But still she wouldn't listen.

When Paula appeared on the set one afternoon, I confronted her. "You know that Marilyn was a star long before she met you and will be a star long after you're gone. She is a consummate film actress, and I doubt that you can teach her very much. So I must tell you, once and for all, stop it!"

I began to feel that some kind of calamity was looming. A few days later, I went to the set to make sure Marilyn went to work. Everything was going fine until Peter Lawford showed up to see her. He was married to Pat Kennedy at the time and was a member of John F. Kennedy's inner circle. I had no idea that Marilyn even knew Lawford, but that turned out to be the least of it. Well, Marilyn went into the dressing room with him in the middle of the day's shoot, and when they came out both of them were loaded, and she walked right off the set with him. He drove her straight to the airport and put her on a special plane to New York so that she could attend a televised birthday celebration for President Kennedy at Madison Square Garden.

The very next evening, while I was watching the telecast of the party, I was shocked and embarrassed to see Marilyn tiptoe into a bright spotlight wearing a nude dress and an outlandish hairstyle. Breathlessly but too loudly, she sang "Happy Birthday, Mr. President." Columnist Dorothy Kilgallen, grasping the implications, described her performance as "making love to the president in the direct view of forty million Americans." About ten days later, alternately laughing and crying—totally out of control—Marilyn called me from the bedroom of her new Brentwood, California, home. I was very cross with her for leaving the set and told her she shouldn't have done it. But it was too late for regrets.

"Fox just fired me!" she cried. As she dissolved in tears, I heard someone's voice in the background.

"Who are you with?" I demanded.

"I'm here with Dr. Greenson."

"Are you sick? The papers said you had a cold."

"No, he's my psychiatrist; I couldn't do without him."

"How long have you been seeing him?"

"Just since I collapsed on the set of *The Misfits*."

Greenson continued to talk, interrupting our conversation. I agonized over the studio's action: If they failed to hire her back, her career might be ruined.

"I'm coming over," I said. "Just stay right there."

I got dressed and a short time later pulled up to the driveway of her mission-style bungalow. I found my way barred by a heavy metal fence. There was no bell and no speaker, and though I shouted a couple of times, nobody answered. With no way to get in, I turned around and drove home, then telephoned her to say, "Marilyn, you're locked up in there. How can I come to see you?"

"It's to keep the photographers out," she mumbled.

I soon learned, however, that her little bungalow had become a prison. Two days later, at about five in the afternoon, I tried again to visit her at home, and this time I was confronted by a pair of very high gates, double-hung and obviously controlled electronically. A tall man stood with folded arms guarding the entrance.

I asked politely, "Can you let me in? I'm here to see Miss Monroe."

"No," he answered. "Nobody sees Miss Monroe. She's with her psychiatrist."

I gave him my name. "At least tell her that I'm here," I said. Looking doubtful, the guard disappeared into the house, and Marilyn soon emerged wearing dark sunglasses and a fedora. She crossed the lawn with some difficulty, leaning on a dour middle-aged man. When she introduced him as Dr. Ralph Greenson, I moved up to get a better look. His gaze was withering, betraying deep hatred for me. His resentment became almost violent when Marilyn threw her arms around me. "Sydney, Sydney, I'm so glad you're here. Please help me."

"Don't worry about anything, dear. I'll have a talk with the studio executives. This thing can be fixed very easily."

Suddenly Dr. Greenson grabbed her arm and hissed, "You're under treatment with me. You must never see this man again."

As he dragged her back into the house, she looked back over her shoulder. It was the last time I ever saw her alive.

On Saturday night, August 4, 1962, exactly eight weeks after Fox fired her, Marilyn telephoned me in despair. She rambled on about being surrounded by danger, about betrayals by "men in high places," about clandestine love affairs hidden even from her friends.

As I tried to calm her, it never occurred to me that I would be one of the last people to speak with her that fateful night.

"What's the matter, dear?" I asked.

Marilyn sounded frantic. "Robert Kennedy was here, threatening me, yelling at me."

"Why was Bobby Kennedy at your house?" I said, thunderstruck. My mind raced: What could the attorney general of the United States have to do with Marilyn?

There was a silence of what I felt was shame. Finally, she blurted, "I'm having an affair with him."

I was shocked. "Marilyn."

"I never told you. I never told anyone. But I had an affair with JFK as well."

"Both of them?" I whispered. I couldn't believe it.

"Both."

I struggled to cope as her words poured out in a torrent of confusion and remorse. She said that Robert Kennedy had journeyed to Los Angeles that afternoon not merely to break off his own affair but to warn Marilyn about ever phoning the White House again. "It's over," he had told her.

"But you promised to divorce Ethel and marry me," Marilyn had replied. Now she was sobbing on the phone. "I'm frightened."

"Is he still there?" I asked.

"He left—with Peter Lawford."

"Well, settle down. You've really put yourself in a trap, dear. What in God's name made you have an affair with the president of the United States? And then to become involved with his brother as well! Did you really think that Bobby was going to divorce his wife with all those children? It's impossible."

Despite all her fame and stardom, Marilyn was really quite naive when it came to men. She wanted so desperately to be loved and to believe in romance that I had no doubt she had believed every word Bobby said. And now he had betrayed her. "I warned him that I could go public," she continued. She told him she could call a press conference.

Bobby had responded, "If you threaten me, Marilyn, there's more than one way to keep you quiet."

I could feel her desperation. "Listen, dear," I said. "He couldn't have meant that. He only said that in anger. Forget it and get some sleep. And just have nothing further to do with them."

When I asked if she had a sleeping pill, Marilyn explained that Dr. Greenson, the analyst who weeks earlier had barred my entrance to her house, had sent over a prescription of Nembutal several hours earlier. "Take one, dear," I advised. "I'll pick you up around noon tomorrow and we'll drive out to Malibu. We'll walk on the beach and talk this whole thing over. You know that you'll never be alone as long as I'm here."

She said yes tearfully, then added a terrifying postscript: "You know, Sydney, I know a lot of secrets about what has gone on in Washington."

"What kind of secrets?" I asked.

"Dangerous ones," she said, then placed the receiver in its cradle.

Disturbed, I slept fitfully. Unaware of the wiretaps on her telephones, I nevertheless sensed she was in danger. When morning finally came, I awoke feeling uneasy. Marilyn's pathetic involvement with the Kennedy brothers continued to trouble me as I drove through the oppressively humid sunshine for an early breakfast in Beverly Hills. "Damn the Kennedys," I said to myself.

Preoccupied with planning a campaign to bring Marilyn around, I ate my omelette in silence, not noticing the subdued air that engulfed my favorite waitress. Instead of her usual cheery manner, she seemed to be tiptoeing around me until I finished my meal.

Then she suddenly grabbed my arm. "Mr. Guilaroff, I waited until you were finished to tell you, but Marilyn Monroe is dead! I'm so awfully, awfully sorry."

Chills ran through me; I still feel them even now as I write these words. I began to cry, then pulled myself together for the drive home, rebuking myself for having recommended that she take sleeping pills the night before—the Nembutal that killed her.

News of her death seemed to be everywhere. Stopping at a supermarket, I saw the huge headline on the front page of the *Los Angeles Times:* MARILYN DEAD! That simple phrase spread across the globe, a public tragedy, a worldwide media event. But at that moment, all I knew was my private grief.

At home I turned on the television set and sat in aching silence. As a telephoto shot showed her shrouded body being wheeled into an ambulance, she was identified coldly as Morgue Number 3895-112. Hours before, she was flesh and blood, the most exciting woman in the world. Now she had been reduced to a mere number.

Knowing that she had no family and that none of her recent bed partners would dare disclose their relationship with her, I called Los Angeles Coroner Thomas Noguchi and offered to arrange a funeral service for my friend. Noguchi said he was sorry, but Joe DiMaggio had claimed the body a half hour earlier. Still later, as newspaper headlines proliferated around the world and broadcasting turned itself over to the subject of her life and death, Inez Melson, Marilyn's manager, called me to relay a request from Joe DiMaggio to dress Marilyn's hair one last time, to make her as beautiful in death as she had been in life.

I accepted without thinking, without reasoning. Only after I hung up the phone did I realize that I simply couldn't bring myself to dress her hair in this state. Instead I brought a beautiful blond wig I had designed for the final scenes in *Something's Got to Give*. On the day of the funeral, shaking and holding back tears, I drove to Westwood Memorial Park and went to a back room where Marilyn lay in a velvet-lined casket. She appeared to be asleep, as beautiful as she had ever been in pictures. The hard edge of reality had been softened. She had already been made up by Whitey Snyder. I dressed her wig so that she looked just as she did in the unfinished film which had led to the downward spiral that ended in her death. I had the attendants remove one of the pillows behind her head because it forced her chin into her neck, making her look fat—which she was not.

On the way to the small chapel, a young man stopped me to pin a white carnation on my lapel. He informed me that DiMaggio had wanted me to be one of Marilyn's pallbearers. I was shocked to discover that except for Whitey Snyder, all the other pallbearers were attendants, employees of the mortuary.

"But she had so many friends," I protested. I was thinking of all the important people—Frank Sinatra, Robert

Mitchum, George Cukor—in her life. "All of them would be honored to serve as pallbearers."

The young man shook his head. "Mr. DiMaggio forbade any stars or celebrities to attend. And no press."

In the chapel, I looked around to see if I knew anybody among the few people who were there. Aside from Pat Newcomb—who, I thought, had failed Marilyn so often in life—I recognized no one else. The service was brief but deeply moving.

I stayed behind as the tiny church emptied out. Finally, only DiMaggio and I remained. He slowly went up to the casket and stood with his hands folded in front of him, sobbing loudly. I was only a few feet behind, wondering whether he was weeping because he was sorry he had beaten her up, or because he still loved her. When he regained control, I approached the casket, bent down, kissed her cold cheek and whispered, "Marilyn, dear, you're finally at peace." She looked so beautiful, so serene, that it was almost impossible to believe she was gone.

The circumstances surrounding Marilyn's death have inspired scores of books and filled many hours of television time. Indeed, there are questions that may never be answered:

- Why would Greenson, knowing better than anyone about Marilyn's precarious mental state, send her 60 powerful pills?
- Marilyn locked her door, obviously so that no one could stop the pills from doing their worst. But who broke in at 4 a.m. to discover she was dead? If it was Greenson, why was he at the house?
- Why did Pat Newcomb, Marilyn's friend and publicist, go to work for the Kennedys shortly after Marilyn's death?

I believe there is no mystery, only an explanation so simple that the world might not accept it. Marilyn killed herself by taking all 60 of the Nembutal pills that Dr. Greenson had sent on that final Saturday afternoon. But then and now I also believe that there was a conspiracy between the Kennedys and Dr. Greenson. He aided JFK and Robert in their confrontations with her, scenes that left Marilyn distraught, confused, frightened and inconsolably lonely. Each man in turn seduced her, then rejected her and finally threatened her. They then provided Marilyn with an easy way out of her despair—60 powerful tranquilizers.

I suspect we will never know all the details of the events that led to her death. But as far as I am concerned, John and Robert Kennedy, aided by Dr. Greenson, murdered Marilyn Monroe just as surely as if they had shot her in the head.

$\mathscr{A}va$

$t$he first time I laid eyes on Ava Gardner, in 1939, she was no more than seventeen years old. She was sitting quietly in a chair, being made up by one of MGM's cosmetologists. With one glance I was swept away by her breathtaking beauty. She didn't even need cosmetics to be stunning. And when she got up from the chair, I saw that Ava also had a graceful and unique way of walking, a rhythmic sway that was incredibly sensual. She was impossible to ignore.

Ava was "discovered" by her brother-in-law, a professional photographer who had shot pictures of her and sent them to MGM's corporate parent, Loews. One look at these images and she was put under contract, initially for six months, with options for the studio to renew if they chose to do so. One of her first pictures was *Sunday Punch*, with William Lundigan and Dan Dailey Jr. It was a story about a boxer, and Ava was cast as a mere face in the ringside crowd. But what a face! The fact that she was given such a small role told me that MGM's movers and shakers didn't have a clue about her potential as a headliner. I was sure I did.

Even before that film was shot, Ava and I had a chance encounter that endeared us to each other forever. While demonstrating hairstyling techniques one morning to some of my junior staff members, I heard an odd, disturbing sound. Turning around, I said, "Whoever that is cracking their gum, please stop." Petrified, Ava actually swallowed the gum! Later that morning, as I approached to help with her hair, I found her crouching down in her chair, cowering in fear lest she arouse my anger. Of course I couldn't stay angry at someone like her. She was such an appealing, unpretentious girl that it was impossible not to care for her.

After a time, it became obvious that Ava's career wasn't moving forward, so I took her under my wing. Her first problem was that she spoke the King's English as a true daughter of the South—no surprise there, since she was born and raised in Smithfield, North Carolina—and her heavy accent was perhaps too great a burden on Northern ears. I saw to it that she took lessons with a voice teacher, who taught her to speak in cultured tones that seemed to have originated somewhere between Oxford and Harvard. Her lovely, low-pitched voice told you right away that you were dealing with someone who was every inch a woman.

Still, Ava remained stuck in small, forgettable parts and was going absolutely nowhere in roles described, for example, as "Girl in the Car." Disheartening as this was to her, I nevertheless took great pains to make her look good, certain that she would begin getting noticed, that she had exceptional talent which would lead her sooner or later to bigger and more important roles.

In 1942 she appeared as a carhop waitress working at a

roadside drive-in cafe in *Kid Glove Killer*, with Van Heflin and Marsha Hunt. Ironically, this was exactly the sort of job taken in real life by young women hoping to be "discovered" by a talent agent or a studio executive. This was followed by *Pilot Number Five*, starring the suavely continental Franchot Tone along with a young Gene Kelly. Once again, however, Ava was little more than an extra. Astonishingly, director George Sidney didn't seem to find her exciting.

Throughout the forties, I guided Ava's career from behind the scenes. When I had a few moments to spare, I would go over to whichever set she was working on to watch and offer moral support. I also made it a point to look at the daily rushes from every film she was shooting. I was friendly with the editors and cutters, and they obliged me by running whatever I asked to see. For lesser pictures, I would watch only Ava's footage.

Whenever she got discouraged, I would reassure her. "You're a natural-born actress," I would say, "and one day you're going to be a great star."

It took a long time before Ava began to believe me, and I don't think she ever really believed that either her looks or her talent were in any way exceptional. But she never forgot that I had paid attention to her when no one else would. Years later, after she had become world famous, she wrote in her memoirs that I was the only sincere person who ever got close to her.

Ava's big break came in 1946. She was on loan to Universal in a co-starring role opposite a young Burt Lancaster in *The Killers*. This is the film that made her famous, but when she returned to MGM the following year to star with Clark Gable in *The Hucksters*, she had to fight for a raise in her salary. Despite her good notices in that film, MGM sent her back to Universal, where a few people had at last begun to sense that Ava might have even greater potential. She was still sure they were interested only in displaying her sensuality. Even though she never thought of herself that way, she did radiate sexuality, and that's why the other studios wanted her.

Her other grievance was that MGM was still paying her at her contract rate, so although other studios paid more to get her services, the difference went into Metro's coffers. All that changed at Universal in 1948 with *One Touch of Venus*, a terrific vehicle for Ava that made her a great star. At last she began getting a star's privileges and was paired with such leading men as Robert Taylor, Gregory Peck and Clark Gable. Peck starred with her in *The Great Sinner*, one of the finest films MGM ever made, a costume picture in which Ava looked exquisite.

She had so much elegance and natural beauty that instinctively she resisted MGM's elaborate makeup process, consenting only to a light coat of Pan-Cake. She applied her own lipstick and added a little mascara to her eyelashes, then powdered down. She rather liked a sheen on her face, a natural tone value, and I admired and encouraged her for that.

As her fame grew, I continued to style her hair and watch over her career. Even when she was filming at another studio, we would take photographs of my hairstyles for her and Ava would bring them along so that the look I had created for her could be duplicated by another stylist. Near the zenith of her stardom, foreign producers and directors asked, "Why do you have to have Sydney do your hair when you're out of the country?"

She replied, "Because he makes me feel beautiful." When that got back to me, I had to smile. It was a touching tribute from a woman who never had any ego whatsoever about her ravishing beauty.

Ava's romantic life became increasingly public, a soap opera filled with outrageous characters and melodramatic events. Her romance with Mickey Rooney, for example, began as a publicity stunt. Studio publicists, following the conventional wisdom of the day, thought that if she was photographed while attending public events with other movie stars, more people would begin to notice her. This attention would translate to higher box-office receipts for her films.

The studio had dubbed Mickey "the All-American Boy." I call him "the All-American Nothing." I found him vulgar, coarse and common, so very obnoxious that I couldn't even talk to him. I didn't like him then, and after knowing him for some 50 years, after watching him prance across the screen, overblown and thoroughly disgusting, my feelings haven't changed a whit.

The minute Mickey saw Ava, he wanted to sleep with her. It was a complication she didn't want or need, but finally she gave in to him, and in 1942 the studio arranged their marriage. After that, however, Rooney paid little or no attention to her, leaving her alone at home most of the time while he went out on the town with his friends. I can understand his wanting to marry her. He was so insecure and driven that he needed constant reassurance, and Ava's phenomenal beauty brought him a great deal of attention. But he used her in the crassest manner and wore her like some gorgeous ornament.

Finally she'd had enough, and they divorced the following year. Early one afternoon she and I were leaving MGM's hairdressing salon arm in arm. I said, "I haven't much to do the rest of the day. Would you care to come with me, dear? We'll go for lunch and have a good time, and if you'd like to, we'll go and see a movie later."

Ava agreed, and as we got into my car, a beautiful green Cadillac convertible, Rooney suddenly appeared from a nearby hallway. When he saw us in my car, his face took on a funny look, as if to say, "What's she doing with him?"

"I wonder if he'll say hello," mused Ava. She looked his way and called, "Hello, Mickey! And goodbye!" When he looked away, Ava seemed delighted, and she laughed as we drove off. "He was just another experience," she said. "I hope life will be better for me from now on."

After her divorce, Ava was pursued by many important men, not the least of whom was Howard Hughes. One of the richest men in Hollywood even then, he gave her a nice little hideaway above Sunset Boulevard. He had girls and houses all over town, and though he really wasn't in the picture very long, he had so much money that he thought of himself as God Almighty, and the idea that any woman would reject him was beyond his comprehension. He called Ava and sent her messages and made demands on her for years, well past the point where she had any lingering interest in him.

Her second marriage was to Artie Shaw, the bandleader. He considered himself an intellectual and helped her to improve her reading skills and polish her manners, but he also got her to begin smoking and drinking. It was Shaw's fifth marriage, so it was hardly a surprise that it was all over in a couple of years.

In 1950 I was about to leave for Rome to work with Deborah Kerr on her hairstyles for one of my biggest films, *Quo Vadis?* Her co-star, Robert Taylor, was at the time married to Barbara Stanwyck. A few days before I left Los Angeles, Barbara telephoned and asked me to come to her house to discuss something very personal.

In her living room, Barbara got straight to the point. She knew that Ava was also going to be in Europe, and, knowing that Ava and I were close, Barbara told me of her concern that Robert, who had once been romantically involved with Ava, might be tempted to resume the affair.

"Would you mind if I asked if you and Robert could take an apartment together in Rome? You two are friends, you could do the cooking, and that way you could look after him for me."

Barbara was a very strong woman, and I knew this was hard for her to ask, so I accepted. Besides, I knew how lonely it could get being away from home. I also cared enough about Ava to not want to witness her getting hurt once again by Robert.

As fate would have it, however, Barbara didn't have to worry about Robert, because Ava never came to Rome but wound up falling for Frank Sinatra. And despite my best efforts, Robert *did* have a dalliance with a beautiful actress he met there, and ended up moving out of our apartment to move in with her.

By the time the movie wrapped and I returned to Los Angeles, Ava's affair with Frank Sinatra was in all the papers. It had even broken up his longtime marriage to his childhood sweetheart. The headlines continued to hound them after she and Frank got married, and it eventually ended in still another divorce. Their stormy relationship has been portrayed as a cruel, tragic union. But in truth, he was very good to her. It's just that they were total opposites. She was at the height of her fame, but she had few friends, rarely entertained and wanted nothing more than to live with her husband and lead a simple and quiet life. Sinatra, in the midst of clawing his way back to movie stardom after falling from the top of the heap, was driven to seek glory, and no amount of fame was ever enough for him. He couldn't stand solitude and surrounded himself with an entourage of friends and hangers-on. Paradoxically, he also couldn't stand being in the public eye, because the press was always looking for a story and all too often he was it.

But if it had not been for Ava, Sinatra might have been forced to content himself with a career as a singer. She appealed to her friend Joan Cohn to ask her husband, Harry, head of Columbia, to cast Sinatra in *From Here to*

Eternity. Ava said, "Do me a favor: Tell your husband that Frank wants the part so badly that he'll work for almost nothing. And ask him to read the book. Frank was born to play the part of Maggio." Reluctantly, Harry listened to his wife, and it turned out to be the break Sinatra needed for his comeback. His performance in *From Here to Eternity* won him an Oscar and put him back on top, this time as a dramatic actor.

By the time Ava called in that favor from Joan Cohn, though, her relationship with Sinatra was already falling apart. Ava had developed a notorious reputation for sexual liaisons with several famous men. But she tried to help younger actresses avoid the kind of mistakes that she had made. She and Grace Kelly, for example, became close friends while in Africa filming *Mogambo.* Ava felt very protective toward her. When co-star Clark Gable made a play for Grace, Ava gave her some advice: "Don't be fooled by his looks or his interest in you! He's been with so many women—you have no idea! I haven't had an affair with him myself, but I know what I'm talking about. Don't fall for it, because he'll cast you aside just as he has all the others. You'll be just another girl to him. He likes to conquer, and when he's done, he's through with them and he leaves them."

Ava was an emotional contradiction. She knew better than to let herself be victimized in a relationship, but she often suffered through heartbreaking experiences with men. One night during her marriage to Sinatra, when something had again gone wrong between them, she came to my house and stood on the lawn with tears in her eyes. She seemed deeply sad, almost at the point of a nervous breakdown, and I said, "Ava, dear, tell me what's wrong? You came here for the comfort of a friend, so tell me what's going on. I'll help you if I can."

"I just can't tell you," she sobbed.

"Won't you at least come inside the house?"

"No, no. I'd just break down, and that's what I'm trying not to do."

So we just stood beside her car in the darkness, and she held her head in her hands while I stroked the back of her neck. Finally I said, "I could insist that you tell me what's distressing you so much, or I could try to pull it out of you. But you have your own way of thinking and feeling, and all I can say is that I'm terribly sorry, but I can't help you if you won't let me."

She said nothing and continued sobbing wordlessly for a long time. Then she kissed the back of my hand and said, "I love you, Sydney, but you can't help me this time. I'll just go back where I came from."

"Please come in," I persisted. "For God's sake, let's sit and talk."

"No," she replied. "It's enough to know you're right here." I went back inside, but for hours I watched her pace up and down in my garden, bathed in moonlight, lost in grief. Eventually she just trudged off into the night.

Some of her worst moments were yet to come during her masochistic relationship with George C. Scott, whom she met while filming *The Bible* in 1965. I had run into him at the studio before he left for Italy and North Africa to begin shooting on location, and innocently I asked him to give Ava a kiss for me when they met. Apparently he did too good a job of it, because almost immediately they fell in love. She telephoned me some time later. "I've fallen for George," she said, "and he's fallen for me. In the early weeks of shooting, we saw a lot of each other off the set. He seems so highly intelligent and civilized, very gentle but with a slightly sardonic sense of humor, which suits me fine. He knows the film world backward and forward, and he's a magnificent, intense actor, too."

I was hurt, as I had grown quite fond of her myself, but

I said nothing about it and tried simply to be there for her as a friend. She needed one.

Several days later, she called back to confide that George had become abusive. After returning from dinner, they had gone to his hotel room for a nightcap. George had already drank quite a lot that night, and after another two or three, he got into one of his rages. "When he began to argue with me, I decided it was time to leave," said Ava.

Then, out of the blue, he smashed her in the face and began to punch her wildly. Instead of screaming or fainting, she tried to reason with him. The result was more punches and a torrent of accusations. "It felt like hours before I managed to get out," she told me tearfully.

When he had sobered up, of course, George was contrite and apologized. But the beatings continued after they returned to Los Angeles, and Ava sought refuge several times with me. One night, while she was staying at the Beverly Hills Hotel with Scott, she came on foot to my home, bruised and terribly unhappy. I could see where he had hit her. I said, "Ava, I just don't understand you, dear. When a man is dangerous like that, walk away from it. Don't even think about it. Don't be taken in by his personality or his talent or whatever you fell in love with at the time." But she just sobbed.

Why did she take such abuse? I've learned that many women will take beatings and refuse to talk about it because they think they're in love. They're very forgiving, and they don't want anybody to know about the abuse. Nowadays everyone knows about the type of man who abuses and batters women, but in those days such things were hushed up; it was a subject never broached. Eventually Ava did leave George, and later she told me that her relationship with him was the most terrifying of her life. "Even today," she said, "If I so much as see him on television, I start to shake all over again and have to turn the set off."

Perhaps that's why Ava finally fell passionately in love with me: I was kind, undemanding, always ready to help. And I fell in love with her. Even though I knew about her marriages and I had heard all the rumors of her other romances, I forgave her and loved her as a human being. I wanted to marry her, but I could never bring myself to press it on her, because I was sure she would refuse and that would be the end of everything between us.

Our affair began in the mid-1960s, soon after Garbo walked away from me, and it involved both tender moments and lighthearted adventures. Before we became physically intimate, we shared an incredible evening in New York City. We somehow found ourselves there at the same time, though I can no longer recall what film I was working on. We were both staying at the Ritz, and Ava wanted to see a particular opera—it might have been *La Traviata*—and afterward we went out for something to eat. By the time we left the restaurant at about two in the morning, it had begun to drizzle a bit, and for some reason there were no taxis available—none, at least, that would stop for us. Finally, as we stood shivering on the curb, waving in vain at passing cabs, a garbage truck came by. The driver stopped, rolled down his window and said, "Hi, Ava, how are you?"

"I'm fine, thanks, how are you?" she replied, as if to an old friend.

"What are you doing?" asked the driver.

"We're stuck here," said Ava. "No cabs."

"We'll take you wherever you want to go," he said.

It was hilarious: Ava dressed in a long, beautiful evening gown, the most glamorous woman ever to ride home in a garbage truck. After I helped her up into the cab, she squeezed in next to the driver. His assistant slid in beside her on the other side, and I wedged myself in against the door. And we all drove off up Park Avenue to the Ritz.

When they let us out in front of the hotel, Ava said, "Fellas, you deserve something for your trouble. Why don't you come on up for a drink?"

We went upstairs to her suite and drank and talked and had a ball until about six in the morning, when the concierge knocked on the door to say, "Miss Gardner, would you mind if I asked your friends to remove the garbage truck from in front of the hotel? Daybreak has come and people will be arriving at any minute."

Ava said goodbye to her new friends, and out they went to reclaim their truck. Then we laughed and laughed until our sides hurt. That was Ava. She was always ready to have fun and never took herself seriously. She had not an ounce of pretense, and that's what I loved about her.

By the time we got together, she had stopped making films in America. So when we were in each other's company it was usually abroad, where for the sake of propriety we took separate but adjacent rooms. We would open the door between the rooms because Ava always slept in my bed.

During her last film, *Harem*, starring Omar Sharif, I stood by on the set to offer encouragement for ten hours at a time. My feet were so sore from a lifetime of standing up that they were often swollen at the end of the day. After a bite to eat, all we wanted to do was go back to our hotel and rest. Ava would say to me, "Oh, your little footsies, they must hurt because you stand up all the time. Let me massage them for you." And she would rub my feet for me. I'd say to her, "You're such an angel. I love you."

But as much as anything about that dear woman, I loved the way she acted with me in public. As we walked together, she'd put her arm in mine, in the way women of her age were brought up to. You used to be able to see that on Easter Sundays in New York City, when everyone dressed up in their finery for the parade down Fifth Avenue, and the women always walked alongside their husbands, but a couple of inches behind, in deference to their maleness. Ava treated me just that way.

I loved her more than I could possibly describe, and I'm sure she felt the same. But as the years went by, our passion mellowed. When you get past a certain age, you don't breathe so hard anymore or become consumed with emotion. You love in a mature way, answering each other's every question only with that love.

In the late sixties, I was still working at MGM when Ava publicly declared that she would never return to America, and certainly not to make any more pictures.

In 1969 I joined her in Paris for the premiere of *Mayerling*. The director, Terence Young, asked me to escort Maria Callas as well. Ava and I shared an appreciation for the wonder of Maria's beautiful voice; she was truly one of the greatest singers of this century. Over dinner—before the thunderous applause both she and Ava would later receive at the theater—Maria bared her soul to us about how Aristotle Onassis broke her heart.

By this time, Jacqueline Kennedy had married the Greek billionaire, and she happened to also be in Paris. Because of this coincidence, I am sure that Maria's pain over losing Onassis to President Kennedy's widow was uppermost in her mind. Frankly, I was stunned that this extraordinary, talented creature was grieving over Onassis' refusal to marry her. He had no appreciation of music at all, and Maria told us that he had asked her to give up her career so that she could be with him all of the time. And for what? So he could dump her for a woman as uninteresting as he was—a woman whose only claim to greatness was that she had been married to the President of the United States. That may have been enough to captivate Onassis, but I could only think that he was a fool to overlook an orchid for a rose.

In May of 1974, Ava agreed to visit Los Angeles for the

opening of *That's Entertainment*, produced by Jack Haley Jr., which became a big hit despite the fact that it was nothing more than a series of film clips featuring a who's who of Hollywood. Ava telephoned me to say, "Honey, I'm coming to America!"

For the premiere, I escorted her to a small art house theater in Beverly Hills. Ava looked dazzling in a white gown designed by a London couturier. She had been away so long that she had begun to take on a certain mystique, and that, combined with her still incredible beauty, made her the star of the evening. Producers and directors and actors of every era craned their necks to get a glimpse of her. After the screening, we followed a red carpet across the street and around the corner to the Beverly Wilshire Hotel for a dinner celebration. The streets were lined with fans, many of them cheering Ava, surprised and delighted to see her once again. It was a triumphant evening. A few days after this event, she returned to London.

A year later Ava called from her home in Europe and asked me to join her in Russia for the first Russian–American co-production, a remake of *The Bluebird*. Her co-stars were Elizabeth Taylor and Jane Fonda. Besides my happiness at the thought of our spending time together—as well as with Elizabeth and Jane, both dear friends—I thought that it would be a fitting tribute to my Russian parents to have my name on the screen in a film made in the land of their birth.

Ava and I shared adjoining suites on the fourth floor of the hotel, down the hall from Elizabeth. By this time, I think Elizabeth knew that Ava and I were intimate, but she never pried. We all had a marvelous time in Moscow, most especially on an evening at the Bolshoi Ballet with director George Cukor. We sat in an ornate box that had once been used by Czar Nicholas and his wife, Alexandra. On days off, Ava and I traveled around Leningrad, and in the evenings, I was happy to treat some of the British journalists covering the film to dinner.

One reporter in particular had become a regular dinner companion, but one day he simply disappeared without even saying goodbye. A few weeks later, a man came up to me in the hotel bar and said, "I just read about you in the *London Times*." I got a copy of the paper and nearly passed out. The journalist I had been friendly with, who had never officially interviewed me, had written an article quoting me about virtually everything we had discussed while dining together—about the film, about Russia and my thoughts about being there.

On orders of the KGB, the writer was forbidden to ever enter the country again, and the movie's public relations man was forced to resign. But thank goodness I had said only wonderful things about the USSR and its people. I even became popular with everyone from the hotel desk clerk to the local florist. After returning home, I mused at how ironic it was that after surviving Hedda, Louella, Walter Winchell and all the other Hollywood gossip writers, I would end up as an unofficial travel guide for the Soviet Union.

In the 1980s, Ava's health began to deteriorate. In an incredibly loving and generous gesture, after she had a stroke, Frank Sinatra—by then remarried to Barbara Marx—had her flown to a specialist in the United States in a specially equipped medical plane at his own expense. When she had recovered sufficiently, Ava returned to her lovely apartment in London's Ennismore Gardens.

For years she called me from there, often in the middle of the night, and because it was her I didn't mind being awakened. But when she called one night in January 1990, she sounded so sick that I said, "Ava, dear, you don't sound good to me. Where is that doctor of yours?"

"Oh, he just comes to tell me I'm okay."

"You don't sound okay to me. Why don't you call Frank and ask him to fly you back here to see that specialist again?"

"I've already imposed on him enough. After all, he's married to someone else now."

"Then meet me in New York and and we'll fly back to Los Angeles together. It's time for you to come home."

"That sounds wonderful, Sydney. Let's do it. But instead of flying back to L.A., let's take the train. We can have our own compartment. I like the clippity-clop of the railroad tracks, and it would make me very happy to hear that sound again."

"What a marvelous idea," I said. "We'll take the train. I love looking out the windows. We can watch the scenery go by and have our meals brought in and just enjoy ourselves alone together all the way across the country."

We talked and laughed and planned the whole trip, and a few nights later, on a Saturday, I called her to talk about our new life together in Los Angeles.

Our reunion never happened. On Monday morning a mutual friend called from London to say that Ava had passed away during the night. I screamed and sobbed in grief, unable, unwilling to believe it. Some precious part of me, the part that loved life and laughter, died with her. That part of me is gone forever. Even now, all these years later, I still dream about her. In one of the dreams, she's running away from me, and I'm running after her, but I can never catch up with her. In another dream, we're younger and walking together in a green park, hand in hand. And that's the dream I want to remember forever.

CHAPTER FIFTEEN

Elizabeth

e lizabeth Taylor was nine years old when I first met her on the MGM lot. I thought at once that she was the most enchanting girl anybody at the studio had ever seen. As nearly everyone knows, she rocketed to stardom in 1944 at age twelve in *National Velvet,* and it was during the making of that film that we bonded.

She was in tears because the director, Clarence Brown, wanted me to shear off her hair to make her look more tomboyish so that her character could pretend to be a boy for the big horse race at the end of the movie. I told her that I had an idea, and not to worry about losing her beautiful long black locks.

Working almost around the clock for an entire week, I wove thousands of individual strands of hair into a short wig—an intricate approximation of what Elizabeth's hair would look like in a boyish bob—and I attached her jockey cap to the wig.

On the day the scene was to be shot, I led Elizabeth and her mother, Sara, onto the set and swore them to secrecy. I then walked over to Clarence and pointed to Elizabeth.

"Will this do?" I asked him.

The three of us held our breath as Clarence ran his fingers through Elizabeth's raven "hair."

"This is more than fine," said Clarence. "This is perfect, an absolutely perfect haircut. But don't cut it another inch."

Elizabeth ran over and threw her arms around me, whispering, "Thank you, Sydney."

Elizabeth's lush mane of hair epitomized her intense longing to escape childhood. Impatient with her greatest asset, her youth, she yearned to be a grown-up. As the only adolescent working among dozens of adults on the lot, she despised being treated like a child. What made things even harder for her was that when *National Velvet* began shooting on location in Walnut, California, Elizabeth already had the ripe body of a full-grown woman. I can't think of another actress whose figure was quite as perfectly beautiful so early in her life.

Most difficult of all for Elizabeth was her parents' separation, which began in the autumn of 1946. At least two biographers have claimed that this breach was caused by her mother's romantic involvement with Michael Curtiz, director of *Life With Father,* in which Elizabeth starred. That may be so, but in the absence of any supporting evidence, it is impossible to assess whether there is any truth to the rumor. What is clear is that a rupture occurred in the Taylor household, and in the summer of 1947, Elizabeth and Sara moved to a beach house in Malibu, while her father, Francis, and her brother, Howard, stayed on in the family home on Elm Drive in Beverly Hills. Consequently, Elizabeth really didn't have a family when she arrived at MGM, and I soon began to serve as a sort of surrogate father in her life. Given Francis Taylor's indifference, my help and concern was both needed and appreciated.

As a young teenager, Elizabeth didn't date; boys her age were so awed and intimidated by her glamour that most believed they wouldn't stand a chance with her. Few dared even to approach her. Except for a handful of child actors at MGM, such as Roddy McDowall, she had no friends her own age. "I rode horses and acted," she recalls of that time. Fond of animals, she even had a pet hamster that she carried around with her at the studio.

So anxious was Elizabeth to begin adulthood that her first dates were with older men. Bill Lyon, a member of the studio's publicity department, escorted Elizabeth to Roddy McDowall's eighteenth birthday party in September 1946, where he noted that she "danced constantly, but with older men." In 1950, hungry for romance and freedom, she married nineteen-year-old hotel heir Nicky Hilton—a union highly favored by MGM management and by Sara Taylor, who thought it fitting that her darling daughter, after a very short engagement, was now wed to the son of an immensely wealthy hotelier.

This was an era when it was not proper for young girls to indulge in sexual relationships before marriage. After their wedding, Nicky, a pampered playboy with many sexual encounters in his past, discovered that Elizabeth not only was a virgin but had no sexual experience whatsoever. Their romance quickly fizzled. Elizabeth was devastated. Like anyone her age in those times, getting married had been one of her lifelong dreams, and she had truly believed it would last forever.

The tension between she and Nicky was almost palpable when she came to see me on the set in Rome, where I was involved in the making of *Quo Vadis?* It was an open set, and the cast, which included mostly British actors, instantly recognized her, though it was quickly apparent that they had no idea whose husband Nicky was. Elizabeth looked so unhappy that I drew her aside and asked what was wrong. She poured out her heart to me: Her marriage was a farce, nothing like the romantic parts she had played on the screen. Real life for her was filled with disappointment and bitterness. She was married to a man who treated her like a child and spent little time with her, preferring to busy himself with his friends and the frivolous pursuits of the idle rich. When she and Nicky returned to Hollywood, she filed for divorce. They had been married for less than a year.

Soon afterward Elizabeth met an elegantly charming, extraordinarily attractive older man, British actor Michael Wilding. Still healing from her painful relationship with Hilton, she was both vulnerable and responsive to his romantic, courtly attentiveness, and she fell for him hard. They got married in 1952 and had two sons, Michael and Christopher.

But while her career continued to blossom, Wilding failed to become a star of her magnitude and began to lose his self-assurance. Elizabeth wanted a man in her life who was stronger than she was, and that was the beginning of the end for them. When the marriage finally collapsed after a few years, again she sought me out for comfort.

"I'll never find anyone, will I, Sydney?" she said sadly.

"Yes, you will, dear," I answered. "The right man will come."

And, of course, it wasn't long before producer Mike Todd, a dynamic giant in the industry, strode into her life and swept her off her feet. He was about 50, old enough to be her father, but that might have been part of the attraction. They fell so deeply in love that Elizabeth even converted to Judaism. They were married in Acapulco on February 2, 1957.

When the Todds returned from their honeymoon, costumer Helen Rose and I gave them a party at my Grecian-style home in Beverly Hills. What started out as an intimate gathering became a party attended by 85 of Hollywood's biggest names, who all showed up to bear witness to what seemed at last a match made in heaven between one of Hollywood's most glamorous stars and one of its most flamboyant showmen.

Despite the huge guest list, I did all the cooking myself. My parties had become a tradition. But this was a night like no other! Elizabeth looked ravishing in the off-the-shoulder black-and-rust taffeta evening gown Helen had designed for her role in the film *The Last Time I Saw Paris*. She was also wearing a stunning pair of diamond earrings that Mike had given her as a wedding present. They were the first of the many gems men would lavish on her in years to come. I had never seen Elizabeth more beautiful or happy as she was that night.

Life with Mike was so pleasurable for Elizabeth—as she traveled with him to promote his Oscar-winning production, *Around the World in 80 Days*—that, after making an average of a picture a year for most of her young life, she was more than willing to retire and simply be Mrs. Mike Todd. She was 25 years old.

Then on March 22, 1958, Mike made ready to depart on a business trip to the East Coast in his private plane. Elizabeth was stricken with a bronchial infection and her doctor had advised her to stay home and rest. When he came to her bedside to say goodbye, Elizabeth grabbed his arm and said impulsively, "Take me anyway."

"No," Mike answered. "You stay home and get well."

He kissed her goodbye six times, each time holding her more tightly.

"Don't go," she insisted. "I don't want you to leave. I have a premonition."

"Nonsense," he said. "I'll be back before you know it."

Four hours later, Mike hopped into his plane, *The Lucky Liz*, and flew off. A few hours later, a furious thunderstorm slammed his plane into a bluff in the New Mexico highlands. He was killed instantly.

Early Saturday morning, after learning of the tragedy, Dick Hanley, Elizabeth's secretary and close friend, along with her physician, Dr. Rex Kennamer, drove to her home on Schuyler Road in Beverly Hills. They wanted to reach her before she saw a newspaper or heard about Mike's death on radio or television. As they entered her bedroom, she looked up from her bed and smiled. Without a word, the doctor moved toward her. The look on his face immediately told her that something terrible had happened.

"Elizabeth, darling—" he began.

"Oh, God!" she screamed. "No! No! It can't be! No! God, I can't live without him!"

Elizabeth bolted from her bed. Clad only in a short nightgown, she tore through the house barefoot, wailing uncontrollably. "She screamed so loud that even the neighbors heard her," reported Hanley. "She went completely hysterical. As she dashed for the front door, Dr. Kennamer grabbed her and took her back up to bed. She submitted to sedatives that eventually quieted her."

News of Todd's death electrified Hollywood. The street outside Elizabeth's house soon filled with camera crews and reporters from all over the world. MGM security guards arrived to bar unauthorized visitors, and studio publicist Bill Lyon tried in vain to handle media relations. Elizabeth shut herself up in her bedroom. "Find Sydney," she said to Hanley. "He'll know what to do."

I was visiting a friend in the hospital when I heard my name over the public address system: "If there's a Mr. Guilaroff in the hospital, please tell him to go to Elizabeth Taylor's home. They need you in a hurry."

Driving through Bel Air toward Beverly Hills, I flicked

Comedy, not drama, was Lucille Ball's forte. I made her a redhead and it became her trademark when she starred in the hugely successful "I Love Lucy."

Kathryn Grayson was one of the greatest singers in the musicals of the 1940s. This "geisha" publicity still is an example of the endless rounds of photo shoots the stars endured under the studio system.

BANQUET
HAIR DRESS
MAKE UP #1

Deborah Kerr's hairstyles for Quo Vadis? *were extremely challenging and required many changes.*

A dinner break during the filming of Green Mansions *in 1956. Audrey Hepburn was already an international star when she glided into my salon chair in a pink Chanel suit and a fashionably short haircut. Seated across from her here is her then-husband, Mel Ferrer.*

This is an actual still from the 1962 film Sweet Bird of Youth. *Director Richard Brooks insisted that I appear in the film as Geraldine Page's hairstylist. Geraldine was thrilled with the non-surgical facelift I gave her.*

Elizabeth Taylor donned a blond wig for her role in Little Women. I argued over changing her hair color and felt blond didn't suit her.

Elizabeth, knowing of my reluctance to have my picture taken, called me into this shot. "Damn it, Sydney. You've never changed in all these years. Now get your ass over here with me." How could I say no? Standing behind Elizabeth is Jorjett Strumme, her very good friend. Photo by Roddy McDowall.

Above: Elizabeth Taylor, standby hairdresser Agnes Flanaghan and myself on the Northern California set of The Sandpiper.

Right: Elizabeth on location in London for a toga test shot for Cleopatra. *Fox drove up the cost of the film by insisting that test shots be taken for every scene. This costume was worn by Elizabeth when she was rolled out to Caesar in a rug.*

20TH CENTURY FOX TEST LONDON TEST
NAME MISS TAYLOR AGE HEIGHT
NAME AGE HEIGHT
WIG #1 46 to 60 70-94. 95
COSTUME Nº 1+2 SCENES 96-97a. 97a
TEST FOR ALT. SKIRT LENGTH

I had great difficulty researching hairstyles for Elizabeth Taylor's role as Cleopatra. As I studied sketches of the real Cleopatra, I discovered how homely she was, and it was beyond me how she seduced two great men. Elizabeth's performance immortalized the Queen of Egypt, and her off-screen affair with Richard Burton captivated the world.

Marilyn never did a picture without insisting I create the styles.

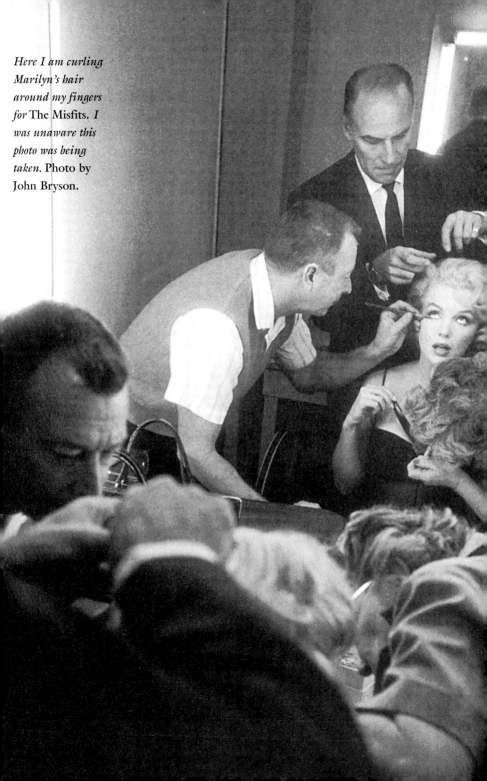

Here I am curling Marilyn's hair around my fingers for The Misfits. *I was unaware this photo was being taken.* Photo by John Bryson.

Even today, it's very difficult for me to look at these test shots of Marilyn for Some Like It Hot. *I loved her very much and am saddened I couldn't do more to help her. I miss her every day of my life.*

Katharine Hepburn has been my friend since 1939. Whenever she calls she always invites me to stay at her townhouse in New York City. "Sydney," she says, "you come stay in the attic above my house. Now, don't think just because it's an attic, it's just an ordinary attic." Nothing about Katharine has ever been ordinary.

Above: This is one of my favorite hairstyles worn by my good friend, Debbie Reynolds. She is as vibrant and entertaining now as she was when I met her during the filming of Singin' in the Rain. *She paid me one of the highest compliments I ever received when she told me that somebody should make a cast of my hands because I had golden fingers.*

Below: Joan Collins was a lot of fun when we worked together during a theatrical revival of The Women. *She was and still is today a great beauty.*

Those legs! Cyd Charisse remains today one of the most elegant stars in Hollywood history. Her dancing is surpassed by no one. She is one of my favorite actors and a dear friend.

At home today in Beverly Hills with my adopted grandson, José, and our keeshond, Lucky.

on the radio in time to hear the first reports of Todd's death. It was as if someone had punched me in the stomach. I pulled the car over to the side of the road for a few minutes to prepare myself for the enormity of what I would face at Elizabeth's home. After struggling through a sea of professional and personal woes, my surrogate daughter had finally found not merely passion but also happiness in the tenderness that Mike Todd concealed behind his blustery manner and take-charge persona. Now, after tasting the intoxicating sweetness of his love, Todd was gone and Elizabeth was once more alone. I could only sigh at how cruel fate could be.

I fought my way through the crowd of newspeople in front of the house and rushed upstairs to Elizabeth's bedroom. I found her sitting up straight in bed, waiting for me, fighting to hold back the torrent of tears that needed to come forth before she could begin to heal.

She was inconsolable, crying until she was too exhausted to speak. I spent every day and night with her for more than two weeks. The studio was very understanding about my absence, because she was one of their biggest stars, and they wanted her back at work. When her screaming finally stopped, Elizabeth retreated into stony silence. She sat for hours without moving a muscle, staring straight ahead, her lovely face absolutely devoid of expression, the inner agony she was enduring visible only in the immobility of her features. She needed sedatives to knock her out each night, but her sleep was interrupted by fitful weeping, by an occasional scream of "Mike, Mike, Mike," and by a constant stream of muttering. All I could do was sleep on a couch next to her bed, rising to kiss her and trying to comfort her whenever things were at their worst.

The funeral was scheduled to take place in Chicago. Although she was still in terrible shape both physically and emotionally, Elizabeth felt she had to go. She wanted a female companion for the journey, and she asked me if it would be all right for her to take her friend Helen Rose along with her to the service. I told her I understood completely and stayed behind in Los Angeles. In retrospect, I'm sorry I didn't go along, because the trip turned ugly. Crowds of people surrounded her, pulling at her clothes and hair, and masses of cameras were pointed at her wherever she went. Her face hidden behind a veil, she didn't complain or protest, and she didn't crack, but the strain took its toll on her, and on the day she returned home, Elizabeth went back to bed—with me on the couch a few feet away.

Later that same day, however, she left her bedroom and started downstairs. In the middle of the staircase she stopped, sat down and called to her children. I joined her, and for the first time since Mike's death, she held and spoke to them. For the past week or so I had been spending a great deal of time with Elizabeth and Mike's seven-month-old daughter, Elizabeth Frances (called Liza), even taking her out shopping with me. It did my heart good to see that Elizabeth was well enough to begin reaching out again. She seemed so glad just to be with them, to watch them and to hear their joyful, childish sounds. Turning to me, she said, "Sydney, I want to ask you something. Should I tell them now that Mike is gone?"

"I think you should, dear," I replied. "He's not here, he's not going to come back, and eventually they'll hear about his death, and it might be in the wrong way. So it's better if you tell them." Perhaps because they were so young, or more likely because of the security provided by their mother's love, the children seemed to handle Mike's death with far less anxiety than she had feared.

Several mornings later, while I was still staying at Elizabeth's, I drove to the drugstore to purchase some razor blades to shave with. I was walking back to my car when I bumped into Lana Turner on her way out of the Pioneer

Hardware store in Beverly Hills. We spoke briefly about Elizabeth; Lana's concern for Elizabeth's pain was heartfelt. "It's horrible, isn't it?" she sighed.

"But what are you doing at Pioneer Hardware?" I asked.

"We needed a new kitchen knife," she said, then quickly returned to the previous subject. "Do you think Elizabeth would like me to come and visit her?"

"I'll tell you what. I'm going right back to her house. Call her anytime, and when I tell her that it's you on the phone, I'm sure she'll be glad to talk to you."

Lana called Elizabeth that very day, expressing her condolences and her hope that Elizabeth was getting better. "I hope every day will help you more and more," said Lana.

The next morning, I heard the stunning news on the radio: Johnny Stompanato, one of mobster Mickey Cohen's former bodyguards, a small-time hoodlum who had become one of Lana's occasional lovers, had been stabbed to death the previous night on the pink rug in Lana's bedroom. The police were holding Cheryl Crane, Lana's thirteen-year-old daughter, as a murder suspect.

I got into my car and flew over to Lana's house. When I arrived, none of her servants was on duty, and Lana herself opened the door. Standing a few feet behind her was an attorney. "Oh, Sydney, I'm so glad you came," she sobbed, falling into my arms.

She wept for a long time. After a while she composed herself a little and began talking. "Did you ever dream that this could have happened?" she sighed. "And with the very knife that I bought just yesterday."

Lana took my hand and led me to a couch. "Johnny was an abuser," she continued. "Last night he was slapping me repeatedly, and at one point he threw me down and began kicking me. But, Sydney, it actually started earlier in the day."

As she went on to explain, the first intimations of the tragedy had begun that afternoon. Two of her friends were in the game room of Lana's sprawling house and heard the whole thing. Stompanato had launched into a violent litany of complaints about slights he felt Lana had dealt him. Grabbing her by the arm and shaking her, he raged, "I'm good enough to do your errands, good enough to sleep with you—but not good enough to take you to the Academy Awards!"

The handsome, well-dressed man she had taken to her bosom when she was lonely and between husbands had revealed himself as a petty tyrant, a dangerous viper who, she told me, had beaten her frequently and now began to threaten her with violence in a manner she found increasingly terrifying. She bolted upstairs with Stompanato right behind her.

"We've been through all this," she cried. "I couldn't have taken somebody like you to the Oscars!"

When Stompanato slammed his fist into the wall, Lana told me she ran back down to her friends. Perhaps because of this audience, Stompanato threw on his coat, muttering that he was going home and would return to take Lana to dinner at eight. After he left, she collapsed into the arms of her friends, confiding that she feared for her life and for her daughter's safety.

Later that evening, after both friends had departed, Stompanato stormed back into the house, and she told me she was frightened to death. A running fight began and soon escalated into a screaming match in Lana's bedroom. As the fight progressed, Cheryl, who had been watching television in her upstairs bedroom, became more and more distraught.

Enraged, Stompanato began shaking Lana by the shoulders, threatening to bash her face until it was permanently disfigured and she could never appear again before a camera. When the brawl moved to the second-floor landing, Stompanato started slapping Lana's face while she hurled expletives at him. Seeing Cheryl standing next to her room in tears, Lana begged, "Please, baby, go back to your room. Don't listen to this. Please, baby!"

Still arguing, Lana and Stompanato moved back into Lana's pink bedroom. Creeping downstairs to get a butcher knife, Cheryl ran back up and stood just outside the bedroom door. Inside, Lana grappled with Stompanato, then began pleading for help.

When Cheryl entered the bedroom, still grasping the butcher knife, he turned to face her, and a moment later the blade was driven deep into Stompanato's abdomen. He bled to death right there on the floor. Sobbing, Cheryl ran back to her room while Lana, in shock, her face ashen, clung to the wall until she thought to claw for the telephone. Her first call was to the studio, but the second was to me.

I couldn't blame Lana for Stompanato's death. Nor could I blame Cheryl, a child defending her mother against a violent monster. The purchase of the long, sharp knife only a day earlier was nothing more than a terrible coincidence.

In the decades since, the events surrounding Stompanato's stabbing have become so clouded with rumor, innuendo and contradictory testimony that except for me, only Cheryl can now say with certainty what really happened. Cheryl was convicted of manslaughter and remanded to the custody of her father, restaurant owner Stephen Crane. Soon after the Stompanato investigation was concluded, Lana herself returned to work, and the entire unfortunate incident was all but forgotten as she went on to box-office acclaim in Ross Hunter's *Imitation of Life*, *Portrait in Black* and *Madame X*.

The twin tragedies of Elizabeth Taylor and Lana Turner were emotionally draining for me. Fortunately, Elizabeth was already on the mend when I had to rush off to comfort Lana. It was shortly after the funeral that Elizabeth asked me, "Do you think I should go back to work?" A few weeks before Mike's death, she had begun shooting a film version of Tennessee Williams's play *Cat on a Hot Tin Roof*, in which she had the plum role of Maggie opposite Paul Newman as Brick..

I said, "Yes, I do. For Mike's sake. He said it was a wonderful part for you, that you might easily win an Academy Award."

Elizabeth thought it over, then kissed me on the cheek. "I guess you're right," she said.

"When would you like to go back to work?"

"I wouldn't mind going back tomorrow."

I called the studio.

Elizabeth's healing accelerated when she returned to the set. I asked director Richard Brooks to tell both cast and crew to act as normal as possible with her, to behave as if nothing had happened; I was worried that any overt expression of sympathy might cause her to break down again. Fortunately, she was able to quickly put herself back into the part of Maggie. With the emotional resonance she brought to the role from her recent tragedy, it was a triumphant performance for Elizabeth, one of the finest of her career.

But her troubles were far from over. As Elizabeth slowly rebuilt her life and career, she began to lean heavily on Eddie Fisher, the popular and gifted crooner who had been Mike Todd's closest friend. He was also the husband of "America's Sweetheart," Debbie Reynolds, with whom he supposedly enjoyed a storybook marriage.

I noticed that something was amiss between Eddie and Debbie when Elizabeth and I joined them one night for dinner. Debbie never said a word about it, but I sensed that she was unhappy, though I couldn't think why until Eddie began paying too much attention to Elizabeth and all but ignored his wife. The evening ended with Eddie driving Elizabeth home and Debbie riding with me; she was ominously silent.

On Sept. 9, 1958, the first of a thousand headlines appeared in New York's *Daily News:* EDDIE FISHER ROMANCE WITH LIZ TAYLOR DENIED. On the advice of MGM, Debbie had reacted angrily to a routine call from a wire-service reporter. "I've never heard of such a thing," she said when asked about Eddie's dalliance with Liz. "I'm so shocked that such stories would be printed that I won't even dignify them with a comment." Debbie told Louella Parsons, "Eddie and Liz are good friends. He was Mike's best friend. I think these stories are disgusting." Meanwhile, Elizabeth told Walter Winchell in New York, "You know I'm a friend of Eddie's. Everybody knows that. We can't help what people say."

Looking to sensationalize the story, reporters began crawling the Beverly Hills neighborhood where Debbie and Eddie shared a house. They quoted neighbors' claims of having overheard fighting between America's most darling couple. Then, on Sept. 11, Elizabeth called Hedda Hopper, the first reporter to interview her when she starred in *Lassie Come Home.* Hedda offered an auntly shoulder, then turned around and wrote about their conversation in her column. Elizabeth later accused her of betraying her confidence. "It was like calling a best friend and having them twist your words against you," she said.

After writing that Elizabeth was dealing with her grief over Mike's death by saying, "Mike's dead, and I'm alive," Hedda publicly crucified her in full view of 35 million readers: "Well, Elizabeth, you'll probably hate me for the rest of your life for this. But I can't help it. I'm afraid you've lost all control over reason. Remember the nights you used to call me at two and three in the morning when you were having a nightmare? You had to talk to somebody, and I let you talk your heart out. What you've just said to me bears not the slightest resemblance to that girl. Where, oh where, has she gone?"

As soon as she saw this in print, Elizabeth telephoned me. "I never said any such thing! How can she be so cruel?" she sobbed. "Sydney, she simply took one of my speeches from *Cat on a Hot Tin Roof* and put it in that article."

I checked and found that it was true: Hedda Hopper rewrote Tennessee Williams's line "Skip's dead, and I'm alive!" and put it in Elizabeth's mouth, then embellished it with a line of her own: "What do you expect me to do, sleep alone?" I don't understand how Hedda could live with herself, unless gossip columnists are immune to the venom they spew.

I wasn't fully aware of the magnitude of this scandal until Debbie Reynolds called a press conference to announce that "Elizabeth has stolen my husband." TV stations coast to coast interrupted their daytime dramas to televise this glimpse into a real-life soap opera. It unleashed a public fury around the world, and both Debbie and Elizabeth found themselves cast in off-screen roles that would haunt them for years to come. Yet the press, the movie fans and the self-righteous women's groups who were denouncing Elizabeth as a Hollywood homewrecker had no idea that they were being manipulated, that the whole affair had begun as a public relations stunt engineered by MGM publicists working with Debbie's own PR staff. Their calculation was that the studio, Debbie and even Liz would reap enormous financial rewards from what appeared to be a marital scandal. But it was about to backfire on all of them.

Two weeks later, Elizabeth and Eddie slipped off to the Adirondacks for a romantic tryst—and a real affair blossomed. "I was lonely," Elizabeth said later in an interview. "Eddie was there. He had been one of Mike's best friends and had idolized Mike to the point of making himself over in his image. Now, I knew Eddie was not very happy. And I knew he loved to talk about Mike almost as much as I did. So we went out in public together several times—and after that all hell broke loose. The press and the public—the whole world, in fact—was convinced that I was breaking up a perfectly happy home."

All along, I understood that it wasn't a question of Elizabeth taking Eddie away from Debbie: No one can take anybody away from her spouse unless he wants to leave in the first place. Whatever it was that Elizabeth saw in Eddie was something he saw in her as well. If his marriage had been as perfect as the press wanted to believe, such a thing never would have happened. The truth was that Debbie and Eddie had been having marital difficulties for more than a year; their closest friends knew the couple was resigned to separate and divorce. Since the marriage would have dissolved on its own, the only effect of Eddie's none-too-private dalliance with Elizabeth was to create a hurricane of publicity. "It didn't seem to matter much that home-loving Debbie and fun-loving Eddie had been squabbling for more than a year," said *Life* magazine. "But then such reality was not in demand."

I felt so sad for Elizabeth. It doesn't make life easy to be written about in such a horrendous manner. Yet it is true that Eddie temporarily filled the void in Elizabeth's life. "Through all those months of grief for Mike, I felt that I had been loved and that there would never be anything like that again in my life," she said. "Eddie, who loved Mike, too, was the one man who could understand that my heart would always belong to the memory of Mike. And Eddie, somehow, made Mike seem more alive."

Later Elizabeth told me, "Maybe with Eddie I was trying to see if I really was alive or dead. Also, for some idiotic reason, I thought he needed me, and I should make *somebody* happy."

The affair that inspired so many mean-spirited comments was as much Eddie's fault as Elizabeth's, and it hurt both of them. Debbie, however, was ultimately the one who was crushed by this unfortunate episode. I felt very sad for her because for a time she believed that she had failed to satisfy her husband, that she had driven him into Elizabeth's arms. Such things can happen to anyone, but when they happen to be famous people, they invite a storm of slanderous comment and gossip. Elizabeth and Eddie, as well as Debbie, however, withstood it bravely and went on with their lives.

Not long after their marriage in 1959, I joined Elizabeth and Eddie in New York City for the filming of *Butterfield 8*, a dark drama about a high-priced call girl, based on the John O'Hara novel of the same title. One day while visiting their hotel suite, I got a call from producer Walter Wanger in California. He said that he was going to make a film about the life of Cleopatra for 20th Century-Fox. Since *Butterfield 8* was the last picture on Elizabeth's MGM contract, and she was free to choose her next film. Wanger wanted her to play the title role but had been unable to reach her. Since he knew she and I were very close, he said he'd send over a copy of the script and asked me to persuade Elizabeth to take the role.

When I replied that I thought the idea sounded very interesting, Wanger added that if I succeeded in getting her to play Cleopatra, I could be assured of working on that picture as well, and at any salary I named. I told Wanger that I was at that moment in the bedroom shared by Elizabeth and Eddie, that his call had been forwarded from my suite to theirs and that I would speak to Elizabeth and call back shortly.

I walked into the living room and told Elizabeth I had just spoken with Walter Wanger. "How would you like to play Cleopatra?" I said. She gave me a funny little smile. She looked at Eddie, then back at me again without saying a word. Finally she replied, "I'll do it...for one million dollars."

My jaw dropped in astonishment. In those days, that was an unheard-of sum for an actress, even one with her beauty and proven box-office appeal. Yet I was surprised that she had agreed, regardless of how much money her request involved. Elizabeth is extremely bright, and I would in time come to understand that she had been secretly pleased to portray such a historic figure, the exotic queen who might have ruled the world if she hadn't been destroyed by love.

When I called Wanger back, he came to the phone quickly, anxiety in his voice. "Walter, she'll do it," I said. I paused, then added slowly, "For one million dollars."

After an ever-so-slight pause, he said, "Thank you, Sydney, thank you very much. We've got a deal. We'll be in touch with Kurt Frings—Elizabeth's agent—and I'll look forward to working with you when we get to England."

I told him I would be returning to California immediately after *Butterfield 8* wrapped, and he asked me to get in touch with him upon my return to discuss my contract and salary. In due course a contract was drawn up whereby I would be paid a certain sum that included all living expenses while working on the film. Although the salary was higher than my usual per-picture fee at MGM, it was the same as what I always got when working overseas; being abroad for months at a time, I still had to bear the expense of maintaining my California home.

Before *Cleopatra* was scheduled to begin production, MGM loaned me to Fox for Marilyn Monroe's picture *The Misfits*, and Walter went to England in preparation for what was to become one of the great film spectacles of its time. Soon, however, I was getting a stream of calls and cables from him, telling me in detail that the British hairdressers union was unhappy about my working in England.

I was born in London and was happy to go there. But although I had worked there before, foreigners are required to obtain a work permit for each film. I had become so well known in my field and was earning so much more than anyone in the British union that several members vowed I would never again be allowed to work in their country. Smoothing this over became a task for Wanger.

I had not yet read a script, so I asked him if there would be any outdoor shots in the film. "Yes, many," he responded.

"Why, then, will you be making this film in England, where weather conditions are rarely favorable?" I said.

Wanger explained that Elizabeth had approved the location, and Fox's top representative in London was delighted with the idea, in part because it lent prestige to him. Still, I wondered about chancing England's notorious rain for a production that was sure to be expensive even without weather delays. Much later I would discover that Fox was hoping to save money by producing in England: If they shot in Britain, using British actors and craftspeople—including Elizabeth, who held dual U.S.–English citizenship—the government would kick in a substantial chunk of cash to offset most of their salaries.

Because of my ongoing difficulties with the union, Wanger asked me to send a copy of my own passport as proof of my place of birth. I did, but it didn't seem to help much. Meanwhile, Elizabeth remained adamant about working with me, insisting that she was entitled to have a stylist who was familiar with her. The wrangle went on and on, and poor Wanger became distracted from his principal job, which was getting the whole film into production. He encountered all sorts of other labor problems, including booking enough hotel rooms for cast and crew. And he couldn't find enough studio space or even electrical generators, or enough skilled plasterers, carpenters and other craftspeople to build *Cleopatra*'s extensive sets, which included replicating part of ancient Alexandria. In the end, the sets wouldn't be finished by the time *Cleopatra* was scheduled to use London's Pinewood Studios. Although I'm not a producer, I should think that someone in Wanger's position would have thought through and confirmed the logistical details of producing an epic such as *Cleopatra* before committing to a particular foreign location. In hindsight, I believe he was in over his head.

For a time it seemed that the studio would try to force Elizabeth to give in on having me, but eventually, they never tried to push her that far. While we waited for union clearance, sets were designed and costumes and script adjustments went forward. Then one day Walter telephoned to say that since I was being held up, he wanted to get started on the wigs. I said that my great preference was for London's Stanley Hall of Wig Creations, one of the all-time great artists of wigmaking. I had worked with him previously on *The Prince and the Showgirl* with Marilyn Monroe.

I find it strange, but dress designers in England also draw hairstyles to accompany each particular dress a star is to wear. At that time hairdressers merely followed these designs instead of creating their own. I felt secure that Stanley would be following whatever Oliver Messel, the dress designer, might suggest, and I would continue when I finally got over there.

I arrived in London near the end of August 1960. Elizabeth and Eddie arrived a few days later. We all stayed at the Dorchester Hotel, where I had resided during the making of *The Prince and the Showgirl*. I took a day to get settled before meeting with Oliver Messel and Stanley Hall. Stanley had indeed followed Oliver's hair designs, but as I looked them over carefully, I realized that Oliver had repeated exactly what he'd done years earlier for Vivien Leigh in *Caesar and Cleopatra*. Although I doubted that they would be suitable for Elizabeth, I kept that thought to myself. Alone with Oliver, I looked at his sketches of gowns, each accompanied by swatches of material to be used for the gowns and shoulder drapes, and I marveled at his impeccable taste. During my entire motion picture career, I had ranked him among the greatest designers of period costumes, so I had no inkling of what was to come.

Before leaving Los Angeles for London, I had scoured the library for clues to hairstyles during Cleopatra's reign, but found nothing. Nor did I find anything useful during a brief stop en route in New York City, where I went to the Carnegie Library. In neither city were there any references to or pictures of the styles or the coiffures of that period.

In London I went to the British Museum, which has an impressive Egyptian wing, and a very intelligent guide there proved helpful. "You won't find Cleopatra in the Egyptian collection," he told me. "She was a Ptolemy—the Greek dynasty that ruled Egypt for centuries—so her proper spot is in our Greco-Roman wing." Sure enough, I found several drawings there, along with one or two headdresses. There were only a few different hairstyles, but one caught my eye: It was a style used on rare religious occasions to suggest that Cleopatra was an incarnation of the goddess Isis. This was extremely informative for me because I felt that I could also design a Grecian hairstyle for the scenes when Cleopatra was at home being attended by handmaidens. I knew the Egyptian and Greco-Roman periods well, and for motion picture purposes, I could draw on my own creativity to show other variations of that period.

While further researching Cleopatra's life, I discovered a number of books written by Anthony Wiegel. They were all historically accurate and quite erudite. But when I finally read the movie script, I could see why the producers were having trouble with it: It bore no resemblance to what was in any of those books. I said nothing at the time, though.

One day Wanger asked me to meet with him at his studio office. Frowning, he said, "Sydney, you know you get four times Oliver's salary, and he was offended by this and protested that he ought to be paid at least what you get."

Walter went on in this vein, insinuating that I had bragged to Oliver about what I was making. My executive salary of $1,500 a week, plus $600 in living expenses, came from an American firm. But in England all actors—whether stars, workers or lesser-known performers—are always paid less than Americans. I replied, "Walter, I haven't been involved with Oliver in any personal matter other than to praise his beautiful costumes. Since the whole studio is in an uproar and we are constantly being threatened with shutdowns, I've been very wary about how to behave."

Suddenly a thought occurred to me. "But it's quite possible," I continued, "that Oliver went to the accountants to learn what my salary and living expenses are." I was angry to think that Walter could have so little confidence in me, but he was clearly distraught, so I forgave him.

A few weeks later, while Elizabeth was ill with a sore throat and a low-grade fever, the studio, trying to stem the production's soaring costs, used the time to rent a London theater for the day to run all the footage of costume and hair tests. In addition to Wanger, Rouben Mamoulian, the director, was there. It went on for two-and-a-half hours, yet it seemed that nothing had been accomplished. We were all extremely frustrated by the end of the screening, and I was discouraged with the way Elizabeth looked in Oliver's hair designs. In close-ups, she looked more like Pocahontas than Cleopatra.

I had known all along that this would happen. Oliver's styles didn't suit her. I left the theater downhearted and returned to my hotel. About an hour later, Rouben called to ask if I would come to his home to discuss the way Elizabeth looked. When I arrived, Rouben came downstairs, shook my hand and then, as if in prayer, put both hands together and said, "Sydney, what can we do to make Elizabeth look good? To make her look like Cleopatra? Those wigs are dreadful, but I know that you were forced to use them to comply with Walter's request for that kind of styling."

I felt deeply for Rouben. I liked the man, a great artist and a great director whose career dated back to the silent era. He was elegant, intellectual and always a gentleman. I replied that the wigs had been cut and styled for all the variations of braids and ornaments in the hair and thus were hopeless—nothing could be done with them. I'd have to have new wigs.

When Rouben asked how many I needed, I told him, "Only two for now. I can vary them with other designs." He asked how long it would take. I said, "With Stanley Hall, in only two weeks we can be ready to test again."

Rouben told me to go ahead and get new wigs. From his home I went to Stanley's place and ordered them. But the next day Wanger called, angry and almost insulting.

"Who gave you permission to buy new wigs?" he demanded to know.

"Where are you calling from?" I asked.

"Rouben's house," he said nastily.

In order to protect Rouben, I said, "I won't tell you who gave me permission, Walter."

"Oh, yeah? Then I'm holding *you* responsible for holding up the entire production."

I finally lost my temper. "Walter, you're lying. I've never

delayed anything. Getting new wigs is a necessity. And while you're at it, if I were you, I would tear up that bum script and follow Anthony Wiegel's books on Antony and Cleopatra. They'll help you to portray an *interesting* version of this great story instead of the tiresome version you're stuck with now." I hung up without saying another word.

Because the union had barred me from the set ever since I set foot in England, I had been preparing Elizabeth's hair in her hotel suite and making minor adjustments to it in her studio dressing room. That day, Elizabeth closed the door to her dressing room, shielding us from the prying eyes of the British hairdressers union spies, and I styled her based on my new idea of how Cleopatra should look. The result was wonderful, just what we had been searching for all along. As we were testing with the new hairdo, as well as with one of Oliver's beautiful costumes, the dresser, a member of another British union, folded a drape over Elizabeth's shoulder. Just before the camera began to roll, the drape fell. The way the unions work in England, everyone does exactly what he or she is supposed to do and not one thing more. When the union dresser made no attempt to fix it, I asked the cameraman to pause so that I could deal with the drape. By union rules, this was an infringement on the dresser's duties, and the incident was duly reported.

Still photographs of the hairdo were taken as usual, and once the test was over, I sat down for a few minutes while Elizabeth changed back into her street clothes. At that moment Oliver came over. He stuttered badly, but somehow he got out his request: "Sydney, you've been very complimentary all along about my costumes. I just saw the gesture you made when the robe on Elizabeth's shoulder fell, and I appreciate that. But I've heard that the picture is going to be moved to Rome, and I'm not going to be there. They've let me go. Would you be a dear and watch my costumes for me the way you have in every test?"

I was so taken aback that for the first time in my life I sank to using vituperative language toward a co-worker. "Oliver, you've been a son of a bitch all the months I've been here. You helped to organize the hairdressers against me, and you've undermined me in every way. You're a goddamned traitor to this production, and now you're pretending to be nice. But I knew what you were doing all of the time. Yes, I'll look after the costumes, but not for your sake. I'll do it because I want Elizabeth to look good. She's the only one I care about in this whole damnable production."

Cleopatra was costing Fox more than $40,000 a day, but by the end of January 1961, Wanger had only ten minutes of usable film. Rouben Mamoulian was allowed to "resign" from the film and was replaced by Joseph Mankiewicz, who soon concluded what I had known all along: The script *was* dreadful, and a rewrite was ordered. Meanwhile, Elizabeth continued to receive her salary, about $2,000 a day.

As the production sputtered onward, I continued to deal with the ongoing campaign by the hairdressers to get rid of me. The union's position was that I couldn't even remain in England, land of my birth, let alone work on the film. They wanted me to leave the country.

Meetings were held with Sir Tom O'Brien, head of the union, and he suggested that I submit an appeal to the hairdressers union. I was brought almost to tears, pleading not for myself but for Elizabeth. I asked if they couldn't find it in their hearts to keep me there, if not in production then merely as her friend. It was a waste of breath. The struggle continued. Nothing I could say would appease them, but I was allowed to stay with Elizabeth through testing.

That worked well until the last test. After shooting one particular costume-and-hair test, Elizabeth asked me to come to her dressing room to make a quick hairdressing change. The female hairdresser standing by on the set at the time followed as swiftly as she could, but once I entered the dressing room, Elizabeth quickly closed the door behind me. The hairdresser chose to believe, or was instructed to think, that *I* had slammed the door in her face, dishonoring her, and she reported me to the union representative, who promptly ordered the production shut down.

Reporting this event, the *London Times* ran a front-page photo of the set, which was a replica of the gates of Cairo. The caption read, "This Is The Set That Mr. Guilaroff Closed Down." That afternoon, a swarm of reporters and photographers descended on the Dorchester, and someone telephoned to ask me to come down. I said, "I don't care for publicity. I'm sorry this thing happened, but I won't come down." About 20 minutes later, a porter came to my suite to hand me a long scroll that looked like parchment. It read, "Dear Mr. Guilaroff, we promise that we won't discuss the trouble that's going on with *Cleopatra*. We would just like to know about your whole career, and how you became so famous. Please come down to see us." Some 20 names were signed at the bottom of the note.

I took a pen with very dark ink and wrote across the note in large letters: "No, Thank You." I thought these people would go away after that, but they were very persistent. My telephone kept ringing with requests for me to meet with the press. Finally I asked the operator not to ring me anymore without asking who was calling. Then I rang the manager of the hotel and asked him if these people were allowed to be in the lobby, because I wanted to go out for dinner and would certainly have to pass through their boisterous ranks. He said, "Mr. Guilaroff, the lobby is a public place. We can't ask them to leave, but we won't allow them to come upstairs either."

I didn't know what to do, so I called Elizabeth, and she

invited me up to her suite for dinner so we could keep each other company. Ironically, she was in the Oliver Messel suite, because in addition to his other talents, Oliver was also a marvelous interior decorator. As we dined together, telephone calls transferred to me continued to come in. This went on through the next day, so we were both trapped. It would have been far worse for Elizabeth, of course, if she had tried to go downstairs or outside. All entrances and exits had been covered by the press.

At one point she said to me in a very sweet way, "Well, Sydney, you're a star at last."

I shook my head. "No, Elizabeth. Without you, they wouldn't be looking for *me*."

We managed to survive that unhappy event, but because it was apparent that we would have constant labor problems if we continued in England, plans were being finalized in California to move the production to Italy. The British unions had won the battle but had lost the war, as the production would have provided hundreds of jobs for British craftspeople.

With the rewrite in progress, Joe Mankiewicz and I remained in London to go through all the test photographs. He tossed out one after another until we came to the last series—the only ones I had been responsible for. He said, "I like these the best." I told him this was how I had wanted Elizabeth to look from the beginning.

Even before the decision had been made to suspend production, streams of telegrams flew back and forth between London and California questioning Elizabeth's long absences from the set. First, Eddie Fisher had to have an emergency appendectomy, and naturally Elizabeth wanted to be at his side. Then she came down with the Asian flu and was confined to her bed at the Dorchester. Gasping for breath as she tossed and turned in the massive bed, she eventually drifted into a tormented sleep. I sat with her, stroking her hand. After about three hours, she squeezed my hand with all the strength she could muster. "Sydney, I can't breathe," she whispered. I telephoned for a private duty nurse, who rushed through banks of fog to reach the hotel. Kneeling at Elizabeth's side, the nurse frowned. "This is serious, Mr. Guilaroff. She's almost suffocating."

Upset about her being ill again, I voiced a thought aloud: "She looks like she's falling asleep."

The nurse shook her head. "No, I think it's more serious than that! She's not breathing normally at all."

We quickly phoned the night clerk, who called back to say that he couldn't locate the hotel doctor. There was, however, a group of physicians staying in the hotel for a medical convention. The clerk asked one of them, Dr. J. Middleton Price, a noted British anesthesiologist, to come up to the suite. Dr. Price found that Elizabeth's breathing passage was almost closed due to inflammation and took her to the hospital for an emergency tracheotomy.

Unfortunately, the desk clerk, who had done such a great service by finding Dr. Price, also had a journalist friend whom he called to report this change in his resident star's condition. The bulletin that reached America via Associated Press wire just two days before the final Oscar ballots were to be mailed sparked headlines in Los Angeles: "LIZ DYING."

By then Dr. Price had moved Elizabeth to the London Clinic, the private hospital where she had been treated for a minor illness the previous year. She was placed in an iron lung developed for polio patients, which took over her breathing and seemed to give her more strength. Yet the doctors weren't optimistic about her chances; one physician gave her only a 50-50 chance of surviving.

Elizabeth's diagnosis was soon confirmed by seven doctors: She was suffering from not only pneumonia but also anemia. A new drug, staphylococcal bacteriophage-lysate, was hand-carried to London by Eddie's agent, Milt Blackstone, and administered to her. Nurse Catherine Morgan described her condition to reporters: "I've been around patients for seventeen years, and during that time I've seen some who died in several days, several hours, several minutes. But in comparison to Miss Taylor, they all looked in bonny health."

"I could feel myself dying," Elizabeth would later say. "I could see a small dot of light far off in the distance. And that was closing up. I remember using all my strength to open up that light again." She added that the experience was not peaceful, it was horrifying.

"There's a saying that when you're drowning, your whole life comes before you," she went on. "It wasn't that way with me. Even though I was suffocating, I dimly knew that I had had some kind of operation. I couldn't make a noise with my throat. When I came back to consciousness, the only questions I wanted to ask were whether or not I was dying and when I would die. I couldn't make myself hear. It seemed to me, though, that I was screaming. I was frightened. But I was angry. I was fierce. I didn't want to die."

Elizabeth told me she had "died" four times during that period. "You feel yourself going, falling into a horrible black pit. You hear a screaming jet noise. Your skin is pulling off. But even when I was unconscious, I had my fists clenched. The doctor told me later that the reason I'm alive is because I fought so hard to live."

I soon became certain that the cause of Elizabeth's problem stemmed from her health having been undermined by drugs given to her by Eddie and his physician, Dr. Max Jacobson—a dreadful man known as "Dr. Feelgood" in certain Hollywood circles. Eddie had brought him along to London so that his own addiction to amphetamines and barbiturates could be satisfied. Unfortunately, Eddie had persuaded Elizabeth to submit to the shots as well. "Dr. Feelgood" also began feeding her Demerol and morphine to ease the chronic pain in her spine and lower back. I can only thank God that prompt medical attention and the new miracle drugs had rescued her from death's door.

The next day at the hospital, I saw Elizabeth wearing a cork in her throat where the incision in her trachea had been made. I said, "Don't try to talk, don't try to do anything. Just rest, dear. I just came to see how you are. I'm glad you're OK." She smiled sweetly and held my hand for a minute or two, letting me know that she appreciated my concern. I stopped by the next day, long enough to ensure that she was well cared for and improving.

After the new antibiotic was administered, Elizabeth was out of danger. But two more days elapsed before her physician allowed me to even kiss her on the cheek. Until then I said "Hello" and just touched her. She could speak again, and she hadn't lost her sense of humor. When she saw me looking at the cork in her throat, she asked, "Do you want to see?"

She yanked the cork out, and now she couldn't talk at all: Air came out through the hole, but not enough to operate her voice box. She replaced the cork and said with a smile, "Well, what do you think of that?"

Queen Elizabeth II herself directed her personal physician to examine her American namesake, and he prescribed a year of rest for my surrogate daughter. Twentieth Century-Fox reluctantly shut down *Cleopatra* and made plans to start from scratch in 1962.

The silver lining in Elizabeth's harrowing tale was that by coming so close to death, she had regained the affection of her peers. As she fought for her life, fellow members of the Academy of Motion Picture Arts and Sciences were mailing in their final ballots for the 1961 Academy

Awards ceremony. She headed home to collect her first Oscar for *Butterfield 8*, the film she despised above all her others. She told me she was sure she had won a "sympathy vote," not only for her brush with death but also in part to make up for the Academy's failure to reward her remarkable performance in *Cat on a Hot Tin Roof*, which Mike Todd had predicted would bring her an Oscar. Elizabeth gushed with gratitude when she accepted her award, but backstage she told me that she didn't care about winning it at all. "I'm just putting on an act," she whispered.

I left *Cleopatra* to return to MGM, where I was needed. When filming resumed in Rome in 1962, I learned that Fox was searching for a new Marc Antony. I advised Elizabeth to take a close look at the work of a Welsh actor named Richard Burton. "Take my advice," I urged. "He's the one."

Elizabeth screened several of Richard's films, then flew to New York to see him in Lerner and Loewe's *Camelot*. "You were right, Sydney," she said. "I'll telephone Fox immediately."

Thus I had unwittingly set in motion a chain of events that led to one of the most scandalous love affairs the movie world has ever seen. Not that Elizabeth and Richard—both married—were entirely at fault. I learned from Elizabeth's secretary, Dick Hanley, that to stir up interest in a film that was millions over budget, the Fox publicists had virtually propelled them into each other's arms. "The studio expected them to fall in love," Hanley wrote me.

The first press releases about an on-camera love scene described it as an "electrifying moment." "Burton even forgot his lines," said *Cleopatra* publicist Nathan Weiss in a telegram to Harry Brand, Fox's Hollywood publicity chief. "He was vulnerable. Elizabeth took his arm and looked directly into his eyes for almost a minute."

Director Joe Mankiewicz later said that "it makes a

love scene much easier when your stars fall in love before your eyes."

The earliest press releases from publicists Weiss and Jack Brodsky, and confidential memos from studio chief Spyros Skouras and other corporate papers, show that Fox had planned for a mere touch of love between the stars: a couple of kisses, a few nights out on Rome's Via Veneto and some titillating items for the gossip columns. Taylor was then supposed to troop dutifully back to her husband, Eddie Fisher, and Burton to his wife, actress Sybil Williams.

In a pig's eye.

Unwisely, Fox publicists had already leaked the story to Sheilah Graham, the globe-trotting doyenne of international gossip. Alerted by Weiss, she swooped down from London and closely monitored the set until the film was completed, and the affair was soon front-page news.

The publicity stunt had crossed over into real life. Hanley told me, "Elizabeth was besotted with Burton—you could see in every look that she was drunk in love."

Eddie Fisher soon recognized the inevitable. "If they had sent an engraved card ordering them to keep their hands off each other, it wouldn't have made any difference," he told an interviewer. "They couldn't stop it. They were powerless."

Personally, I thought the affair was fueled by alcohol. From what Hanley told me, both Elizabeth and Richard were drinking pretty hard at the time.

By late April the affair had been inflated to such colossal proportions by the media that Elizabeth—not Richard—was in danger of being expelled from male-chauvinist Italy as an "undesirable person." Vatican Radio, which beamed broadcasts to almost a million listeners, began editorializing against the affair, depicting her as "morally bankrupt." Then the weekly Vatican newspaper, *L'Osservatore della Domenica*, with a circulation of more than 100,000 Catholic leaders, published an "open letter" to Elizabeth and 20th Century-Fox, in which she was accused of "erotic vagrancy" and being an "unfit mother."

Because these editorials were personally approved by Pope John XXIII, Fox production chief Peter Levathes was certain that the condemnation would spread around the world. "It was so serious that we took a look at the morals clauses in the Burton and Taylor contracts," he said.

The scandal reached its apex with the filming of Cleopatra's entrance into Rome, in which 7,000 Catholic extras portrayed the Roman masses of ancient times. Concern for Elizabeth's safety was so great that teams of sharpshooters from Rome's elite police antiterrorist squad were stationed on the rooftops of the *Cleopatra* set. Other troopers, costumed in Roman wigs and togas, were hidden behind columns or positioned among the crowd of extras. But the scenes were filmed without incident.

Back in Hollywood, I monitored the growing scandal in Rome, desperately worried about Elizabeth's emotional health. I sensed that she was taking too many drugs and joining Richard in the decadent world of Roman nightclubs as he encouraged her to stay out all night drinking.

But I didn't learn until later that even worse things were happening. Overwhelmed by the emotional roller-coaster of her affair with Burton, Elizabeth was either late or absent for 99 of the 101 shooting days in Rome, and, on more than one occasion, she even attempted suicide, prompting the production's insurance carriers to refuse to risk their money on her delicate health. If she had died, Fox would have lost its entire investment.

After her first suicide attempt, in March, *Il Tempo* scoffed at Fox's claim that its star had been laid low by a case of food poisoning. The newspaper noted that "police stormed the villa to investigate suicide charges." This moved Wanger to jump in with a statement noting that he himself had taken ill from spoiled food. "It was the bad bully beef we ate at lunch," he insisted.

Cleopatra cost a fortune. Even by today's standards, the entire debacle would be outrageously expensive, but in 1961 the costs were staggering. The film finally went on to make money and has become successful in the home video market, but at the time it was considered the biggest financial failure in the history of filmmaking. Between *Cleopatra* and Marilyn Monroe's never-completed last picture, *Something's Got to Give*, 20th Century-Fox was starved for cash.

The end of this production, however, was not the end of poor Elizabeth's problems. After Burton threatened to return to Sybil, Elizabeth apparently tried to kill herself yet again. According to reports attributed to Spyros Skouras, she swallowed a massive dose of sleeping medication, probably Nembutal and Seconal. In Burton's diary, released in 1988, the actor said that she had told him, "I love you so much, I'm prepared to die for you."

"Go ahead!" he had said in return.

I believe that these were halfhearted suicide attempts, desperate calls for attention and understanding as she grappled with divorce proceedings against Eddie Fisher and fought to win custody of Maria, the German child she had adopted with him in 1961.

But I cannot condemn my dear friend for her tumultuous relationship with Burton. To me it was just another case of Elizabeth falling in love once again with the wrong man. And no matter what the Church of Rome thought, or what the public thought, or what the scandal-mongering media chose to print, when she was in love with somebody, she wanted to be married.

After divorcing their spouses, Elizabeth and Richard married each other in 1964. They divorced once and remarried, but the second marriage was short-lived. Still, I predict that their passionate yet stormy relationship will go down in history as the greatest love affair of the twentieth century.

Despite all her misfortunes, I admire Elizabeth without reservation. She has a sincere spirituality and many deeply held convictions that she feels are nobody's business but her own. If she weren't so incredibly beautiful or so famous, few would care about her private life, and fewer would profess shock at her behavior. Let's face it: Millions of Americans get married and divorced over and over again. Even more don't bother with the legal formalities; they just cheat on their spouses. Elizabeth, for all her fame, is no less human, no less able to love, but far more willing to risk everything for it than anyone else I've ever known.

CHAPTER SIXTEEN

Judy

Until she came to my office one day in 1938, I had only the briefest contact with Judy Garland. As a child star in her early films, including the Andy Hardy series and the others in which she co-starred with Mickey Rooney, her hair needs were modest and were easily met by one of MGM's assistant stylists. When she finally stopped in to see me, it was at the suggestion of my old friend George Cukor, who hoped that I could create some very special styles for this young woman of seventeen, who would be playing a girl of eleven in a movie called *The Wizard of Oz*.

During the seven years that this classic-to-be had been in development by Louis B. Mayer, he had visualized the film as a Shirley Temple musical, a sort of overripe stage play with cutesy songs and peculiar sets that evoked, rather than simulated, the Land of Oz. Mayer offered to lend Clark Gable and Jean Harlow to 20th Century-Fox in exchange for Shirley's services, a deal ultimately rejected by

Fox production chief Darryl F. Zanuck. Reluctantly, Mayer gave the part of Dorothy to Judy, ordering Jack Dawn to make her look "as much like Temple as possible." Dawn's approach to this request was merely to supply Judy with an ill-fitting wig of blond moppet curls.

Cukor, who was a consulting director on the film at the time, was appalled. He called me to say, "Sydney, this is a big film and this girl is now a star. She deserves the best. See what you can do." Parting her hair down the middle, I pulled it back from her face and shaped it into soft curls hanging down her back. It was a pretty but youthful style for a performance that would make her one of MGM's biggest stars.

But when Judy first came to see me, she seemed very nervous—distracted and shrill. I'd seen people suffering from drug addictions before, but never one so young, and I failed to recognize that something was seriously wrong. I would later find out that Judy was displaying the classic symptoms of amphetamine dependence. It would be years before I learned that MGM itself, through its doctors and production assistants, had supplied Judy with drugs, so I could do little but stand by helplessly, watching her career and her talent unravel before my eyes. With the support and consent of Judy's mother, Ethel Gumm, the studio was supplying this child with Dexedrine and sometimes the even stronger Benzedrine to keep her performing through one film after another with little or no rest in between.

What I didn't realize at the time was that MGM had assigned Judy an assistant makeup artist and dresser who was notorious on the lot for supplying contract players with all sorts of drugs. Since I felt that Judy had been too young to know enough about these poisons even to ask for them, at first I blamed only her mother. A few years afterward, however, during a string of films Judy made in the 1940s, I noticed studio doctors strolling in twice a day to administer what were described as "vitamin shots." These so-called vitamin B-12 injections were actually a Benzedrine/Dexedrine cocktail, enhanced with morphine derivatives, designed to stifle her appetite and keep her thin while rendering her calm yet energetic enough to perform.

The World War II years were a hectic era, one in which MGM made more films than at any other time in its history. It was during this time that Mayer insisted on trying to transform Judy into a great beauty. And while I was creating distinctive hairstyles for an entirely new generation of stars—Ava Gardner, Greer Garson, Cyd Charisse and Kathryn Grayson, among dozens of others—I continued to work with Judy now and then. I designed her trendsetting styles for *Meet Me in St. Louis* and her period image for *The Harvey Girls*.

In 1947 I designed Judy's hairstyles for a big-budget musical called *The Pirate*. At an early stage of production for this fateful film, three different designs had been prepared for a bridal-veil headdress that went with a wedding gown that Judy was to wear in the film. The designs hadn't been sewn yet because no one—not Judy, her outspoken co-star Gene Kelly or even director Vincente Minnelli, who was Judy's husband at the time—liked the styles that the costume designer, Madame Korenska, had chosen for her. To break the impasse, Korenska said, "You know what? This has to do with the hair. Let's get that genius Sydney Guilaroff over here. He'll know what to do."

I have never thought of myself as anything more than a creative artist, but I must admit that I was flattered by that description, and I was walking on air as I went over to see Judy in the gown. Korenska showed me three different bridal veils she had designed for the wedding scene, and I thought I could do something interesting with the third one. I described my notion of weaving the veil through long swatches of hair intertwined with Judy's own. Korenska said, "See, I told you. He knows."

As I instructed the standby hairdresser in what to do with the veil, I glanced at Judy. Her head had slumped and her chin was buried in her chest. She was so much under the influence of drugs that she was barely able to sit up.

By 1949, after a dozen years constantly under the influence of various drugs, Judy was scheduled to appear in two big-budget MGM musicals back to back: *Annie Get Your Gun,* a $3 million production directed by Busby Berkeley, and *Summer Stock,* which reunited her with Gene Kelly. Even before the first production started, she was already so exhausted from completing *Easter Parade* and *In the Good Old Summertime*—also back to back—that what MGM's publicists described as a "complete nervous collapse" had forced her to drop out of a role opposite Fred Astaire in *The Barkleys of Broadway.*

Annie Get Your Gun, a Broadway smash with Ethel Merman and music and lyrics by Irving Berlin, should have been a triumph for Judy, who seemed happy, even enthusiastic, as I designed her elaborate and flattering hairstyles for this showcase role, which would take her from untutored hillbilly to chic international star of the Wild West rodeo circuit. This was the biggest, most expensive musical at this point in MGM's history, rewritten and tailored for Judy and meant to be the crowning moment of her career.

Scared out of her wits, however, and gulping Benzedrine by the handful, she reported to MGM's recording studio to dub the musical tracks and consumed six torturous weeks to produce fifteen mediocre songs. Her once thrilling voice emerged as a terrible moan, drifting off-key dozens of times in the course of recording an album that was a pitiful portrait of a woman beyond all help. It was never released to the general public.

Down to only 90 pounds, Judy faced her first day before Berkeley's cameras in pitiful condition. Her eyes dull and unfocused, she could barely muster the strength to lean against her makeup trailer. Finally Berkeley began shouting at the four children and a group of extras hired to back her up as she sang "Doin' What Comes Naturally." Judy left the set, the production ground to a halt and, for the next 72 hours, she surfed a wave of drugs, staying up with Benzedrine, then coming down with Seconal. On one day alone, according to an MGM makeup artist who counted them, she gulped more than a hundred pills of all types.

Just before sunrise, around 4:30 a.m. on the next day of shooting, she called one of the assistant directors to ask what kind of day he thought it would be. "If only the sun would shine," she said cryptically. After a bit, she called again, and again, and then a fourth time. By 7 a.m., according to assistant director Al Jennings, she admitted the real reason for her concern: "Al, I don't think I'm going to be any good today." Then she hung up the phone.

Somehow she managed to return to work in a few days, and the production resumed. But three weeks into the shooting schedule, Judy went to MGM's executive projection room for the first screening of "Doin' What Comes Naturally." Watching the screen with horror, she slid down into her seat, squirming with embarrassment. Finally she rushed outside to a water fountain and gulped down a fistful of Benzedrine. "How could you make me look so bad?" she hissed at Berkeley.

I couldn't stand watching her like this. I knew she suffered from deep anxieties about her talent, so I told her constantly how great she was. But Judy tearfully confessed to me that she was terrified at the thought of filling Ethel Merman's shoes in this movie. All I could do was encourage her. "You have the voice, the warmth, the believability," I told her. "You'll make this picture even greater than Merman could have ever done."

She was beyond convincing, and Busby Berkeley's manner on the set did nothing to build her confidence. When a take failed to please him, instead of telling her what was wrong, he merely barked, "Again! Again! Again!" In fact, he never told anyone what he had in mind—he just said "Again!" Perhaps he really didn't know, or maybe he lacked the ability to communicate, but in any case, even as an observer I felt frustrated. Imagine how Judy must have felt, bone tired, strung out and unable to please him or to understand just what he wanted. I was often on the set, watching while poor Judy struggled on. She could be brilliant one day and dreadful the next. Rolling her eyes during a performance of "I'm an Indian Too," she grew disoriented and finally couldn't even open her mouth. I heard constant rumblings about her drug abuse, but in those years I was still naive about such things. I didn't know that one of the sure signs of advanced amphetamine addiction is hair loss. So when she began to lose her hair, I designed several wigs for her, without understanding the reasons.

Through it all, she was always very dear and kind to me; she never raised her voice, she never played games. As strung out as she had become, as frightened and insecure as a dozen years of drug abuse had made her, I could see that she was trying desperately to do her job. We kept working together on the film, but I didn't know how much longer she would be able to keep going.

Neither did the studio executives. If they had been willing to give the poor girl a few months to rest, with wholesome food and no drugs, she might have been able to finish the film. But when co-star Howard Keel broke his ankle, his scenes were rescheduled and the brunt of the film rested on Judy's thin shoulders for six long weeks.

She couldn't hold up under the strain. One day, with executive producer Arthur Freed on the set, Judy was playing a simple love scene with Keel. Suddenly she collapsed and slid out of his arms and onto the ground, tears staining her face. While others in the cast wept for her, Freed rushed over and shook Judy hard. "What's the matter with you? Get up off your ass and let's film this scene." Fortunately, she was too far gone to care.

Metro finally borrowed Betty Hutton from Paramount to replace Judy in the film, and belatedly they hired Dr. Fred Pobirs to cure her drug addiction. Sequestered in a private clinic in Santa Barbara, she was treated with an anti-psychotic drug. But the publicity surrounding her dismissal attracted the attention of Harry J. Anslinger, director of the Federal Bureau of Narcotics, who proceeded to fine MGM for "perpetuating Judy Garland's drug abuse as far back as *The Wizard of Oz*."

Despite all her troubles, MGM brought Judy back for *Summer Stock*, to be produced by Joe Pasternak. But during the six-month shoot, she gained 45 pounds while gulping enormous quantities of drugs, and before its finale could be shot, the film was halted for nine weeks while she went to yet another clinic. Once she returned to the set, though, she was still so high that no one dared approach her. Locked in her dressing room, she ignored the knocking and pounding from cast and crew trying to communicate with her. When notes were passed under the door, she screamed at everyone to leave her alone.

Finally director Chuck Walters, anxious to film the movie's last musical number, came to her door, but Judy wouldn't speak to him either. In desperation, Chuck asked me, "Do you think Judy would let *you* in her dressing room?"

I agreed to try. I went to her door and knocked gently. "Judy? Judy, this is Sydney. Would you let me in, please, dear? I want to speak to you." There was dead silence for what seemed like an eternity. I knocked again. "Judy, did you hear me?"

At last she replied in a low voice, "Wait a moment, I'll

unlock the door. But don't come in until I tell you to!"

I waited until she called out, "Come in," and entered to find her on the floor, wearing only a wrinkled dressing gown. In shock, I saw that she had been tearing her hair out—it was strewn all over the floor. I picked her up, kissed her and sat her on the couch.

"Everyone is against me here!" she wailed. "I know they're trying to get rid of me. Nobody cares about me! Nobody!"

I wrapped my arms around her and said, "Now, Judy, darling, you are a wonderful person and a great talent. You've been a great entertainer your whole life. Everyone here at the studio holds you in the highest possible regard." In truth, she had become so obnoxious that everyone was completely fed up with her. That could all be remedied, I was sure, if she would just come back to what she had always been—a simple, good-hearted young woman. But she seemed to be beyond that, weeping in fear and frustration about what she and her life had become.

After my many attempts to console her, she asked, "What am I here for, anyway?"

This was my first opportunity to tell her that the company was waiting to shoot her last number, "Get Happy," a woefully ironic song title in light of her circumstances.

"What am I supposed to do?" she asked.

"First of all," I said, "let's tell the company that you want to do the song, and then we'll make preparations to get you ready. OK?"

Judy remained quiet as I called the director to say, "Judy will do the number. At least she'll give it a try. She's a wreck, but I'll call the makeup and wardrobe people so we can get to work."

While she was being made up, I looked over her costume and took the young woman from wardrobe aside to ask, "Marie, does she have only black silk tights, black jacket and black high heels to wear for this number?"

"Yes, that's all."

I told her there was no possibility that I could make Judy's hair look good in the amount of time that we had, and I asked her to bring me two or three black fedora hats from wardrobe for Judy to try on so I could see which fit her best. Then I would tuck her mangled hair underneath it. Dot, the makeup girl, did a good job on Judy's face, considering that her star's head kept bobbing around and she couldn't keep her eyes open. Marie returned with several hats, and one of them fit remarkably well. When Marie got Judy dressed in her costume, Judy looked absolutely adorable even in her sorry state, and I felt a glimmer of hope that she might actually be able to do her number.

She was quiet, seemingly dazed, as we went to the set, and our arrival was met with a sudden hush. Crew and company had been waiting over three hours for Judy, and it was almost time to break for lunch. But the director wisely chose to postpone lunch and film Judy without further delay.

Everything was in place and properly lit; Judy's stand-in had done her job. Gently, with Marie's help, we got Judy on stage and on her mark. I said, "Before we begin, do you think you'd like to hear a few bars of the music, dear?"

Flashing her first smile of the day, she said, "Yes, I think I would."

"All right, Marie will stay with you while I go tell Chuck to have them play a little of the song." When I returned, I held Judy's hand as we listened to the music, and after a bit she brightened.

"Is that enough, Judy?" I asked.

She nodded that it was, and I waved my hand to stop the music.

"Judy, dear," I continued, "the music will start and I'm going to leave you on stage. Just stand here and look straight ahead at the camera. Can you see it, darling?" I pointed through the lights. When she nodded, I kissed her and said, "Do it, Judy, do it!"

"Action!" Chuck called. The opening bars of the song began, and Judy came in on cue. Despite the deleterious effects of years of drug and alcohol abuse, all her genius burst to the forefront. We went through the entire number, note for note, word for word, every gesture and every movement, and she was perfection, everything any director could have wished for—and all in one take. When Chuck yelled "Cut!" the entire crew broke into genuine applause, and this dazzling, classic performance of "Get Happy" became one of her most famous musical numbers.

But *Summer Stock* was Judy's last picture with MGM. After that she drifted, singing in live performances all over the world. Throughout her turbulent life, she remained a devoted mother and was loved and admired by millions. In 1954 she returned to the screen with great success opposite James Mason in *A Star Is Born*, which earned her an Academy Award nomination. To commemorate the occasion, I wrote this poem in her honor:

You have to find a sense of security within yourself.
Fame can sometimes bring tragedy in one's life.
To acquire the happiness we all search for,
We must lead our path based on the
Ultimate simplicity which is the nature
Of our being.

My final contact with Judy was in June 1969, when I went to London to help Ava Gardner prepare for a film. We went to a party given by Bumble Dawson, England's foremost motion picture dress costumer, who had designed costumes for Marilyn Monroe in *The Prince and the Showgirl*. Ava and I had been there for about an hour when Judy arrived, looking extremely thin in an odd getup that made her look like a hippie: large, floppy hat, blouse, vest and a long, full skirt. When Bumble told her that Ava was sitting on the floor near the fireplace, she walked right over and sank to her knees. They immediately hugged and kissed. Then someone told Judy that I was present, and she got up and threw her arms around me, too.

We reminisced for a while about the movies we had made together, but I could see that Judy was in very low spirits. When Ava and I told her that we had plans to visit Paris for a week of costume fittings, she said, "I've been so lonely I wish you and Ava would come to my house after the party so we can have some time alone to talk." Our hearts went out to her, and we decided to take her up on the invitation.

Her home was in a narrow two-story mews, very dreary and practically devoid of furnishings. The walls were bare, without a single picture hanging on them. With one glance I knew that she was down and out financially, and that saddened me. In all the years we had known each other, I had never seen her in such poor condition.

After we walked in, she began crying. "I wish you weren't going away," she lamented.

"Don't worry, darling," said Ava. "We'll be back from Paris next Saturday night, and we'll call you the moment we get back."

Ava did telephone Judy when we returned, but there was no answer. The very next morning the headlines in the *London Times* announced that she had been found dead in the bathroom of that dreary flat. We were stunned, in shock. Such tremendous talent, such a marvelous soul, such a delight and inspiration to people of all ages throughout the world—destroyed by drugs and alcohol. How terribly tragic. Judy had given Hollywood everything she had, but it wasn't enough.

CHAPTER SEVENTEEN

Bouquets

*A*s the decades passed and MGM faded into just another movie studio, slowly I became one of the few living vestiges of the studio's glory years and, until my retirement, its last link to the days of Thalberg. By outliving so many of my peers and colleagues, I emerged as the studio's elder statesman. This book tells my story, but my true legacy will always be the 1,200 motion pictures that display my hairstyling creations. These include not only MGM films, but also dozens made while I was on loanout to every other major Hollywood studio up until the late 1980s. Because of home video and cable television, many of these classics will continue to delight audiences for centuries.

From the first, I was fascinated with faces. To me, they are the most interesting aspect of any human being, the key to expressing the innermost qualities of each character, to peering into the deepest recesses of one's soul. This was my gift, and with it I was fortunate enough to build a career during an era when movie stars personified a mystique of beauty that left the entire world enthralled. I met, befriended and worked with literally thousands of actors and actresses, among them the most famous, the most beautiful, the most talented of Hollywood's Golden Age. After all these years, I find myself forgetting names—never faces—but there is hardly room between the covers of a book to describe all my encounters with the celebrated stars who turned Hollywood into the capital of glamour. I will, however, mention a few who remain vivid in my memory.

Of all the stars with whom I worked, none depended more on makeup and hairstyling than the legendary Marlene Dietrich. Yet for three decades our relationship was a closely guarded secret. There was never any written contract, all payments for my services were in cash and everything was done in the privacy of Marlene's dressing room.

Our relationship began in 1938 with a telephone call from Universal, where, after being declared box-office poison by theater owners around the country, Marlene was attempting a comeback by appearing opposite James Stewart in *Destry Rides Again*. It was a Western, explained her assistant, and the elegant actress had no clue as to how her hair ought to be styled. Her character was Frenchy, a patrician European woman who had fallen on hard times and was trying to survive by running a rowdy saloon in the Old West. I spent a week looking through library books and screening films until I realized that the usual approach in Westerns was to create an elaborate style or a top-heavy wig. Neither really suited her look, so Marlene and I worked together to create a crown of small ringlets that tossed effectively about her head as she strutted atop a bar crooning "See What the Boys in the Back Room Will Have."

That singular look became her standard for *Destry Rides Again* and for a number of Westerns that followed, and these films brought stardom back to Marlene. But we didn't work together again until 1943, when she came to MGM to star opposite the suave Ronald Colman in *Kismet*, a glossy extravaganza loosely based on the classic fable *A Thousand and One Arabian Nights*.

Creating a Middle Eastern harem-girl look for Marlene was a challenge. I finally came up with a series of gold-toned wigs, braids and twists of hair that sat atop her head. She loved the look. For the final touch, I suggested that she spray some sort of metallic sprinkles on her hair to give it more of a shimmer under the lights. Marlene one-upped me, going to Tiffany's to have real gold ground into a fine powder, and at a total cost of $12,000, she sprayed her hair every morning before stepping in front of the cameras.

One day in the dressing room during the filming of *Kismet,* several of the stars and supporting players from various pictures were complaining about their husbands and boyfriends, and Marlene decided to join the conversation. Sounding almost bored, with half-closed eyes, gesturing casually with a limp hand, Marlene announced, "If any of you ladies have men who claim they are impotent, just send him to me and he'll find he isn't impotent any longer." I burst out laughing.

I didn't hear from her again until 1956, when she was slated for a cameo—as yet another saloonkeeper—in Mike Todd's Oscar-winning *Around the World in Eighty Days*. I crafted a tight-fitting platinum wig with ringlets cascading down her neck. By now Father Time had begun closing in on her, but I knew that Marlene wanted to appear as youthful as she had in all those Westerns, so I devised a series of tiny hooks and tapes that, hidden in the wig, stretched her skin taut. Thanks to this nonsurgical facelift, she really looked 20 years younger. On the set and ready to step under the lights, she paused to whisper in my ear, "Guilaroff, we really have cheated time, haven't we?!" She continued to use that hooked wig, or one just like it, throughout the rest of her career.

Although my relationship with Marlene was warm, we never saw enough of each other to grow close. In contrast, I became dear friends with Grace Kelly, the reigning beauty of a later era, though she didn't remain in Hollywood very long. Few events—and few films—required more of my attention than her 1956 wedding to Prince Rainier of Monaco. And few events captivated the public imagination in such a grand manner. Everybody in Hollywood wanted to be invited, of course, but Grace chose only a special few to attend. Cary Grant, Frank Sinatra, Rita Gam (one of Grace's bridesmaids) and I were honored to witness the couple take their vows at the ceremony in Monaco.

Before I even left for the wedding, MGM's publicity man, Howard Strickling, wired the studio from Monaco to say, "You cannot imagine the pandemonium here!" The press had converged on the tiny principality in droves. Even Gloria Swanson was there, covering the event on special assignment. I was held up in customs in London and almost didn't arrive in time, but I finally made it.

Grace looked every inch a real-life princess. I designed a special hairstyle for her, and I also made her a toque, a small, round, close-fitting hat. When she met with her mother in New York City en route to the wedding, she was wearing a fur coat and the toque adorned with three roses. *Women's Wear*, a popular newspaper declared: "Grace Kelly looking lovely. Hats this spring will be toques, with roses." And of course, the whole of the high-fashion world continued to follow her tastes for many years afterward.

After their wedding, Grace Kelly became Princess Grace of Monaco, and if ever there was a woman born to be royalty, she was it. She had the manners, the elegance, the beauty, the sweetness and the character. Grace knew who her friends were, and even after she became Rainier's consort, she remained loyal to them—one of many things I adored about her. Every year she sent me a unique, book-sized Christmas card with a beautiful family photograph.

Grace missed Hollywood and film work, though, and she was constantly bombarded with scripts by producers hopeful that she might come out of "retirement" and return to the screen. But Rainier would not allow it; it was years before Grace resigned herself to remaining only a wife and mother. She understood the public demands of her position and always maintained her duties graciously.

Following the birth of her third child, Stephanie, I went to lunch with her, the prince and their other two children. After the meal, the prince excused himself and I asked to hold the baby. "Do you think she will cry?" I asked.

"No, she's very good-natured," said Grace, and put her in my arms. She sat on my lap, absolutely adorable, smiling and cooing. We had a wonderful time that day, but not long afterward Grace telephoned me, distressed. She confessed she had learned that the prince was being unfaithful to her. "I know he has affairs with other women. That's very frustrating to me, and it makes me very, very unhappy," she sighed. She said he had even slept with her personal secretary, a woman whom Grace had trained and groomed. Eventually she managed to get the secretary out of the palace, but she was miserable about it.

Eventually, Grace came to terms with her lot: She resolved to build her life around her children and her subjects, and Rainier would do whatever he chose, but discreetly. We had many more long conversations over the years, but the one that stays in my mind took place in 1982. It was about happiness and how each person has a different perspective on life. Grace said, "You know, happiness comes and goes, it's there sometimes and then it isn't."

Not long after that sad conversation, I called the palace to speak to Grace, but she was out. A few days went by and I wondered why she didn't call me back. Then I heard the news: She had died from injuries sustained in a horrible car crash. After the shock wore off, I was left with a sense of incompleteness, as though important things had been left unsaid, that issues were left dangling and would never be resolved.

Many of my other friendships have happier endings. I was fortunate enough to make friends with Vivien Leigh, whom I met during the filming of *Gone With the Wind*. I found her to be charming and soft-spoken. Working on my own time, I often went to her Beverly Hills house to design hairdos to match her dresses. We then sent stills back to stylists on the set. So many of Scarlett's distinctive designs were created by me. I didn't get a credit, but because of my friendship with Vivien, it didn't bother me in the least.

Sometimes, instead of taking lunch in the commissary, we ate at the Selznick Studios, which were part of the MGM lot. One day at lunch, near the start of filming, she said suddenly, "I don't know what to do with my part."

"What do you mean by that?" I asked.

"Look at the cast," she explained. "There's Olivia de Havilland, Leslie Howard, Clark Gable and me. Any woman, even Scarlett, would choose Gable over Leslie Howard. Why would she fall in love with Ashley over Rhett Butler? And all that business about how she'll 'think about it tomorrow at Tara.' I think Scarlett's a twit!"

"Don't worry about that," I told her. "It's the whole picture that's going to count in the end. And you can't say it's not a good story."

Eventually, Vivien put aside her reservations and threw herself into the role. And twit or not, she went on to huge success.

Not all my Hollywood relationships were so friendly. I may even have alienated a few people along the way, partly because I refuse to allow people to run roughshod over those I care about. In 1958, for example, while I was working on the set of *Gigi*, actress Isabel Jeans complained to me that her hair had been colored purple, and she hated it. I told her it didn't have to be purple. "I'll get this color out of the wig and restyle it," I said, adding that I would also lift her face, as I had for Marlene Dietrich.

When I had finished, Isabel, who was at least 65 at the time, looked wonderfully young—45 at most. Upon hearing of this conversation, however, dress designer Cecil Beaton immediately phoned producer Arthur Freed and complained: "Guilaroff changed the color from purple and it doesn't make her look any better. She was more startling with purple hair."

Cecil considered himself a man who knew everything about everything. What all this was really about, of course, was that Cecil was jealous of the affection so many actresses felt toward me because I made them look beautiful and was always respectful toward them.

The first I heard of this animosity was when Arthur Freed brought him down to Hair and Makeup. I had heard so much about Cecil, who had created so many wonderful sets for so many great British films. I held out my hand and was very cordial until he began berating me about the purple wig and my changes to a couple of hairdos that he had designed.

I wrote a letter to Cecil reminding him that my wigs and hairstyles encompassed every era from the Etruscan period to the modern era, and I ended the letter by saying, "Cecil, as far as I can tell, everything you do resembles a Victorian piss pot, and that's as far as you go with your eye for historical replications! So from now on, I would thank you not to interfere with my work."

Arthur called me later to say, "I hear you're not getting along with Cecil."

"He's telling everybody what to do," I fumed. "He even told the set designer how to change the furniture! Nobody in the company likes him. Do I have to like him?"

"No, you don't have to like him. But we've got him, so do please try to get along with him, that's all."

So I wrote Cecil another note: "At first I thought it was an honor to meet you, but it's no honor at all, believe me. He didn't reply. A few years later, when Cecil was at Warner Bros. during the filming of *My Fair Lady*, he did a complete turnaround by insisting that the studio get me to style Audrey Hepburn's hair for that picture. This just goes to show the utter hypocrisy of some individuals in this industry.

Although I had established my Hollywood reputation by making lovely women even lovelier, there were a few times when I was challenged to turn a duckling into a swan. One of these occasions came about when Ava Gardner turned down *Sweet Bird of Youth*; in her place was cast the gifted stage actress Geraldine Page, who had created the role on Broadway. Even though producer Pandro Berman and director Richard Brooks felt she was too ordinary-looking, they were confident that I could transform her into a beauty on the screen. Brooks tracked me to the house in Italy that I was then sharing with Ava while we were working on the film *The Angel Wore Red* with Dirk Bogarde, and asked me to come back to help with Geraldine. "You can make her look better than anyone else can. So we'll wait until you get back," he said.

Three weeks later, after finishing Ava's movie, I was waiting in my MGM salon when Miss Page appeared. She beckoned me to come close and whispered, "I know I can play this part very well, Mr. Guilaroff, but I need your help."

She was right. I knew I would face a challenge to make her look stunning and beautiful. When Brooks and I met, I told him that I would have some wigs made for Geraldine. "When I'm through with her," I said, "you won't recognize her."

This wasn't arrogance; I knew I could do something for her. Viewing her screen test, I noted a shadow over her cheeks, which were very full. She also moved her mouth with too much expression. This is useful for stage performances, in which the audience is some distance away, but not for movies. I knew immediately that changing that one thing would make a big difference in her screen appearance.

For her wig color I chose a muted shade of auburn that had a lifelike look. In a different way than I had done with Marlene Dietrich, I devised a system of elastic bands that gripped Geraldine's own tightly braided hair, lifting her face and gathering the loose skin at the top of her head under the wig. With both sides lifted, her face lost the bulge that had thrown a shadow across her cheeks. I also stretched back the skin from behind each ear, which eliminated a slight looseness in her jawline so that the camera could capture her high cheekbones and the bone structure of her face.

After makeup was applied, I put the wig on. The difference was electrifying: Geraldine looked glamorous. I called Brooks to come in and take a look, and the transformation was so complete that it almost took his breath away. *Sweet Bird of Youth* was an enormous success, and Geraldine Page was nominated for an Oscar.

Yet despite my gilding of the lily, Geraldine preferred to dress in a rather Bohemian fashion offscreen. On the day of the Academy Awards ceremonies, I got a panicked call from the film's publicist insisting that I meet him at the airport where Geraldine's plane had landed. I was told she looked too ghastly to be photographed by a hungry press corps waiting to record her arrival in Los Angeles. Luckily, I had an extra wig from *Sweet Bird of Youth*, so I raced to the airport, went aboard the plane and performed my magic one last time on Geraldine.

Another stage actress who was challenged by the harsh demands of the camera was Judy Holliday, who became justly famous for her role in *Born Yesterday*, a hit Broadway play. Harry Cohn at Columbia bought the rights to the play and began looking around for someone to star in the screen version. Judy came out to California for an audition, but from the beginning it was plain that Cohn didn't want her. Director George Cukor was sure she was perfect for the role, because while *Born Yesterday* didn't require a glamorous star for the lead, it did require an actress with a lot of talent.

Judy was young, sweet-natured and interesting-looking, but she was not what one would call a pretty woman. George persuaded Harry to let him make a test with Judy, and he asked me to do her hair and direct her makeup as well. I had much more to work with than I'd had with Geraldine Page, so when the test was finished, Harry was astonished. He couldn't believe the transformation. Judy got the part and went on to become a major star.

In addition to Judy and Geraldine, I was privileged to work with an actress and singer who was one of the greatest talents of her day, but one who had to struggle so hard against prejudice and bigotry that she never succeeded to the degree she might have if she hadn't been born with black skin. Despite all the glory of MGM's golden era, the studio's treatment of Lena Horne was unforgivable. When I was a little boy growing up in Canada, I had more than a few black friends, and I had never believed that a black person was any different from you or me. But in 1943, not one of my hairdressers at MGM would so much as touch her, and as head of the department, I was appalled by such rudeness directed against anyone of any color.

In order to serve Lena's needs as an actress, I had to beg a woman named Priscilla, one of the leaders of the hairdressing and makeup union, to get me the finest black hairdresser she could find to become Lena's standby, the artist who remained on the set to maintain the style I gave Lena each morning for that day's particular scene. The person hired became the first black hairstylist in the history of MGM to serve in this capacity.

To try to compensate for the obvious racial hostility that Lena had to endure, I worked very intimately with her, ensuring that all her styles were of the highest quality. I gave her a sleek, upswept look for *Thousands Cheer,* and the curls for *Till the Clouds Roll By* that would become her classic preferred look for many years to come.

Although Lena had been exposed to prejudice for most of her life, its depth and virulence sometimes shocked even her. One afternoon she came into the MGM commissary carrying a newspaper, and as she stood waiting to be seated, she held it up, pretending to read. When she put it down, I waved to her. I thought she didn't see me, because she never acknowledged me, even though I waved three or four times. She stood there for a long time, and no one offered her a table.

I kept waving until a producer sitting next to me said, "Sydney, I wouldn't do that if I were you. Not everybody feels the way you do."

Shocked and angry, I replied, "Well, I don't care whether everybody does or not, I don't give a damn. And I don't have to sit here either."

I rose from my table, walked over to Lena and asked, "Would you like to join me for lunch, dear?"

She said, "Oh, yes, I would! Very much so. I'd be very happy to."

I looked around the room and saw a table where some people had finished, then told the hostess, "Would you please see to it that this table is cleared, because Miss Horne and I are going to have lunch together."

When the table was ready, we sat down and had an enjoyable conversation while we waited for our food to be served. Later I excused myself for a moment to speak with the hostess. I told her, "I don't want you to do this ever again to Miss Horne. She is just as important as—if not more important than—most of the people you've seated at any of the tables here, and that includes the executive table. But because she's black, you let her stand around waiting until a table is absolutely clear of everyone so that she can't possibly sit with a white person. If you ever do that to her again, please believe that I have enough authority to report it to the top. I don't believe the executives at MGM want it known that the studio discriminates against blacks."

The hostess apologized, and from that day on, at least in the commissary, Lena was treated no differently from any white actress. Many years later, when she was invited to sing in *That's Entertainment III,* she told the producer, "If Sydney Guilaroff's alive, please get him to do my hair. And if he's dead, I'm not coming." We had a wonderful reunion.

The irony of racial prejudice in Hollywood was that, at this time in history, all of America had mobilized to fight Hitler, in part because he was an avowed racist. During the World War II years, Bette Davis and others started the Hollywood Canteen, where servicemen could enjoy meals and entertainment. Each night after feeding my children, I said goodbye to them, then rushed off to my "second job" as a volunteer waiter at the Canteen, arriving just before 8 p.m. There was no time to rest; it was all I could do just to keep abreast of my tables. That is why, to this day, I feel very sympathetic toward any waiter or waitress who serves me.

I was only one of many who helped out, including quite a few celebrities too old or infirm to serve in the armed forces themselves. Sometimes the second shift, from 10 to midnight, didn't show up and I'd have to stay on. By the time I got home I had been on my feet most of the day and was worn out. But I was glad to do it. All the kids at the Canteen were going to fight overseas, so it was the least I could do. All the food and drink was free to them, and under Bette's leadership, all of us chipped in enough money to keep the Canteen going until the war ended. I even persuaded Cary Grant to do his bit on the home front. I asked him one evening, "Could I enlist your aid in a little matter?"

"Why sure, Sydney, anything for you," he told me.

"How about coming down to the Farmer's Market for a fund-raiser? They'd like you to sit on a huge heap of potatoes and sell them for two fifty apiece to help raise money for the war effort."

That was lot of money in those days, but people gladly contributed even more than that, and by golly, Cary stayed until every last potato was sold. He managed to raise thousands of dollars that night.

One new star of that wartime era, June Allyson, owed much of her success to her flippy hairdo and her husky voice. Both had been carefully developed. We first met informally, between takes on one of her first pictures, *Girl Crazy*. June saw me enter the set and ran over. She knew little about what I did or what I could do to help her, but she was very ambitious and very bright.

"Do you ever go to the rushes?" she asked. In those days, few stars were allowed to see their own rushes.

"Yes, I do," I answered.

"Well," she continued, "how am I doing? Did you notice me?"

"Yes, I noticed. You're doing very well. Unless I'm mistaken, you're going to become a star."

"You're kidding! You're kidding me, aren't you?"

"No, I'm not kidding you. I think you're going to be a star."

June had a definite star quality that came across on the screen. She soon developed a deeper, distinctive tone to her voice that gave it more personality. Achieving this was risky and dangerous; each morning she would get into her car, roll the windows up and scream at the top of her lungs from the time she left home until she got to the studio.

For all her sweetness on-screen, however, June was often temperamental. During filming of *The Opposite Sex*, a remake of *The Women*, director David Miller and I agreed that she ought to look different to play the role of Mary Haines, which Norma Shearer had created in the original. I had a wig made for her, one with a little sophistication, an adult look that wasn't at all like the "girl next door" image that had brought her to the brink of stardom.

She hated it. At first she rebelled, complaining to Miller, "I don't like to wear a wig! I'd rather wear my own hair." But eventually she submitted, and her new look became her trademark. To this day she wears the same basic style, with bangs and her hair turned under.

Because I often sensed star quality almost at first glance, I tried to nurture it whenever I could. Thus when an unknown named Rita Hayworth captured a tiny part in *Susan and God*, directed by George Cukor, I picked her out of a group of people and said, "I'll do her personally." I wanted her to stand out from the crowd, and after what I did for her, she was indeed noticed. On the set one day, I saw her doing needlework on the sidelines. I came up and remarked, "What beautiful needlepoint!"

She was making an afghan. "Would you like to have it?" she offered.

"I wouldn't want to take it away from you."

"You've been so sweet to me that I'd be very proud to let you have it when I finish." So I accepted it and had a favorite chair upholstered with it.

A few years later, before she became a big star, I saw Rita in a nightclub with her husband, businessman Edward Judson. She looked lonely and unhappy, so I excused myself from my companions, Hedy Lamarr and Constance Bennett, walked over to her table and said hello. After introducing myself to her husband, I asked his permission to dance with her.

While we danced, I asked if she was unhappy. She said yes, and after that neither of us said another word for a long time as we continued to dance. Finally I spoke. "I have a feeling something has gone wrong, and I'm not trying to make you tell me anything about your personal life. But I promise you that you're going to get somewhere in this business, dear. You will." And of course, she did.

As Rita's years of struggle proved, it takes a long time to become an overnight success. And even then, the biggest stars still are often beset with problems. Many are quite lonely, as I discovered during production of *North by Northwest*. Passing Cary Grant one afternoon, I said, quite casually, "How are things going?"

"I don't know," he replied, downcast.

I stepped up, put my arms around him and said, "Don't be unhappy about it. We can talk later."

I was on my way to help co-star Eva Marie Saint, but I promised to come back and talk in a short while. But before I had finished touching up Eva Marie, Cary came over from his portable dressing room nearby. When she felt his presence, she snapped, "What are you doing over here? We're not wanted yet."

He said, "Oh, I'm just lonesome. I guess I need a little mothering."

"Well, I'll be darned," I said. "I thought I'd given you enough fathering to hold you for a while. And now you need some mothering."

Unfortunately, Cary suffered from what would today be called clinical depression, and I was told he was so miserable that he had resorted to taking LSD under a doctor's supervision. If this had happened in the nineties, he would have been openly prescribed an antidepressant like Prozac. But back then, in the fifties, he would have been ostracized if it had leaked out that he was taking psychedelic drugs.

At the opposite end of the emotional spectrum, young Shirley MacLaine, whom I worked with for the first time in 1958 on location in a small Indiana town for the film *Some Came Running,* never acted like she needed mothering or fathering. She was sweet, but even before she became a star, Shirley displayed an extremely self-assured and independent air. She had wonderful hair, which I cut into a pretty, layered look with bangs for *Some Came Running.* Several years later, for *The Yellow Rolls Royce,* I created a different look for the bangs and brought her hair forward to rest softly on her cheeks, pointed toward her mouth.

For *Sweet Charity,* Shirley started with medium-length, light brown hair. Edith Head had designed a red dress for her, but after a test, director Bob Fosse said he didn't like it. Edith was crushed; the dress was scheduled to be used in a scene to be shot the very next day, and no one seemed to know what to do. I didn't want Edith to bear all the blame for what I could see was going to be an ugly exercise in finger-pointing, so I said, "I don't think it's the dress at all. It's the color of Shirley's hair. It doesn't go with that dress."

As they all just stood there with their mouths open, I went on. "I think she shouldn't be brown-haired. With that red dress, she needs more flash to her personality for this picture, so I'd like to make her a redhead."

Actually, I was thinking aloud and really didn't know what color I had in mind. So when someone challenged me on that, I replied, "I don't mean red red, I mean a sort of soft, golden red."

"But we have to shoot it tomorrow," said the producer.

"We can do the hair tonight," I countered.

"Yes, but if you do it tonight, we won't be able to see it until it's time to shoot."

"Well, what have you got me here for? Either you have confidence in me or you haven't got confidence in me."

The producer gave in. "OK, then, make her a redhead."

Shirley loved it—they all loved it. It became her new color, the shade that she used in picture after picture. She also became a wonderful friend and asked for me on every film. We're still close, and I've always enjoyed being with someone who's interested in so many things: politics, acting, dancing, spirituality. Shirley can do anything and everything. One of her greatest performances was the title role in *Madame Sousatzka,* the touching tale of a piano teacher and her gifted pupils.

Though I was seldom wrong either about a young actress's potential or, as with Shirley, about how best to enhance it with my art, not all of my best work was appreciated. David Selznick, for example, paid an unprecedented $3,000 for my trend-setting haircut for Ingrid Bergman in *For Whom the Bell Tolls.* Bergman was so nervous about having her hair worked on that I decided to proceed very gradually. I tried about five different lengths and six different looks until we agreed on which one was the best. It was short, and I curled it very loosely, ruffling it with my hands to make it look very natural and extraordinarily feminine. Bergman, who had worn pants well before most women wore them onscreen, looked for the first time like a girl instead of a woman dressed like a man. Alas, Selznick wouldn't leave it that way; he ordered her hair curled more tightly, and that ruined it.

One of my offhand choices, however, turned into the signature color for one of the world's most beloved actresses. I first met Lucille Ball when she reported to MGM for a singing part in yet another film adapted from Broadway, *Du Barry Was a Lady*, in which she reprised the role that Ethel Merman had created on stage. It was the sort of big-budget musical that could make a star—or break one—and despite Lucy's pedestrian talent as a singer, she won a Metro contract from her appearance in the film.

In the 1946 film *Ziegfeld Follies*, Lucy wore an apricot dress and a pompadour hairstyle and cracked a whip over the heads of chorines in cat costumes that sparkled with sequins and jet beads. I felt she needed to stand out, so I mixed a variety of hair dyes into a henna rinse that transformed her into a shimmering golden redhead. That formula became the basis for her on-screen persona throughout a fabulous career that took her from queen of the B's to television stardom in the all-time sitcom hit, "I Love Lucy."

All that was still years ahead of her when I went along on the promotional tour for *Ziegfeld Follies*. She had married Desi Arnaz in 1941, but as we waited backstage at Radio City Music Hall, I was agonized to see this young, good-looking Cuban musician flirting outrageously with every one of the Rockettes. Lucy blushed but kept her composure and her silence. I felt very sad for her. Everyone in Hollywood knew that Desi was a womanizer of the first rank.

Many years later, after she had won practically every honor television could bestow and was as widely beloved a figure as any woman in America, she invited one of my oldest friends, Joan Crawford, to guest on her TV show. I came along to do Joan's hair and was astonished to notice that she was actually shaking with stage fright. In rehearsals Lucy was merciless, belittling Joan by screaming, "I knew I should have gotten Gloria Swanson—she's a professional!"

When it was time for taping, Joan rose to the occasion, as always. She was magnificent. Afterward, Lucy tried to make up for her rudeness by inviting her to dinner. "I have other plans," said Joan with icy primness.

Not long after, when Lucy's guests were Elizabeth Taylor and Richard Burton, Lucy was so abrasive that Burton almost walked off the set. When Elizabeth appeared in her stunning Balenciaga gown, adorned with a king's ransom in jewels and the special "movie queen" hairstyle I created for the occasion, it was Lucy's turn to stew in silence. My conclusion was that power corrupts, and even Lucy was not immune. To be fair, I also realized that her television show had become her entire life, though that is not reason enough to change from a sweet-tempered girl into a terror.

Another actress whose real personality belied her public image was Irene Dunne, the great star of such classics as *Show Boat, Roberta* and *The Awful Truth*. When she came to MGM in 1943 to make the World War II drama *The White Cliffs of Dover,* I was very excited; from the films I had seen, I expected a woman who not only was quite beautiful but also exuded sophistication and breeding and was the personification of goodness. But after I worked night and day on her hairstyles, she told director Clarence Brown that she didn't like any of them and demanded a new stylist.

I didn't understand, but what could I do? I sent over another stylist, a woman Miss Dunne loathed on sight, though I will never know why. I sent a third stylist, a man who was rejected almost as quickly. I warned Clarence about Dunne, and finally he screened all three hairstyle tests for her. Before the lights came back on in the screening room, she declared, "Why, Mr. Guilaroff's styles are the best! I will work only with him."

My styles won her many accolades, but during the filming, which experienced many delays resulting from Dunne's temper tantrums, Clarence confided in me. "You were correct, Sydney," he said. "The woman is a bitch." I later learned Irene did this on purpose because it was in her contract that she made an additional $10,000 every time she was called in for tests.

In total contrast to Dunne was Esther Williams, the all-American bathing beauty who had been discovered modeling hats at Robinson's department store by the legendary Broadway showman Billy Rose. She was no more than seventeen when she came to MGM in 1940 for a screen test, and as I styled her hair for that test, I saw that she was trembling with fear.

Esther wasn't afraid of the camera. What had shaken her up was the prospect of doing her test with Clark Gable. But Gable was gracious and charming and stayed on through several takes of each shot. When she muffed her lines for the fourth time and the director called for still another take, I came over to fix her hair.

"Are you married?" I asked.

"Yes."

"What does your husband do for a living?"

"He's a doctor."

"Listen to me, dear," I said. "I have only your interests at heart. Why don't you just get up and go home and forget this business? The rise is wonderful, but the fall is terrible."

Looking back, I find it remarkable that I said what I did, because Esther was quite stunning and a fine actress. But she seemed so young and vulnerable, and I was worried that the business would ruin her life. It's just as well that she didn't take my advice. Esther accepted an MGM contract and remained a star for nearly 20 years. Along the way, however, she shed her husband, Dr. Ben Gage, and married actor Fernando Lamas.

A champion swimmer, Esther became a unique star, appearing in movie after movie doing aquatic ballets. It almost drove me crazy, because I virtually had to reinvent the art of hairstyling to accommodate the demands of her underwater activities. She kept her hair relatively short, a godsend because I had to cover it with olive oil so it wouldn't move and so water wouldn't penetrate it. I adorned her hair with faux hairpieces and ornaments, including a series of sequined headdresses.

One of her most challenging scenes involved a dive from the high board into a circle of swimmers. After she hit the water, they were all supposed to submerge just as she surfaced. This called for complex choreography and precision swimming. Esther did it in one take, the camera following her all the way down and then pulling back—a remarkable scene. Afterward, as she did every night, she spent hours removing the olive oil and chlorine from her hair. Despite all that, we're still great friends.

Another MGM musical star I befriended was the beautiful balletic dancer, Cyd Charisse. Like me, she came from a humble background—as Tula Ellice Finklea in Amarillo, Texas. She was in the midst of her first picture, *Ziegfeld Follies*, when we met in 1945. I styled her hair for a disastrous dance number with Fred Astaire in which she was supposed to tiptoe down a mountain through water and bubbles created by a huge bubble machine backstage. The scene never worked right, and it was cut from the movie, but Astaire was so impressed with Cyd that he called her "leggy dynamite."

It was 1952's *Singin' in the Rain* that really showcased Cyd's marvelous dancing talent for the first time and made her into a star. But my fondest memories of her have to be from the filming of *Two Weeks in Another Town* in Rome. Her co-star was Kirk Douglas and it was a breakthrough role for her as a dramatic actress. It was my great pleasure to style her hair for the part in a silken gold to go with a breathtaking bottle-green silk evening gown adorned with coque feathers.

While we were in Rome, a party was given in honor of Kirk Douglas and his wife Anne. Since *Cleopatra* was also in production in Rome, Elizabeth Taylor was there with Eddie Fisher, as was Richard Burton and his wife Sybil. I remember the electricity in the room when Elizabeth and Richard left their partners to dance one number together. Cyd, dancing nearby with her husband Tony Martin, felt it too, for she glanced over at Elizabeth with a soft, knowing smile while they glided by.

Cyd and Tony and I had become good friends by this time, and we had enormous fun going out to dinner together during the making of that picture. We've spent many unforgettable evenings since then, and our relationship has endured through the years. So has her classic beauty. She is still a stunning woman, a portrait of elegance, the epitome of refinement and I am honored to count myself among her loyal friends.

Another lifelong friend, who also happens to be one of the greatest musical stars of all time, is Debbie Reynolds, a versatile talent and a truly remarkable woman. She and I got off to a rocky start, though. We first met in 1951 during the filming of *Singin' in the Rain* with Gene Kelly and Donald O'Connor. Since she was still a teenager at the time, we tested various hairstyles on Debbie to make her appear a little older for the role. Producer Arthur Freed and I decided on a simple hairdo with an extension added at the back of her neck to make her hair look fuller.

Arthur was pleased, but Debbie was furious. She thought she should look softer and more glamorous. On the first day of shooting, as I was doing her hair, she looked at me in the mirror and, in what she undoubtedly considered a very grown-up manner, said to me, "I'd like to have a word with you in private."

I took her to one of the empty makeup rooms and sat down, but she stood over me and shouted, "You know, it's your fault that I look this awful! And if you hadn't done this style for me, I wouldn't look so old. I don't care what Mr. Freed says. I blame you!"

I took her comments in stride, knowing that she was still a child, and I explained to her why she had to look more mature in order to be accepted by audiences as a dancing partner to her older co-stars, and as Gene Kelly's love interest in the picture.

She finally relented, huffing, "Well, it's done now. But I won't forget you—and what you made me look like! That's all I have to say to you."

In time, she came to appreciate not only my work but also me as a person, and we've been wonderful friends in all the years since.

Helping young people find their way in the motion picture business was always very important to me, and I have particularly fond memories of two second-generation stars, both of whom I have known since they were small children: Liza Minnelli and Jane Fonda.

Back in 1948, Judy Garland's daughter Liza toddled into my hairstyling department for the first time as a wide-eyed two-and-a-half-year-old gripping the hand of her father, director Vincente Minnelli.

"I don't know what to do with her," Vincente said to me. "We've cast her in the final scene of *In the Good Old Summertime*, but Judy sent me to ask if you could do something about her hair. She cries every time I try to brush it. Judy, Van Johnson and three hundred extras are waiting on the set!"

I winked at Vincente and asked him to leave me alone with Liza. As we walked toward the salon chair, I told her how I had made her mother's hair pretty when she was a little girl, and I'd love to do the same for her. For a moment she seemed willing until I actually had her seated in the chair. She began squirming and put her hands over her ears, but with patience I managed to soothe her as I untangled her wavy curls, and she never uttered a single "ouch" while I brushed her out. By the time I had removed all the snarls, she and I had bonded. Grateful, Vincente brought her back to me often after that until she was on her own in grade school.

I carried that image of her with me for many years, like a photograph of my own child, and the memory was still vivid almost 30 years later in 1977 as I stood gazing at a ten-foot billboard on Broadway in New York City. It was a giant portrait of Liza in a stunning red dress for her one-woman show, *The Act*. On the bottom line were the words "Hairstyles for Miss Minnelli by Sydney Guilaroff." I smiled and thought, Liza dear, we've both come a long, long way.

I had known Jane Fonda since she was a young woman of 20, trying to break into the movies and hoping to escape the long shadow of her legendary father, Henry. The moment I saw the rushes for 1960's *Tall Story*, her first film, I whispered to her, "Jane, don't worry, dear, you might even turn out bigger than your father. Just wait."

By the time I designed the daring hairstyles for Jane's film *They Shoot Horses, Don't They?* in 1969, she had become an international star and was a major force in French films, thanks to her husband, director Roger Vadim, who had turned her into an on-screen sex kitten. But Jane had her own ideas. While filming *Horses* I sensed her marriage to Roger was in trouble. Despite her personal problems, though, she was completely engulfed in this role, and she would study her lines intensely as I did her hair at her home in Malibu for the next day's shoot.

Because the film was about a dance marathon during the Depression, I reached back into the past, resurrecting hairstyles I had designed during that era, and Jane loved them. I put cold waves in her hair, and I had to keep redoing it as the style deteriorated from her perspiration during the marathon. I tried to show her character's mental and physical self-destruction by using the hair design as an outward sign of her inner feelings. It was quite a challenge, but she seemed to feel I was successful, and so did director Sydney Pollack. After watching the daily rushes, she would ask me, "Well, what do you think?" I always told her the truth: that she was marvelous. It was this Academy Award-nominated performance that established her overnight as one of the premier dramatic actresses of her generation.

Another star who matured into an actress of genuine depth and range was my beloved Natalie Wood, who to this day tugs at my heart. A kinder and more compassionate woman I have never known. She was a great beauty with an exquisite body, but there was no pretense about her. And she was extremely generous and protective toward her family and all her friends. When Tony Curtis made derogatory remarks about her friend Marilyn Monroe after working with Marilyn in *Some Like It Hot*, Natalie scolded him gently for being so uncharitable. Though she divorced Robert Wagner (affectionately known as R.J.) after falling in love with Warren Beatty, she later remarried him and I truly believe he was the love of her life.

It was in 1958 that this handsome young couple first arrived at MGM when Natalie was cast in *Marjorie Morningstar*. I designed her hairstyles for that film, and we became dear friends. Natalie, Robert and I worked together many more times after that, and they asked for me no matter what studio they were working for.

In 1981 my heart sank when I heard the news that she had drowned in the waters off Catalina Island. She had been cut down in the prime of her life—so beautiful, so gifted. I was going to miss her deeply. The very next day Robert called me to ask if I would do Natalie's hair for the funeral. I said yes, of course, but I wept the entire time as I swept her hair back. She looked so angelic lying there, as if she were only sleeping.

One day not long afterward, while I was out on a drive, I put my hand out the window to signal a left-hand turn, and my watch fell off my wrist into the street. It was a beautiful watch that Robert and Natalie had given to me after I worked with her on *Gypsy*. They had inscribed on the back, "With love to you, dear Sydney, from Natalie and R.J." I stopped and retrieved the watch, but the crystal had been shattered. At a party a few nights later, R.J. noticed I wasn't wearing it and asked me where it was. When I told him, he asked me to give the watch back to him, and a few days later it was returned to me with a new crystal on it—and a new inscription: "Dear Sydney, Natalie loved you, and so do I. R.J."

After outliving so many wonderful friends over the years, I'm grateful for those close to me who are still alive, and there is none I cherish more than Angela Lansbury. I had worked for several years at MGM with her mother, a fine actress named Moyna MacGill, but it wasn't until 1943 that I learned she had a seventeen-year-old daughter with acting aspirations of her own. The studio was looking for a teenage girl to play a secondary role in an Ingrid Bergman–Charles Boyer film called *Gaslight*, and she was one of the girls we tested. After director George Cukor ran the footage, he asked me which one I liked best, and I said, "Angela Lansbury. She has a perky look and an impertinent way about her that's exactly what you need for the part."

She got the part and delivered a memorably provocative, Oscar-nominated performance that won her more prominent roles in *The Picture of Dorian Gray* and *National Velvet*. Those films elevated her to stardom and launched an extraordinary career that took her to the Broadway stage in *Mame*—for which I styled her hair—and finally to television in the long-running hit "Murder, She Wrote."

From the very beginning, she was a charming woman, extremely intelligent and articulate, but with a disarmingly sweet and modest nature. We became fast friends and have remained so to this day. When her husband, Peter Shaw, was hired to run the talent division of MGM in the seventies, he called me to his office to show me a telegram he'd received from John O'Brien, head of Loews Incorporated. It read: "There is a man by the name of Sydney Guilaroff who is very valuable to everybody at the studio. Please see if you can get him to sign a ten-year contract."

I was flattered, of course, but I had never worked under a contract and had no desire to come out of retirement and begin doing so now. Peter was quite persuasive, however, and I was so fond of him and Angela that I decided to oblige him and continued working at MGM for another decade.

Another dear friend of mine is Stefanie Powers, whom I first met at a party soon after she had fallen deeply in love with William Holden. She and I hit it off immediately, and we have remained close ever since, particularly in the wake of Holden's death in 1981. She and I were born on the same day, November 2, and each year we celebrate our mutual birthdays with my adopted grandson, José, and Stefanie's husband, Count de las Chesnias.

A beloved friend, and a star whose gifts have never been fully acknowledged by the industry, is Ann-Margret.

I first worked with her on *Viva Las Vegas*, where I turned her hair into a pale golden red tumble to match the exuberant choreography and her outrageous on-screen relationship with co-star Elvis Presley. Despite her tremendous talents as a singer and dancer, I was most interested in the film's dramatic scenes; from her presence and passion, I saw that she would become one of the great actresses of the modern era.

She struggled for years against being typecast as a sex kitten and finally broke through with a wonderful performance in *Carnal Knowledge* opposite Jack Nicholson, Art Garfunkel and Candice Bergen. I worked on that picture, but director Mike Nichols and I disagreed strongly over the way Ann-Margret should look in the film, so I left and caught a plane back to California from Vancouver, where the film was being shot. A few days later, however, Nichols called me back. He had turned his star into a brunette, and it wasn't working. I was asked to take on the difficult task of removing coarse brown dye and bringing back Ann-Margret's natural golden-red look. Since the dye had damaged her hair and huge clumps of it had fallen out, I was forced to weave hairpieces of appropriate color into her real hair.

I worked with Ann-Margret throughout the seventies, but by the time the 1988 television version of *A Streetcar Named Desire* came along, which would become her greatest triumph, I had retired. I was astonished when she called to say that although playwright Tennessee Williams himself had personally asked her to take the role of Blanche DuBois, she would not accept it unless I agreed to come out of retirement. "You're the only one who can do my hair," she said. "But more than that, I need you for moral support and artistic guidance. I can't do it without you."

The choice of Treat Williams as the oafish Stanley

Kowalski was equally inspiring; he brought to the role a joie de vivre that Marlon Brando had lacked. He stayed in character for nearly the whole production, talking as Stanley might, common as dirt, and eating with the grace and manners of a half-starved street hustler. Yet Treat is a lovely, warm-hearted, modest man, one of the most unusual and gifted actors I've ever come across.

Ann-Margret became so engrossed in her role that she was on the set practically all the time. I was always nearby, standing behind the camera whenever she was on. One day, associate producer Greg Baumgarten showed up with a couple of personal friends. It was a mistake; they were a distraction on the set of this very serious production. Director John Erman told his first assistant to clear the set. He asked me to leave as well.

I protested, "This is a very intense moment, and she's nervous about playing it and would like me to stay."

"It's nothing personal," said John in a nice way. "It's just that no one is allowed here except the cast and crew."

Reluctantly, I left the soundstage. Five minutes later, an assistant director came looking for me. Ann-Margret was ready to shoot her scene but wouldn't do it without me. "I lose confidence when I don't see him behind the camera," she insisted. So I came back.

Toward the end of the film is the famous scene in which the fearful Blanche is raped by Stanley, her sister's husband. When I saw the rushes, though, I was very disappointed. The close-ups didn't capture the sheer horror of that terrible experience. I told John Erman about this, and he shrugged. "Well, what can I do?" he asked. "The producers don't want to pay for an extra day."

"Let's tell them that it has to be done," I said, "because what we have is not good. This is the scene that provides the reason why Blanche is taken away at the end of the picture. It foreshadows the tragic ending, and it has to be done right or the ending doesn't work. We've got to see her, to feel the horror we see on her face."

John seemed unwilling to press the matter with his bosses, so I took it on myself to speak with Greg Baumgarten. "We have not asked for many retakes on this production because everything has gone wonderfully," I explained. "But this scene just isn't good enough—you must see the terror on the face of this woman. This is the moment that drives her absolutely mad."

"It costs a lot to do a setup like that again," said Greg. "We'd have to have the whole crew again for that shot."

"I know what it takes. I've been around a long time. But it should be done, it really should."

Finally, Greg agreed to reshoot, and it was worth every penny. Ann-Margret did it perfectly in just one take. Fifty million viewers tuned in to watch *A Streetcar Named Desire*. The production won rave reviews, and Ann-Margret was nominated for an Emmy. But she didn't win. She hadn't won an Emmy the previous year for her nominated performance in *Who Will Love My Children?* and when she was nominated a third time the following year for the TV movie *The Two Mrs. Grenvilles,* she was again ignored. Even Barbara Stanwyck, who took home an Emmy for her role in *The Thorn Birds,* felt that Ann-Margret should have won, and she went so far as to use her acceptance speech to pay tribute to her. I feel strongly that the reason Ann-Margret didn't win was purely political: She and her husband, Roger Smith, have never run with Hollywood's fast crowd. They don't frequent industry functions, and they surround themselves not with glitz and phoniness but with real people whom they care about.

So when I was awarded the Emmy for hairstyling and makeup for *The Two Mrs. Grenvilles,* I not only boycotted the awards ceremony but refused to accept the statue. When the Academy of Television Arts and Sciences called to say they had an Emmy for me, I told them to keep it. They wanted to know why, so I told them: because Ann-Margret had been denied the Emmy that was rightfully hers, and until that was rectified, I didn't think enough of the award to trouble myself with collecting it.

Following *The Two Mrs. Grenvilles*, I returned to retirement and to reflecting on my years at MGM. Those were years thronged with a larger-than-life cast of characters. But the most unusual and memorable of all never set foot in front of a camera—and I never touched his hair. There has never been another tycoon quite like Louis B. Mayer. The highest-paid businessman in all America for some time, he was invited to the White House long before such nods to the industry became fashionable. Despite our many differences, I always knew that he had achieved something quite special at MGM.

Over the years Mayer became very close to writer-turned-producer Dore Schary and considered him a member of his own family, a sort of adopted son. Then in 1951 Schary cast a young Oklahoma boy named Audie Murphy in the film version of Stephen Crane's *The Red Badge of Courage*. Murphy had never been in front of a camera but had won the Congressional Medal of Honor at Anzio and was the most decorated soldier of World War II. Perhaps Schary thought that this was inspired casting, a real war hero in a story about courage in war, but in reality this Civil War tale is about the futility of war. Mayer, an ardent Republican and a sincere patriot, thought that the move was too political, that Murphy might be perceived as an insult to the U.S. government or to the American people.

One afternoon Schary visited my office. I was shocked to see how everyone—writers, producers, directors—flocked around him, trying to curry favor. Schary and I had been friendly, and for a time I went to his home on social occasions. But soon I began seeing the very same people who had once carried the banner of L.B. Mayer, except now they were "yessing" Dore Schary and I lost my feeling of friendship for him.

Once Nick Schenck, head of Loews, learned how many MGM bigwigs had deserted Mayer, he took Schary's side. By this time, Schenck was more than a little tired of Mayer, who supposedly worked for him but made more money and got much more publicity than he did. In backing Schary, he put Mayer on the spot, and finally Mayer said that if *The Red Badge of Courage* was made at MGM, he would resign.

When I heard about this, I sat down and wrote L.B. a long letter, in which I said, among other things, that "none of us would be here if it weren't for you. The very sets we walk on, the cobblestone streets, the soundstages that you caused to be built—all reflect your vision. Kings don't resign, they pass away. Please don't resign, Mr. Mayer. I'm sure you can overcome Dore Schary eventually. This is just one picture; close your eyes to it, but don't resign."

He replied, "Guilaroff, only two people wrote to me. I never dreamed you would be one of them. It was like rats leaving a sinking ship." The other letter he received was from director Mervyn LeRoy. Nevertheless, L.B. Mayer did resign in 1951, forced out of the very studio he created. After he left, MGM was never the same, and neither was my life there. I went on working for the studio for many more years, but for me and for the moviegoing public, it was truly the end of an era.

Epilogue

*t*he world of movies, in which I lived and worked for more than 60 years, was a golden age, a time when American films represented this country at its best, when audiences expected to be thrilled and entertained with romance and glamour in stories that embodied humankind's highest aspirations. The films made in those years promoted and displayed standards of beauty, romance, pride and hard work that people sought to emulate in their daily lives. It was an industry of visionaries, a business of high artistic standards, and at MGM, at least, greatest of all the studios, a family of craftspeople, artisans, performers and executives worked together with love and care, which is still evident in each frame of every movie. They will live forever.

But that world and that age are long gone. I can think of hardly more than a handful of films made in recent years that will stand up for another half century. The reasons are not hard to understand: The motion picture industry was founded by entrepreneurs, small businessmen who had come from other backgrounds. They were inventing a new art form even as they built their studios. The best survived into the era in which I was fortunate enough to play my own small role. And because their personal values reflected a simpler and more congenial age, they often treated their employees with the sort of respect and devotion otherwise found only in extended families.

Today, however, the studios are owned by huge and impersonal multinational corporations that have sacrificed art on the altar of profit. Their films are too often triumphs of technology, bursting with elaborate special effects but sadly lacking in stories that celebrate human values, promote culture or elevate the spirit. Instead, most Hollywood films now are aimed at the lowest common denominator, glorifying greed, lust and violence, the basest aspects of human nature. Audiences now expect and accept wildly exaggerated tales featuring totally unbelievable characters, and the life expectancy of each $40 million epic is determined week after week solely by its box office receipts.

Even worse, those who appear in today's films are a different breed. Movie stars were once admired and emulated by people around the world. Now the so-called superstars look much like their audiences. Their public behavior is frequently despicable and unprincipled: top-billed actors bashing automobiles with golf clubs over traffic disputes or consorting publicly with the most sordid of prostitutes; actresses proudly bearing babies whose father's names they cannot even recall; screen stars ingesting all manner of illicit drugs and behaving like spoiled children instead of public figures. They demand wealth and fame as their due for working in the cinema, but they do little in return for the moviegoing public except provide the worst examples of human misconduct.

And so I present this book as a record of what the movie business once was and as an inspiration to those who would seek to better themselves in any field. Although I have made my share of mistakes, I have also learned from them. I hope this account of my life has shown that with perseverance, with heartfelt convictions, with respect for oneself and for others, even an uneducated person from a poor family can build a rich and satisfying life for himself or herself. If you're willing to make sacrifices, to always do the very best you're capable of and to treasure your individuality above all else, there is no limit to what you can accomplish in this life.